Two Worlds

One Light

A Memoir of a Medium

Robin H. Lysne, Ph.D.
White Turtle Woman

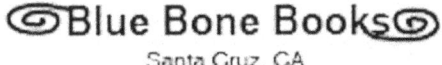

Santa Cruz, CA

Publication Page

Two Worlds One Light: The Memoir of a Medium
Book Four: Ancestor Women Series

Copyright 2023
Robin H. Lysne, M.A., M.F.A., Ph.D.

Cover: Painting by Robin H. Lysne

Blue Bone Books
300 Jims Road
Ben Lomond, CA 95005
United States of America

Blue Bone Books is a cooperative poetry and literary press. All rights reserved under the U.S.Copyright Act of 1976. No part of the publication may be reproduced, distributed, or transmitted in any form or by any means of stored in a database or retireval system without the prior written permission of the publisher or the copyright holder.

ISBN#: 9781948675178

Library of Congress#: 2023924306

Ebook: 978-1-948675-18-5

*This book is dedicated to
all those who are coming into
their intuition, or mediumistic skills.
May it help you own
your gifts and talents
and release all fear so you may
serve others with clarity of sight
and a heart full of Love.*

Robin Lysne, Ph.D. is an intuitive of the highest caliber with a calming presence and precise insights. Her insights have helped me make positive life decisions for over a decade across career, relationships and finances. I highly recommend a session with her to guide you to better outcomes in life.

A. Lal
VP of Product Marketing

I am thrilled to endorse Robin Heerens Lysne's publication, Two Worlds One Light: A Memoir of a Medium! Robin's thoughtful, informative account of her journey as a medium is inspirational. It is filled with detailed examples of her many and varied experiences. Her book is filled with highly practical advice for anyone on a similar journey. Two Worlds One Light: A Memoir of a Medium is a MUST READ for people who are experienced mediums, those who are learning to become mediums, and those who find the topic of interest.

Bonnie Baker Berg, Ph.D., CCC-SLP
Professor Emerita
Minnesota State University, Mankato

Two Worlds, One Light
A Memoir of a Medium

CONTENTS

Introduction - 1

Section One: Growing Up Naturally as a Medium: - 2

Chapter One - Another Day at Work - 2
Grandpa's Crossing - 4
Early Years - 10
Summer Camp and Colorado - 18
Near Death Experience - 21

Chapter Two - Launching Into My Life - 33
Beginning Medium - Suicide of a Friend - 43
Outing Myself as a Medium-Another kind of Wedding - 45

Chapter Three - Hiking Slowly Up the Mountain - 58
Moving to California and Grad School - 68
Meeting a Master-Da Free John -71

Section Two: Native American Wisdom- Discovering Earth-based Traditions - 76

Chapter Four -Beginning Native American Path - 76
The Woman's Ceremony - 76
My First Native American Dances - 79

Chapter Five - Beginning My Work - 88
Gold Miner's Ghosts - 88
Medium with a Massage Practice - 92

Chapter Six - Mom's Story - 96
Leaving and Arriving The First Book Tour -105
Trip Home from Rockford via Norway -117

Chapter Seven - Landing in Santa Cruz and Cutting the ties that Bind - 129
Adventures on Mt. Madonna - 134
Alfonzo and I begin our Life Together - 143
Recovering and Starting a Practice -158

Chapter Eight - More Native Ceremonies - 165
The Ogitchidaah Ceremony - 165
Troll of the Willows - 170
Journey to Canada - 175

Chapter Nine - Brazil and Another Kind of Earth-Based Ceremony - 181
Umbanda Initiations - 181
Condomblé Ceremonies - 193

Section Three: Mediumistic Work - 200

Chapter Ten - Stories from a Medium's Work - 200
Readings and Healings - 200
Stacy's Story - 201
An Unwanted Visit - 206
When to Call a Loved One - 207
Sasha and her Lover - 209
Ninja Healing – Takuma's Story - 215
Irma's Pain -217
Carl's Request -218
Flight #237 - 223

Chapter Eleven - The Awakening - 227
Transition- 2nd Saturn Return - 230
Kisti's Crossing - 231
Starting Over - Back to School - 237
Channeling - 239

Chapter Twelve - What I learned from House Clearings - 242
A San Francisco Apartment Building Nightmare - 246
Beach Boardwalk House - 249
Burial Ground House - 253
Spirit Possession Jan's Story - 256
The Case of Harrold - 260

Chapter Thirteen - Conclusion: - 264
Dad's Crossing - 264
Finding My Teacher - 273

Biography - 278
Blue Bone Books Publications - 280
Endorsements - 281

Two Worlds

One Light

A Memoir of a Medium

Robin H. Lysne, Ph.D.
White Turtle Woman

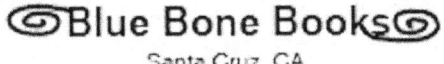

Santa Cruz, CA

Two Worlds One Light
A Memoir of a Medium

Introduction

This book was written with very strong guidance from my Spirit Guides. It took me three months to do the initial manuscript, which is a very short time. However, as I started writing, I felt the reasons why I was guided to write this book.

My intention is to help people. Some people are aware of their intuition, accept their gifts and find ways to help others. Everyone is intuitive, whether it is a gut feeling of doing this rather than that, or whether one sees, feels, hears or tastes what is occurring. It is also important for anyone who is curious about the energy of the world and how it impacts all of us. I hope this book supports those who read it to give up their fears and live their heart calling through love.

Like many people I have inherited my intuition from my family line. My mother, her sister, and her parents were both quite intuitive. Mother saw entities and energies like I did, and we often sat in church and looked at the spirits floating around the room comparing notes of what we were experiencing. (see Chapter One, Early Years.)

It was as natural as any other talent one inherits. There was nothing special about it growing up. It wasn't until I was in my 30's that I realized I could help people with my gifts.

Now after living my destiny, I hope my story will help others live out theirs destiny. Each person has guidance, and each of us can use our intuition to help the world, whether it is as a professional like myself, or as helping ourselves find our path, or guiding children to grow to their true potential. May you enjoy the true stories, and may it help you find your own true heart-loving path.

Section One:
Growing Up as a Medium:

Chapter One
Another Day at Work

Be thirsty for the ultimate water, and then be ready for what will come pouring from the spring. –Rumi

It is another day at work. My client Lynn and I are standing in her large spacious bedroom as I wave my feather fan over the smoking wooden bowl that holds burning sage. I am feeling into the energy as I sweep the room from side to side with the smoke and fan. Looking around at the contemporary furnishings and up to the cathedral ceiling, the energy seems pretty clear in the bedroom. Next, I move into her bathroom.

The large white-tiled bathroom has twin sinks, a shower stall with a clear glass door, and a jacuzzi tub that floats like a swan on one end of the room. As I enter the room, sage lit and smoking in my wooden bowl, I wave my owl wing over the sage. The smoke wafts up to the spirit hiding in the high cathedral ceiling above the sinks.

"She is up here hiding near the ceiling in the bathroom," I tell my client. I feel the air, smoke, and tips of my feather fan catch a shadow of a spirit hovering in one corner.

"That was her bedroom before the remodel," Lynn says.

"You stay here in the bedroom. I don't want her to come after you." I said.

In the fourteen-foot ceiling bathroom, I extend my

spirit stretching to reach her above me. The smoke helps me perceive her more clearly and move her on. She is still in her hospital bed, only near the ceiling where she is trying to hide. She is old and not able to do much. She is angry and keeps saying to me,

"This is MY house! Go AWAY!"

I try to calm her down, and soon she is moaning.

"Dear heart this is not your house anymore," I say to her in my mind. "You died over three years ago, and now it is time to move on. It is okay, it won't hurt at all; in fact it can be quite a relief for you."

"I don't want to leave!" She crosses her arms and looks away to the wall.

"I know, it is not fun to transition to the spirit world, but here you are!" I try to reassure her that she is and will be safe and that I have brought in some friends to help.

"Look, here is your Guardian Angel." Slowly she turns to the angel and sees her for the first time. The angel reaches out to her. She is like a child turning towards her mother's loving face, and the woman is finally able to leave. She is surrounded in the bright light of the angel that has come to help her. Suddenly, as she crosses over into a bright golden beam, the room feels immediately different and I am relieved to feel her out of her misery.

"What did you do?!" The new owner of the house says startled.

"She's gone, she won't cause any more trouble. I just sent her on her way. She won't bother you anymore."

My client's face has shock and relief written all over it.

This is a typical day at work. Though there are really no "typical" days. Sometimes I sit in my living room and talk to people on the other side of the country or the world through Zoom. Other days I go to my office for in-person sessions. Sometimes I am traveling from place to place, clearing out spirits and ghosts. Other times, when I have people come to my home, we sit in my living room and have a cup of tea. They tell me their stories, and I help them let go or expand more fully into their more authentic loving presence.

When I think about how all of this started, I go back to my first mediumistic experience as an adult. Of course, I had these experiences as a child, too, but this next memory as a young adult is burned into my mind and heart.

Grandpa's Crossing

It was the middle of the night and my grandfather was pounding up and down the floor, pacing like I had never seen him do before. His footsteps, filled with anger and frustration, woke me up. Grandma, who was sleeping in the next room, began to stir.

"Joe, I need to go to the bathroom," she said. I got up to check on her.

"I've got her Gramps, please don't worry. She'll be okay," I said as I passed him.

"But I can't do it anymore," he said. "Who is going to step in?"

"Don't worry Gramps, really."

I helped Grandma get up to use the commode and got her back into bed. She moaned some but was fine. I think she thought I was Grandpa. "Good night, Grandma, I love you," I said to her, closing the door slightly.

On my way to the bathroom to empty the pan, Grandpa began pacing and pounding around again. He was always such a jovial man, and he did funny things to make us laugh. But this was not funny. His spirit was showing more of him than I had seen before.

"Gramps, really, she will be okay. Bob—Dad will find a way to manage her care. Now please just relax, it is okay. We've got her."

I went back to bed on the rollaway they had moved into the dining room where Grandpa had slept. It had been his bed while they were dealing with a new guest bedroom mattress and finding ways for both of them to get some sleep. The walls of the dining room had large green and white floral wallpaper and a white painted built-in sideboard. The mirror in the back of the sideboard reflected me in my nightie and the piano and furniture in the living room. My grandparents had lived in this two-flat apartment building for over forty years. They rented the upstairs apartment and lived on the first floor.

Grandpa woke me up several more times that night. Finally, about an hour before dawn, I was awakened again by his shouting and pounding around on the floor beside me.

"I can't do anything now," he shouted. "Who's going to take care of her?!"

"Grandpa, it's okay. Robert, Trudy, and Joe agreed that they would take her to Rockford. It is okay. They are making a plan in the next few days."

He looked right at me and said, "Robert and Joe and Trudy, they will take care of her?"

"Yes Gramps, they are going to take her to Rockford, under Dad's—Robert's care. You died Gramps, you are on the other side and it is time to move on into the spirit world. This life with Grandma is over now. You need to go to the light. Now just let go Gramps. We've got her."

At that, I watched as my Grandfather's spirit moved into a tunnel of light that was made for him as soon as he realized there was nothing more he could do. I watched him disappear into it and out of the place where he and Grandma had lived through most of their married life. I saw others greet him in a golden glow of light. 'That must be his brothers and sisters and parents' I thought. Then the vortex closed, and he was gone.

Grandpa's tunnel of light was no different than the one I had experienced with my own near-death six years earlier. At age seventeen, I had somehow contracted meningitis and slipped into a coma. I found myself wandering to the end of a long tunnel of light. However, at the end of the tunnel I passed through, a spirit stood there blocking my way.

"You can leave now, but you will have to come back, and it will be much harder," the man said gently and firmly. He was an elderly man with a very long white beard, wearing white. He didn't tell me his name, but his authority was unmistakable. I was slightly disappointed that he looked so typically God-like. I was expecting to be surprised. Perhaps this image of the man with a white beard was created by my own imagination to receive his message.

"Harder! No way, life has been hard enough!" I said in exasperation.

At that, I instantly went back, as if I was sucked through a "vacuum tube" of light, and woke up in my hospital bed with tubes and I.V.s everywhere.

After meeting him, and hearing that I have work to do here, I knew I had some kind of purpose to do on planet earth. It was a long recovery road, after the meningitis, but I had a new determination to find my purpose. I had no idea at the time that I would become a medium, or that I had any gifts at all, except in art. So I had set out to art school, and finished two years of high school and four years later with a degree in painting and drawing, I was working now in Milwaukee at a needle point shop, and had taken the train down to visit my grandparents in Evanston, Illinois, as I sometimes liked to do.

Now, at twenty-three, a year out of school, as I witnessed Grandpa leave, my tunnel memory came back to me. Grandpa's tunnel was just like mine, with lots of gold light; except that his tunnel had choirs of singing voices like nothing I had ever heard before. It was quite beautiful to watch him go, even though I was sad to lose my Grandpa.

I sat on the bed and cried. But it was more relief than grief. Grandpa had insisted on taking care of Grandma, despite the fact that it was wearing him out. It finally did wear him out completely and there was nothing any of us could do about it.

The rest of the night was more peaceful, and Grandma settled down to sleep. I was sleeping in the bed where he had slept twenty-four hours before, alive and fully in his body. He had his heart attack that afternoon in the bathroom, and we had spent the rest of the day taking care of Grandma, calling family members and making plans for his funeral.

Grandpa's death was my first realization that I could help people, living and dead, with my ability to see spirits. It was as natural as rain for me to speak to him, and he could hear me and talk to me. I did not think of it as anything special or unusual. I had seen spirits since I was a small child. They were a part of my life, and I thought everyone could see them, until that day. All of us were still in shock from his death. No one else had experienced Grandpa's ghost and communicated with him as I had. That really surprised me.

In the morning, Mom and my two sisters and brothers-in-law came over from our aunt and uncle's houses. Mom fixed breakfast for Grandma and me and the rest of the family. They had stayed with my aunts and uncles in Palatine and Park Ridge, outside Evanston, where my grandparents lived. As Mom cooked, I talked to her about Grandpa Heerens spirit.

"Mom, he was pounding around all night. He woke me up several times, and then I told him he was dead and that it was time to move on, and he finally left. But I had to tell him what Dad's plans were to take care of Grandma, over and over, and it wasn't until I convinced him that Bob and Aunt Trudy and Uncle Joe would take care of her before he let go."

"Just don't tell your father dear, he is upset enough as it is. He just lost his own father. You know how close they were," Mom said as she flipped the pancakes and the bacon. "It seems like it was good you were here, Robby."

"Yes, it seemed meant to be, I guess. His whole Norwegian family was on the other side, Mom."

Mom could see spirits, too. The ability came on her family line. Her mother read signs from animals and her father could see energies and entities that were all around us. Grandpa Lysne, Mom's father, was a retired chiropractor, a Mason and a Son of Norway. His Masonic group in North Carolina where they moved after he retired, tried to find lost children and pets with their psychic abilities. My maternal grandparents understood my abilities.

It was odd that the one I helped across was Grandpa Heerens, a dyed-in-the-wool Baptist. Grandma would never know what happened with Grandpa's spirit the night of his passing. She was a strict Danish Lutheran. If I told her about it, she would think it was the work of the devil or something odd that did not align with Lutheranism. It was better for her not to know.

Just the morning before, I had come south on the train from Milwaukee to Evanston. Mom and two of my sisters and their husbands had chosen that day to sort through the items in Aunt Lily's house. Grandpa's sister, Lily, had been moved into a nursing home, at age 94. We were invited to go through her house to see what we needed. All of us had new apartments or houses. My two sisters were newly married, and I was just out of college living on my own.

When we arrived in Evanston, we were all shocked to see how tired Grandpa Heerens was, though he was still in high spirits. Occasionally, he got up to play a little tune on the upright piano. He played a hymn for the luncheon blessing and talked the whole time we had lunch. He mentioned how his parents had died in their seventies. At eighty-seven, he had lived a whole decade longer than his parents. "That is pretty good, don't you think?" he said, beaming through his exhaustion.

After we finished lunch, Grandpa played his ragtime selections. He carried little cards with him with musical chords and the names of the song above on the cards. The cards were small, about the size of a business card. He kept his stack of a hundred or so cards in his foot-long change purse, which he folded up and kept in his pocket, along with Cracker Jack prizes, little tops, paper clips, and loose change that he gave to his grandchildren when we visited. Even in my twenties, we asked him what prizes he had saved for us. He was always chuckling and making little jokes. He was quite fun to be around.

On the way, Mom had picked up Kentucky Fried Chicken and we made a salad. But I could not eat a thing. I was too fixated by Grandpa's aura. It was totally black. I was so shocked to see this, since I had never seen a black aura before, I lost my appetite. I could not tell anyone. It was too difficult to see, and I did not want anyone else to feel as bad as I did that afternoon.

After lunch, Mom and my sister Nancy and her husband Ralph, who was a doctor, took both my grandparents to their doctor for a check-up. The rest of us went over to Lily's to collect our new teapots, platters, and kitchen items from Great Aunt Lily's house.

When Grandma and Grandpa returned from the doctor, Grandpa suddenly had to go to the bathroom and ran inside. Grandma was having a hard time getting up the steep grey steps, so she sat down half way up. Mom and my sister Nancy and her husband Ralph were left trying to get Grandma inside. Grandma was exhausted from visiting the doctor. Just that much of a trip was too much for her. Nancy ran in to check on Grandpa after hearing something bang to the ground.

Ralph heard Nancy shout for him. When he got to the bathroom, he saw Nancy bending over Grandpa checking his pulse. He was dead of a sudden heart attack, just as his father had died before him.

Nancy and Ralph left his body in the bathroom and pulled a mattress from one room across the entryway to the dining room to block the view from Grandma until they could move him into the bedroom and lay him out. This way we could all be around her on the couch when we told her the difficult news.

Ralph had told us this story when he came to get the rest of us at Lily's and drove us back to our grandparent's flat. As we walked into the living room, we found Mom with Nancy and Grandma sitting together on the couch.

Mom looked at us, startled, and said, "We just witnessed a miracle! Just now, a very large man walked by and asked if he could help. He lifted Grandma effortlessly and set her in on the couch in the living room. Then he tipped his hat and left." Mom's eyes were huge as she spoke to us of what just happened.

Nan and Ralph went into the bathroom to move Grandpa's body and lay him on their bed. When they returned, and we were all around Grandma, Mom held Grandma's hands and told her the news of Grandpa's sudden death. It was such a shock for her, as it was for all of us. She kept saying, "What?! Joe, dead? He can't be! No. No. No. He was just here! Joe, where are you?" Then we took her to their bedroom so she could see his body.

We spent the day after Grandpa's death getting things ready for the funeral, and getting ready to move Grandma to Rockford. My aunt and uncle would spend the next few nights with Grandma before she would be transported to Rockford to a nursing home. Dad would make arrangements for her arrival. This way my physician father could take care of her and keep a close watch over her care. Grandpa's death was the first death in our immediate family and the first dead body I had ever seen.

Early Years

The home where I grew up was in the midwestern town of Rockford, Illinois, outside of Chicago about two hours to the downtown. The town was divided by the Rock River, on the east side mostly Swedish and Italians, with African Americans who lived on the westside. We were a fairly normal family, mostly Norwegian, with Danish and Scottish Grandmothers. As most families, we had all its foibles and complicated relationships.

I am the fourth of five daughters. We lived on busy Route 20, or State Street, on the corner of State and London Avenue. Then, as now, Route 20 was constantly full of traffic that traveled between downtown Rockford and Chicago.

Our home was a federal style two-story house with dark, almost black-brown bricks and white trim. We lived there until I was five with my four sisters and parents. My younger sister Sara and I shared a room, as did my sisters Jill and Nancy. Kisti, my oldest sister, always had her own room. The house had one bathroom up stairs with the four bedrooms, and a living room, dining room, kitchen, and den downstairs. There was also a screened-in porch in back and a small yard with an alley running behind the house with a detached garage.

My father was a young family physician, and Mom's job was to take care of us and the house, as was typical for women in the 1940s and 50s. She certainly had her hands full with five daughters.

When I was only 15 or 16 months old, my mother had

an episode that I witnessed and no one else in my family did, except my father. This memory came to me only in my fifties. Though I had an earlier memory about the same time, the actual memory of the whole event came later.

My father's aunt and uncle came to visit, then they got the flu. My mother was pregnant with my younger sister Sara, and Mom was trotting up and down two flights of stairs taking care of them with dirty sheets from their diarrhea and vomiting. Since she was a nurse, she knew how, but since the washer and dryer was in the basement, she had to run up and down two flights of stairs.

Then one afternoon, she broke down and had a migraine that was so bad, she could not see. It was called, in those days, hysterical blindness. Today they would say she had a nervous break down. She began to stab a cutting board with a large knife and started screaming, "I can't see, I can't do anything, I can't see." I was in my playpen in the den off the kitchen watching the whole thing. My father came home for lunch, as his office was just a few minutes away. He took the knife out of her hand, and stopped her, holding on to her telling her she was going to be all right. He set her down, called the babysitter, and ran upstairs and told his aunt and uncle they had to go home that Marty was going to the hospital.

The baby sitter came, Mrs. Dorr, and Mom and Dad left for the hospital. After that, Mom was in the hospital for the rest of her pregnancy. Sara was delivered June 18th, 1954. I did not see her until she came back, and then she had another child with her who had colic. This impacted me and Mom for the rest of my life. This story was confirmed by both Mom and Dad when I was in my 30's after an E.S.T. (Erhard Seminar Training) that I attended where another memory came to the foreground. A memory of Mom falling or being hurt and me trying to help her as a tiny child, at the time, what I had remembered. They looked at each other, and both my parents acknowledged the aunt and uncle, their illness and mom going in the hospital with 'hysterical blindness.' She had migraines the rest of her life, when she was under stress.

My mother often told me another story that I have a vague memory of from my childhood. One day, at age two, I climbed up the kitchen drawers in our old State Street house, using them like steps. Reaching the counter top in my footy pajamas, on the way to my goal—the top of the refrigerator—I grabbed a large knife from the knife rack and climbed up to sit on top of my imaginary mountain. As I was waving my arms with the large knife in one hand, and singing a song to myself at the top of my lungs, my mother came in to answer the phone.

"Oh hi, Shirley, I just wanted to—" She turned around when she heard me singing. "Wait just a minute," she said to her friend. "I have to get Robby off the top of the refrigerator . . . I will call you right back."

I remember Mom setting the receiver down and taking the knife out of my hand, then carefully lifting me off to top of my mountain.

"How did you get up there?" She was equal parts amused and alarmed. Even at age two, I knew that my life was about climbing the mountain, and dancing and singing to life. However, Illinois was flat, and I had never seen a mountain anywhere at that age even in pictures. It was not until much later that I would learn what it meant to climb to new heights and "be the mountain."

As a small child, my imaginary friends, or spirit guides (as I later understood), were very vivid to me. They looked like grownups and took the shape of humans, but they were light-filled. There were at least five or six of them, as I recall, both male and female. When I think of them sitting with me one winter afternoon, I can still see their faces, and their glowing hair, and their beautiful light. They must have enjoyed themselves sitting with a three-year-old, cutting out paper dolls with me, and laughing at how bossy I must have been. I do not know if they came as a result of the trauma, or if they were just with me always. They were with me always, but I saw them after the traumatic event mom had.

"Now do it like this. No, no, not that, like this…" I did

their cutting for them, and used the best scissors, straight ones with sharp points, not my play scissors with rounded ends. Mom had collected all the scissors I could use as a three year old and set them in the circle as I sat with my guides.

We sat together by the radiator under the window between the living room and the den, with the sunlight streaming in on the worn gray carpet in the winter. Our house was old, but cozy. I cut out my paper dolls, and then theirs; we each cut out different family members.

They were not in my imagination—they were actually sitting around me in a circle. I did not conjure them up. They were simply there. Mom called them my imaginary friends. But to me they were not imaginary. They were real, and very kind and loving. I knew I had come from where they lived. We were in two different realities. But I could see them and remember them as my light family. We were one light, even though in two different worlds.

One day, I realized that I was doing all the cutting of paper dolls myself and I got angry. I said to them, "What good are you if you can't even cut out paper dolls! I am doing all the cutting! I don't want to play with you any more." After that, I would never see them as vividly as I had that day until much later. Until then, I was aware that they were still around, but not in the Technicolor I had experienced before when we sat together in the light of the sun and the heat of the radiator.

I did not realize at the time that I had actually sent them away. What I did realize, however, was that I was not alone. I had very loving beings that were with me all the time ready to talk with me whenever I needed them, even if they were hiding in the invisible side of the world. As a small child I never experienced any spirits that wanted to harm me. Somehow, I knew they couldn't hurt me anyway. Even so, I was still affected by my fear of scary things that might get me at night.

One creature that made a big difference on State Street was our neighbor's dog Rusty. Rusty and I took naps together when I was three or four years old. Whenever she was around the house, I would play with her. She would often lay under the giant elm trees that lined the street along the side of our house. I would lay down on Rusty's belly and take a nap with her. I also talked with Rusty, and he/she seemed to intuitively talk back. That dog was the most gentle and kind dog I have ever had the pleasure of knowing. In hindsight, I am amazed that my mother never called me away from Rusty. Perhaps she remembered how much she loved her own dog when she was a child.

My extended family on my father's side was made up of mostly conservative Lutheran and Baptist Christians. On my mother's side, my grandparents were Christian Scientists and metaphysicians. They believed in God, in a broader sense—God is everything in nature; God as the Great Spirit, God as us. They believed in reincarnation and avidly studied the work of many spiritual teachers, including Paramhansa Yogananda, and western mystics such as Edgar Casey, Madam Blavatsky, the Ukrainian born medium, and many others. Grandpa Lysne was fascinated by Native Americans especially Red Cloud. He even painted his portrait and felt he had been him in a past life. He was fluent in Civil War history and the great Indian wars. He spoke of this when we visited, but not in front of my father or his more conservative family. I learned early on that there were things you spoke of with certain members of the family, and things you did not with others.

Two other vivid memories have stayed with me from my early years. My older sisters, who were four, six, and eight years older than me, took Sally and I around the outside of the house to see where they had stuck fairy house doors made out of cardboard in the roots of the old Elm trees. They had created these doors for the fairies while my younger sister Sara (then she was called Sally) and I were taking a nap. They did the same in Evanston, at the house where our Heerens grandparents lived.

There were huge Elm trees out front between the sidewalk and the road. When all the doors were in place and we woke from our naps, we opened the front door to fairy houses in the trees roots and pretended to play with the tree divas. It was so much fun. My sisters did not realize that the fairies were really there. I saw them, and I was actually playing with fairies and divas at that very young age. I thought that we all were enjoying the fairies and not just pretending.

Grandma Heerens always had crayons ready, as well as glitter, glue, and craft paper, for us to create things. Often, we made Grandma ornaments for her Christmas tree. But I remember the fairy house doors the best—the fairies were actually there, I did not imagine it; they spoke to me. Mostly they were glad someone could hear them. They were very beautiful with dresses and clothes that blended in with the hydrangeas, hostas, and lily of the valley flowers. The tree spirits were dressed in green and brown.

On another day, when my mother had gone out to get groceries, my older sisters took Sara and me with them to a very haunted house a few blocks from where we lived. My sisters wanted to visit this house where a murder had taken place the week before.

A man who had brought vegetables to sell to his neighbors (including us) had lived in this house with his mother. He had killed his mother with an ax and cut her up and put her in the oven. Blood was all over the kitchen. The murder was all over the news. Always the explorers, my sisters, wanted to peek in the windows of the house, and so they sat Sara and me by the curb and told us to stay there. They did not intend for either of us to be scared by the experience, I am sure of that. But we were too little, as neither of us had been this far from our house before. I was maybe three or four, and my sister Sara about two or three.

After my older sisters disappeared around the house, they seemed to be gone a long time, so I got up to look for them. They were somewhere on the other side of it, but everything was so large that I got lost and didn't know if this was the house or not. I saw the yellow tape across the doors. Then I looked up into the windows of the kitchen and saw the blood on the ceiling and blood on the walls inside the house. I cried and cried, I was so scared, and when my sisters heard me, they came running around the corner. Sally was crying too, sitting on the curb. Sara was really small and I don't think she came with me, even though she was afraid of being alone.

I remember seeing a woman park her car on the street nearby; she must have wondered what the hell two small children were doing sitting on the curb at this horrible house. I think she knew us, and she made sure all of us went home to our own house.

After that I remember I was too scared to go to sleep that night and I must have cried for hours when Mom got home. I remember Mom being extremely angry with Nancy and Jill. I don't remember if Kisti was there or not. I do remember that when I looked in the kitchen and saw the blood in that house, I "saw" the whole incident.

Years later, after the man got convicted and executed or put in jail, there was a reenactment of the whole murder shown on T.V. I had nightmares for weeks after that. The man's mother wasn't doing anything but cooking. Who knows what she said to him, or whether she provoked him? This was in the 1950s, which was long before any real understanding of psychology had hit the mainstream mindset. Though I am fascinated with television shows that depict forensic pathology, I have never been drawn to becoming a forensic medium. I am certain that my experience witnessing that scene is probably why.

Recently, I uncovered a deep fear of ever damaging a child. I don't think I could ever forgive myself if my words or deeds impacted their behavior towards others, as in the case of a serial killer, or pathological predator. I know this visit to the bloody house contributed to that fear and perhaps set the direction for my life course. I identified somehow with that murdered mother. I don't blame my sisters. They were only seven and eight years old. They really were just curious and had no intention of harming us. A deep fear of being murdered with my mother by an insane man, was part of my early psychic awareness, and I am sure I was reliving a past life, or just had absorbed the energy of that murder.

Soon we moved into a new house on Bradley Road, which was out in the country quite a ways from where we lived on State Street. With the help of an architect, my parents designed and built the house of their dreams: a large four-bedroom colonial. Sally and I had our own room with lots of room for toys and games. The house had a utility room with washer and dryer, a pantry joining the kitchen, and a mudroom off the garage, where we could sit and take off boots. It had laundry shoots and two and a half baths, and a huge backyard. We had a full basement, and a room for canned goods that we called "the bomb shelter," where we could stay in case of nuclear war. There were enough shelves for all seven of us to sleep on, or so my sisters and I imagined. In reality, the shelves were only about a foot wide, but we pictured our family surviving there for some time.

The girls' bathroom was right off our bedroom. It had a door that went from our room to the bathtub area. As you entered the bathroom from the hallway, it had two sinks and mirrors on three sides, so the girls could all work on their hair and makeup at the same time. It had two sliding doors, one dividing the sinks from the toilet area, with another one from the toilet area separating the closet, shower and bathtub area. The door to our room was across from the closet. This was a bathroom that five girls could use simultaneously. This was a far-cry from the single bathroom for everybody on State Street with one small mirror over the sink, and a huge claw-footed tub and shower.

Soon after our arrival to the new house, I remember vividly getting into the bathtub one night, with my mother helping Sally and me bathe. I sat down between my "imaginary friends," Diane and Frieda, in the warm bath water. My sister Sara tried to come in after me and I shooed her out of the tub, "You are stepping on Diane and Frieda!" I shouted at her.

My mother calmly asked me, "Who are Diane and Frieda?"

I said, "They are my friends, can't you see them?! They are right here!" I showed them where they were sitting. Sally stood up, shocked, and my mother wrapped her in a towel and held her.

"Okay, then, Sally get in over here." Mom said, pointing away from where I indicated my guides were. Diane and Frieda moved around, and then Sally got in a little bit more carefully. I was fine as long as she didn't step on them. Mom asked me what they looked like and how long they had been around me.

"They came when we moved here," I said. "Diane has blonde hair and Frieda has braids, like me."

Later on, I was quite grateful that my mother never judged me or told me I was crazy, like some of my medium friends who were admonished in their childhoods. She just listened and acknowledged my experience.

The Bradley Road house had lots of trees around it, and a creek down the road. Other houses had just been built and still others were being built on our street and behind our house on Orchard Way. Large oak trees were all around the house. One was on each corner of the property in the back and one in the front, along with a large tree my parents preserved to shade the patio. The back yards of the houses on the two streets made a kind of green beltway that ran down to the creek, which was down the hill in the woods.

Nature was the main theme for me as a child on Bradley Road. My best days were spent outside, whether in summer or winter, playing with my sisters and the neighborhood children. We were outside in the summer from sun up to sun down, breaking only for lunch. It was a wonderful life on Bradley Road. Throughout that time and into high school, I felt spirits around me. Mostly I ignored them or just said, "hi", acknowledging them but not engaging them in conversation.

Summer Camp and Colorado

During the summer vacation between my sophomore and junior year in High School, my oldest sister Kisti, who had married Sidney Beckwith from Michigan, had the first grandchild in the family. They named her Lysne. My parents decided we should go as a family to visit Kisti, Sid, and Lysne, who lived in Crested Butte, Colorado.

Sometime before visiting Colorado, I had written my will; somehow I knew that I would die soon. I didn't tell anyone I did this. But I left it in the top drawer of my bedroom desk for my mother to find when they cleaned out my room after my death.

That Summer, Sara and I were going to a Lutheran camp in South Dakota first and we would take the bus to Colorado Springs, where we would meet Kisti and Sid, then Mom and

Dad would join us later. During my time at the camp, I experienced for the first time, how nature and spirituality work together.

The camp in the Black Hills outside of Custer, South Dakota was set up like a fort with teepees nearby. The camp had two areas you could stay in, the teepees or the fort. I was in the fort with a group of four other girls. Sara was in another tower of the fort. We were very close to Crazy Horse Memorial, which was just getting underway at the time. We took a ten-mile hike through the woods to the memorial on one of the days. It was beautiful with pine trees and birch trees scattered everywhere over hills and valleys.

During that week Margo, a friend at the camp, felt moved to get baptized. She asked if I would go with her and be a witness for her baptism. I felt honored, so I told her yes of course. Later that afternoon, with the wind howling and an icy chill coming from the mountains, we followed the minister and his wife and a few camp counselors into the woods. The birch forest we wandered into was beautiful, with white bark against a roiling gray sky. It was a blustery and cold day for the summer. The wind howled through the trees, and we had to wear coats that day, the chill was biting.

When we arrived at a small clearing, the minister gathered the six of us into a circle. As soon as the minister opened the service for Margo, the wind stopped immediately. There was not a breath of wind. We could hear it below in the valley, but it was not coming into the birches. We were able to carry on the service with still silence all around. At the end, as he declared that my friend had been received into the company of Christ and then ended the ceremony, that very second, the wind began again as fiercely as it had been before. We all noted the change before heading back to the camp. As we walked in silence back to the Fort, I was in awe. This was the power of nature working in cooperation with us.

Later that week, we enacted the crucifixion of Christ, which was held outside. The storms came up as the crosses were being erected, and 'Jesus', one of the counselors, was tied to the cross. We walked up a hill to the crosses, but with a flash of lightning, the camp leaders thought it too dangerous to complete the event; instead we all ran for cover. I remember them getting 'Jesus' down really fast, as he was a sitting duck up on that hill! Nature was speaking to us. Something wasn't right about the attitude of the participants to carry out such an important reenactment. I remember being secretly glad to hear the rain pelt the roof overhead as we sat inside the dining hall.

At the end of the camp session, Sara and I were dropped off at a bus stop in Custer, South Dakota late at night. The bus was later than expected and picked us up at 2 a.m.!

It was a long bus ride from Custer to Colorado Springs. After many stops on the way, we found ourselves in Colorado Springs the next afternoon, and disembarked with crying babies and old drunks. Kisti and Sid picked us up and we drove up the mountain to Crested Butte. Sara and I were discovering Colorado for the first time.

Crested Butte was a small mountain town with a lot of hippies and artists living there. My sister Kisti was an artist. She and Sid had traveled in a hippie van from San Francisco to Colorado. They had been living in San Francisco with others of their generation and decided to leave the madness of the city when Lysne was about six months old, after a break-in. Kisti and Lysne were held at gunpoint in their apartment as the robber took their stereo and other valuables in the Height/Ashbury district. Sid packed them up that night and they left for Colorado the next day.

We spent a week with them hiking trails and exploring Crested Butte. It would be the first of several vacations I would take to Colorado to visit Kisti and Sid. During that visit, Kisti took us to the Ruby Queen Mine up in the mountains. There was a cemetery there, and we wandered through it looking at graves.

At the Ruby Queen mine cemetery, I had the strangest experience. I found my grave from a previous life! I was quite startled. I said nothing except to Kisti, but decided to join my family to see the mineshaft and the mechanics of a gold mine.

After we looked around, we were invited to the miner's office by a lone miner who was working the mine. When I looked out the window of his office, I could see there had been a landslide that covered the town. He then showed us a picture of the valley. On the table before the window was a picture of the town of Ruby Queen that existed in the 1880s. Suddenly, I felt choked by dust, and I could "see" that I had died in the town. My Grandfather Lysne, who was my father in that life, owned a grocery store. I was working in the store sweeping it, when everything happened so fast that we could not get out in time. None of us could. We all perished in the tumbling rocks and dust. I was eighteen in that lifetime when I died in the landslide near the Ruby Queen mine.

Finding my grave was quite an experience, and I was shaken by it for some time. I also realized that reincarnation was real, and I had just had a confirmation of it. I thought perhaps that finding my grave at the Ruby Queen mine was the impending death that I knew would soon occur in my current life. Part of me was relieved. Another part wondered if I might die soon anyway.

I told Kisti about the grave in the cemetery in Ruby Queen, and she confirmed that there were lots of ghosts around there. She could sense them, though she did not "see" their energy.

Near Death Experience

That fall of 1969, in my junior year in high school, some boys I knew gave me a sick mouse. They had found it in the parking lot of Guilford High School. I asked the Biology teacher, who was my teacher the previous year, if I could keep it in the lab until I could take it home. He agreed. After school, I packed the mouse in a perforated shoebox with some shredded toilet paper and took it home. I fed it with an eyedropper and tried to keep it alive. It died in my room at home next to my bed that weekend. The shoebox was less than a foot from my head.

We buried it in the back yard. That was the same weekend Senator Kennedy drove with Mary Jo Kopechne off a bridge in Connecticut. I named the mouse Mary Jo, after her. We buried the mouse on Monday in our backyard herb garden in a solemn ceremony with several of my sisters in attendance. Shortly afterwards, Nancy and Jill left to return to college in Iowa.

I started feeling bad right after we buried Mary Jo. At first it felt like the flu, then I felt dizzy and got a terrible headache. Neither aspirin nor ibuprofen seemed to cut the pain.

It was beginning of the semester at Guilford High School, and I had just completed a week or two of school. My boyfriend Jeremy was getting ready to leave for prep school on the East Coast. On Wednesday, Jeremy came over to say goodbye. I remember him being there, but I could barely see him. He appeared double and blurry. He was very worried about me because I was not getting better, I was getting sicker. I don't remember anything beyond Wednesday. I did not get out of bed for two days.

By Friday, I was in a coma. Mom found me in bed unconscious laying in my urine. She called an ambulance and rushed me to the hospital. I did not come out of the coma for a several more days. It was very odd to lose time like that, as I did not know how long I was in a comma.

Sometime during the next few days during the coma, I remember walking down a long white tunnel that was swirling and spinning. I saw the man at the end of the white swirling tunnel who told me it would be harder in the next life if I left now. "Harder! No way! How could it be harder! I am going back to finish what I came to do!" I said to him.

The next thing I knew, I was waking up in an old Swedish-American hospital room with a twenty-foot ceilings. I did not like that room, as it reminded me of the State Street house, probably built in the same era, and just a few blocks from where I had lived the first few years of my life.

I found myself with wires and tubes everywhere. I pulled everything out and went to the bathroom. All I knew was that I had to pee really badly; I didn't realize that they'd put in a catheter. My mother came in and asked the nurse what the hell I was doing out of bed. I could hear them arguing in the hall, and it felt like my head was inside a tin pan and they were banging on it, the sound was excruciating. I was crying and pleaded for them to stop shouting.

I was escorted back to bed by an angry nurse and an angrier mother, and didn't know where the hell I was. Dad came in and was trying to calm the whole situation down. I remember his calming voice, and tucking me back into bed.

"Where am I Dad?" I asked holding my head.

"You are at Sweds, Robby, in intensive care," he replied.

"Oh, what am I doing here?" I don't recall his answer and fell back to sleep again for some time. The next thing I remember was my Grandmother Lysne standing at the end of the bed wringing her hands. My sister Nancy was standing next to her. Nancy was supposed to be at college; she had just left the week before. This was so confusing. She was looking at me, calling my name.

I opened my eyes, and she said quietly, "Jeremy called." I didn't know who Jeremy was. It took me a minute. Then I remembered him, "Oh, I am suppose to be in love with him, aren't I?" I remember saying. I felt quite disconnected from my feelings. Then a second later, the feelings flooded in and I remembered I did love him. My nervous system was reawakening as the feelings flooded in. It was as if the electrical wires were coming back alive.

"Good Lord, she is awake!" Grandma Lysne shouted in her southern accent. She started to cry. I had never seen her cry before and could not understand why she would cry at the end of my bed. It made no sense to me. I was fine. I just had a terrible headache and a backache.

I had to re-remember everyone that came in to visit. It took a minute followed by a flood of feeling and memories. My synapses were coming back to life. Later, I realize that my physical body had died, and I was stirring back to life a little at a time as I remembered who people were, and in what context I knew them.

They moved me out of intensive care and down to another floor a day or two later, though I do not remember it. I just woke up in another room. Friends came in to visit and I had to remember them. It was so embarrassing, because these were my really good friends and I could not remember their names or who they were in relation to me until they gave me a get-well card with their names on it. Then I remembered them—Donna, Paula, Chris, Linda . . . Again, I experienced a flood of feelings and memories and then I could remember who they were. We had a "potluck" group that met every month. 'Of course,' I thought, 'that is who they are!' More flooding of memories came back as my synapses woke up. By the end of their visit, I knew who they were and had put the pieces back together again.

After a week in the hospital, it took me five more weeks to come back from that illness. I had been diagnosed with meningitis. (Inflammation of the layer around the brain and spine.)

When I returned to school five weeks after I came down with meningitis, I felt overwhelmed with sound and noise. I got sick to my stomach walking down the hall. Spirits were everywhere and it was quite overwhelming. Headaches and migraines occurred frequently. With the energy of 3,000 kids in one school, and all the dynamics of a high school clicks with boys and girls hormones running wildly, I think I was probably overwhelmed by poltergeists. Poltergeists are negative spirits that hang around teens with high and low emotions.

I started talking to my parents about going to prep school like Jeremy. My parents were dead set against it. They had two girls in private colleges, the oldest had just graduated from Kalamazoo College, in Michigan, and both Sara and I had just gotten out of a private junior high school at Keith Country Day School in Rockford. It would be like adding another year of college for me. But I was determined not to go back to Guilford. I just couldn't stand it. I really felt as though I would die if I stayed there. It was simply too overwhelming.

Finally, my sister Nancy talked to them about sending me away. Nancy showed them that I had needs that were different from the rest of my sisters and somehow she convinced them. I have no idea what she said to them, but they softened to the idea.

Jeremy came home for Thanksgiving break that fall. One afternoon we were sitting in their library at his house, and his mother Janelle overheard us talking. I was upset and crying because my parents were still against me going to prep school. Jeremy's mother walked in and took a book off the shelf and handed it to me: *Lovejoy's Guide to Prep Schools*. She helped me find some schools, write down the information, and we chose some possibilities together. I was so grateful to her.

When I returned home with *Love Joy's* in hand and my list, my mother gritted her teeth, and then she said, "Okay, but you will have to do this on your own, find the schools and figure out what you want, write and schedule the interviews. If you get in, I will drive you to the interviews, but not until then!" I think she was angry that I had this idea at all and probably did not know how to go about finding a prep school for me that would suit my needs. My parents were also very egalitarian raising the five of us. They wanted to treat all of us the same. So, what they did for one, they did for the rest of us. They were dead set against playing favorites and this was at the root of their resistance to prep school.

So I wrote to two schools and got the information and sent in my applications. I got into both schools. My poor Mother was as shocked as I was, since my grades were average, but she kept her promise and drove me to the schools for my interviews.

The Prairie school in Steven's Point, Wisconsin wanted me to go back a year. That was not going to work for me since I had a younger sister just one year behind me. So I decided on the more conservative school with uniforms, no boys, no cars, and a smaller student body. I wanted to focus on my studies and not be distracted by the partying and drugs and alcohol that were so rampant in the public schools. My class at Guilford High School was the first one where drugs were added to alcohol as favorite experimental experiences for teens in the late 1960's including acid. It created a lot of chaos.

The next prep school we attended was Kemper Hall in Kenosha, Wisconsin. There were nine seniors, counting me, and four students in the junior class, with less than one hundred in the whole school, kindergarten to grade twelve. I was so grateful. I knew in my gut that Kemper Hall would be a great experience for me.

Kemper was like Hogwarts in Harry Potter stories. The main house was the Kemper Hall Durkee Mansion, a three-story federal style brick structure with a spooky basement. Kemper Hall sat on Lake Michigan along 3rd Avenue in Kenosha. The school campus was composed of several brick buildings that had been built in different periods, all tacked together with odd hallways and stairs going up and down and crooked doors to match the warped floorboards. The result was a lot of stairs going in different directions and hallways that seemed to twist and turn for no reason. It seemed they were built as an afterthought connecting one building to another like a maze.

The school started in 1865 and became an Episcopal Girl's School and convent for Episcopal Nuns. At the time I attended it was co-ed until 7th grade, and a girl's prep-school through grade twelve. We were not being groomed for the convent. That ideology had been left behind years before. However, there were retired nuns that had taught and then lived in the convent section of the structure away from the school. Also our graduation gowns were reminiscent of the old convent "bride of Christ" idea as we wore white dresses and white veils for graduation.

An archway went through the building between the gym and the dining hall. The whole complex was built right on Lake Michigan. It was and is a gorgeous setting on about 25 acres of trees and athletic field. Most of the building was covered in ivy. The lake was like an ocean that crashed as we slept in our beds. The whole place shook in big storms. But I loved the buildings and felt safe in the storms even so.

When I entered Kemper, I felt I was in heaven. The ivy-covered arched driveway went through the building between the gym and the dining hall contrasted sharply from Guilford High's long modern barren halls with little history in them made of cement and steel. My sister Jill was in the first graduating class just a few years before I attended Guilford.

At Kemper, there was a haunted observatory that began in the basement and followed up the spiral staircase ending above the 4th floor. I loved the odd halls and funny doors and the four-story spiral staircase to the observatory. Kemper was haunted, there is no doubt about it, but all the spirits were benign, except for the one in the observatory, which we all avoided like the plague. We all heeded the warnings about trying to go to the observatory—as the warnings were given to us by the science teacher. Perhaps she did not want us messing with equipment, but I felt that she was even more scared about going up there than we were.

I could see the observatory from my bedroom window. My room was in the attic of the Durkee mansion where the seniors resided. My room had a round window complete with a custom-made screen. I sat in the window for hours watching the birds and reading or doing my homework. I loved the place and soaked in each day I was there like a sponge. I could stick my feet out the window on the sill and the heat would rise and keep them warm from the radiator as the draft went out the window into Wisconsin winter and pulled the heat with it. Radiators clanked loudly as they heated up from the basement. Those old radiator were either on or off. There was no thermostat. Hot or cold, that was it.

It was nice not to be competing with clothes, cars and boys with the other girls. We held dances, and organized events with local schools where there were boys however, and we made sure of that! I was on the committee to organize the events. Of course we snuck in alcohol and pot smoking by a few of us seniors occasionally.

It was at Kemper that I recall feeling/seeing spirits again, at least to some extent. There were presences everywhere. I remember sitting in the living room of the Durkee Mansion and seeing whole scenes pop into view with "Cotillions" or social dances and gatherings going back one-hundred years. The energies of those dances and the good times were still there playing on in the living room! Sometimes I heard the piano playing in the front room. Others did not seem to hear it. But I knew there was someone there from the past whom had probably died some time ago, still living as though it was going on. One girl from the class before us had died in a car accident the summer before I started school, so I wondered if it had been her.

That was the hardest and best year of my life school-wise. I had five subjects, I was the yearbook co-editor, and I was vice-president of the senior class, vice-president of student council and on the fire council. I had never been part of the school politics before. It was great, as they 'needed' me because we had such small classes. It was the best year of school with friends that I have ever had up until that point of my education.

Near the spring break of his school, Jeremy came to visit me at Kemper, and he broke up with me. We agreed to stay friends, and we did, even to this day.

I had never felt such an instant affinity with other students, until years later in my 30's when I attended graduate school in California, where 90 students bonded over the material we studied at Mathew Fox's Institute in Culture and Creation Spirituality (ICCS) at Holy Names College, in Oakland, California. That was also an amazing year.

Living at Kemper you could feel the transition from the past to the future, the senior tea, the dances, the plays, had all been done by all the other classes since the beginning one-hundred and one years before. We did Brecht on Brecht, and hemmed our dresses like mini-skirts. We had formal teas where we needed to wear white gloves, hats and dresses. I sewed my own uniforms for dining hall, and I bought the navy blue pleated wool skirts and my Kemper Hall blazer with the gold emblem on its breast pocket. We had few clothes with us, beyond our uniforms, a few dresses and skirts, boots and mini-skirts, however we rarely wore them except to go out on Friday or Saturday nights when we had to be chaperoned by a teacher or an adult.

There were rituals and traditions that we followed. I felt

the solemnity of them. I learned about the importance of ritual at Kemper Hall and from the girls at the school. We had two school teams, the Sisis and the Kukus. Some of us, to this day, identify with one team or the other. Many of the girls then are still some of my dearest women friends today.

One of them was Mary Ann Godfrey. She was the first girl I met there, and became my best friend almost immediately. Mary was full-blooded Lakota Sioux Native American. She and I smoked cigarettes together at night, usually in her room, as it had two small rectangular attic windows close to the floor. Her room was less visible to the night guards, as her windows faced the chapel roof. We sat by the window in the dark. The small window ledge perfectly held the can with water we used to douse our cigarette butts when we were finished or when the guard came by outside the windows.

In our late-night rendezvous, I often asked her about her family, her tribal traditions, and what they practiced at home. But she was raised Episcopal, so she was not familiar with Lakota traditions. When she went home for breaks, she began to ask her grandfather things about their tradition. When she returned she would tell me stories.

Two weeks before we graduated, I met a new guy, and started dating him. He went to a private school in Racine that we had come for a dance at Kemper. We stayed together all through college. His name was Peter and his family lived a few blocks away in Kenosha.

After graduating from Kemper, Mary Ann went to Europe as a foreign exchange student in Germany. Germans love Native Americans, so she was asked even more questions that year. When she went back to South Dakota she sat her grandfather down and he told her more stories. Then she got involved in the Native community when she returned to the states. The Wounded-Knee takeover occurred for a short time while she was gone and the whole year after she returned from Germany.

In the spring of my sophomore year and her freshman year in college, she invited me to visit her in South Dakota during spring break. I was going to the University of Wisconsin,

Milwaukee, she was going to Lower Brule Community College, in Lower Brule, S.D.

I drove out to South Dakota alone in my mother's "banana boat," a Chevy Impala, which had a yellow body and black roof, and visited Mary. It was my first road trip on my own and my first experience of native ceremonies.

That same year I learned to meditate through Transcendental Meditation techniques of Maharishi Mahesh Yogi. The two spiritual practices seemed to be a part of my life from that very early time, meditation and Native American lodges and ceremonies, sky-based, and earth-based respectively.

The week that I was with her was the most amazing week for me up until that time of my life. I was immersed in meeting her friends, most of whom were Lakota. In 1973 when this took place, a lot of young men had long "hippie" hair. But all of the native men had long hair, even older ones. It was a form of pride, as traditional native men did not cut their hair.

At the time, I thought their black hair was beautiful. I still find myself attracted to darker complexioned men with longer hair to this day. I did not know it then, but later I learned that many Native American men were forced to cut their hair when whites occupied their lands and they were put onto reservations. Perhaps this was a throwback to biblical Samson myths, where men were forced to cut their power when they cut their hair.

While I visited Mary in South Dakota, many people came from Wounded Knee to report on what was happening in the siege. A child was born and someone was killed inside the schoolhouse that the Oglala Sioux were occupying on the Pine Ridge Reservation on the other side of the state. An FBI agent was killed too. That was the week I was in South Dakota with Mary, out near Brule River Reservation, close to the Eastern Boarder of South Dakota.

We did my first Native American sweat lodge together during the week I was there, and I will never forget it. The lodge was a dome made of willows covered in canvas. Inside was space to sit around an empty pit that would receive hot rocks for this ancient purification ceremony. Outside the lodge a fire was heating up hot stones. We changed into shorts and tee-shirts, and went inside the sacred lodge with towels wrapped around us.

Somehow, they were able to get the lodge leader out of jail to do the ceremony. I don't recall his name, nor what he was in jail for, but it was common for young men of color to be in and out of jail at that time. He wore long raven black hair and had beautiful skin. He was not happy to do this sacred ceremony for a white girl. But Mary was clear that she wanted to share this with me, and I was very glad to share the experience with her.

Inside the lodge, I remember hearing songs and the drum, and I remember chanting and saying prayers. It was hot and dark, like returning to the womb of the Earth. I felt at home and yet in an entirely new place at the same time. It was a strange feeling.

Something in me felt I had done this before. It was very confusing for me because I was white, but I was home nevertheless. That was my first sweat lodge or sacred lodge experience. I don't recall specific spirits, but I do remember the energies as we sat in the dark. That is, energy swirled inside the lodge with the prayers. Today I would say that the forces of nature were swirling inside that lodge with our prayers.

It would take another fourteen years before I did another sacred lodge at a woman's retreat in Canada with a Native American woman and my friend and teacher. That Fall, after I had my first lodge with Mary Ann in 1973, I would start attending lodges once a week for the whole year of graduate school in my mid-thirties in 1987.

Aside from my experience with the ghosts at Kemper Hall, I pretty much ignored my psychic gifts until I was out of college and living on my own. However, as an art major, I often drew and painted the energy in clouds with oil, pastel, or watercolor. And I was excited to express the energy of the air, even in white on white paintings with pale watercolor washes. To me it was about energy and entities that lived around us, but I never told anyone about that inspiration.

After graduating from the University of Wisconsin-Milwaukee with a B.F.A. in painting and drawing, I lived in Milwaukee with two friends from Kemper Hall, then with my college boyfriend and another roommate who was a friend of ours. I found a job working at a needlepoint shop painting canvas designs. My boyfriend was getting ready to go to work and would move home with his parents to Kenosha for a while. I began thinking about going on another adventure--perhaps on a charter sailing boat--maybe I could crew aboard someone's boat!

Often I took the train south to Evanston to see my elderly grandparents during college. One of those adventures was to visit Grandma and Grandpa Heerens before I decided on the next steps. That was the last trip I would take to Evanston—it was the week Grandpa died.

Grandpa Heerens, cousins Karen, sisters Jill, Nancy, Grandma Heerens, Robin, cousin Wanda, sisters Sally, Kisti

Grandma and Grandpa Heerens

Grandpa Heerens and baby Robin

Chapter Two
Launching into My Life

The summer after my Grandpa's death in the spring, I found myself heading for a party at a swimming pond in central Michigan with my mother and sister Kisti. I had moved out of my rental place in Milwaukee, broke it off with my boyfriend who I had since Kemper Hall for five years, and was living temporarily at my parents' home. Mom and I were visiting my sister Kisti and her husband Sid and their three kids. The party was being held at an old gristmill owned by their friend Dewey and his brother Timmy Carter, who were launching the reopening of the Waterloo Grist Mill. This time it would be named Carter Mill Works. Timmy was opening a shop to make custom furniture for people. At least that was his plan, as he had just began.

I had met Dewey several years before at a Thanksgiving gathering at Hatsy's and Pappy's Beckwith's house, Sidney's parents. They lived on a small farm at the edge of Stockbridge, Michigan about fifteen miles from Waterloo where the Mill was located. Kisti and Sid had bought a property on the other side of the county about forty-five minutes from Waterloo and were building their own house while raising their three children. At the time, they lived in Eaton Rapids, Michigan, about a half hour away from the Mill.

This was the first time I visited Waterloo, which really was more of a state of mind than a town. There was no central main street, just the junction of three roads that wound around the kidney shaped pond from different directions.

Back when the Mill was operating to grind flour for the community, the pond had been emptied weekly. Old timers reported to us that when the pond was drained, that it stunk to high heaven, until the pond filled up again. Now there was a steady release of water over the dam, which not only made an ideal sound, it also kept the pond at a good depth for swimming. It also housed fish, turtles, garfish, and kingfishers who flew over the pond every morning.

When we arrived for the party, the Mill Pond was still, except for people splashing in the water and jumping off the dam. Lily pads were growing in the water beyond the dam, and blooms dotted the surface. There were about five houses visible around the pond. Trees and shrubs lined the water, and the rolling countryside, with trees and green hills surrounding the Village of Waterloo, which consisted of a country store across the water from the mill and the few houses we could see around the pond.

Since I knew very few people at this party and loved to swim, I decided to join them in the pond. I dove in as soon as I could, and found an inner tube and floated out far away from the thirty or so people gathering for a potluck and conversations.

As I was struggling to get inside the giant tractor tube, Dewey's brother Timmy, who I hadn't yet met, swam up to me and held one side of the tractor tube and said,

"You better be careful, the garfish bite."

"Garfish do not bite!" I slid into the inner tube and swam away. Actually, I did not know what garfish were.

For some reason, my dismissal drew him closer, and he started flirting with me out in the middle of the pond. His girlfriend gave us contemptible looks from shore and obviously was not happy about our connecting. We spent most of the time talking to one another during the rest of the party, and Timmy did not seem too concerned about her jealousy. I did meet a lot of other nice people that my sister knew at that party besides Timmy and Dewey.

As it turned out, Timmy had traveled to Florida and Europe working as a square rigger in the North Sea on ships with names like The Black Pearl. I was fascinated and somewhat smitten. I told him about my dream to crew on a charter boat and he started helping me make plans. He was not holding on, he was encouraging me to follow my dreams. 'Okay, this is a man I could be with,' I thought. 'Besides the fact that he has a girlfriend.'

Mom and I stayed at Kisti's and Sid's until the end of the week. We drove to the Mill once more for a brief afternoon visit. Mom had left a dish there and wanted to retrieve it. Timmy and I took off and went for a long walk while Mom and Kisti visited with Dewey. They were having tea and Dewey showed them around the Mill.

The floor was newly laid with red bricks that Timmy and Dewey had scavenged from old buildings. The beams were exposed and contrasted beautifully with the white plaster walls inside. I fell in love with the place. Some of the old beams were 14 to 18 inches square. These were old growth trees cut for the mill's construction. Everything was pegged; there was not a nail in the place except for the siding that was nailed with square, forged nails. Later I found out it was built in 1837, one of the first places built in the area. Every village needed a mill to grind grain and the Waterloo mill and pond were constructed for that purpose.

Timmy and I connected quite well as we went on a long walk in the woods, and we decided to stay in touch after that. In those days you had to exchange landline phone numbers, and write letters, as there were no cell phones.

After I returned to Illinois with my mom, Timmy and I continued to talk to each other by phone. A few weeks later, I left on a bus to get to the airport to go to Fort Lauderdale, Florida. My parents gave me their blessing, and I took the money I had saved from my work in the needlepoint shop and left for Florida with an extra $300 my Dad slipped to me as I got on the bus. His vote of confidence in me with the cash was unlike my mother's worry. I felt great support from both in different ways.

In Fort Lauderdale, I got a room at a Motel 6 and ate next door at Denny's. My waitress, Suzie, was very friendly. We struck up a friendship, as I came back to eat at Denny's every day. Her boyfriend Skipper was a charter boat captain off Bimini and taught people how to dive. After talking with Captain Skipper, he hired me as a cook on his scuba charter. They would not be ready to leave for several months, so I found a place to rent by the week.

As it turned out, Suzie and Skipper needed me to housesit and babysit for Skip's twelve-year-old daughter while they took care of business in another state. They paid me for the week, and I was settled in within two weeks of being in Florida at Suzie's and Skipper's house.

Their house was just a few blocks from the Unity Church, which had welcomed me earlier that month. It was the first place I headed for after landing in Ft. Lauderdale. It seemed like a good place to meet like-minded folks. While there, I met Rick and Jenny (Jeni) Prigmore at a healing service. Rick was a bit like my Grandpa Lysne. He was a large man with big warm hands. He was also a minister and hands-on healer. Jenny was lovely and very caring woman who worked as a dental hygienist. Rick was running a healing church service for anyone who needed it.

I was really happy being on my own. I was housesitting and taking care of Jackie, Skipper's daughter, and he gave me a van to drive us around. I was settled in for now, but I could hardly wait for my adventure with Captain Skip and Suzie.

To my surprise, Timmy wanted to come down to Florida a month after I got settled. I was glad he wanted to come, and shocked when he actually did it. After picking up Timmy at the airport and spending a few days together, Timmy proposed! I was quite startled, and felt a lot for him, but I wasn't sure I could just up and marry him. We had known each other for just over two months total, mostly getting acquainted by phone.

Before I decided whether or not to marry him, I felt the need to take a walk by myself, without him, to decide what to do. I had thought this was the time for an adventure on my own. I wanted to explore the world. I loved him, or so I thought. We were certainly passionate. But was the timing right? Was I supposed to marry him? What about my new job?

I really wanted to learn how to scuba dive and cook for Captain Skipper's charter boat.

It was just before Halloween. I walked to the parking lot of the Unity Church just down the street. Night blooming jasmine flowers were fragrant in the yards of neighbors. As I sat on the curb in the dark, I decided to ask the universe, God, whatever was out there, should I marry Timmy?

As I prayed, I suddenly felt a group of Native American spirits join me in a kind of waking dream. We were inside a teepee smoking a sacred pipe, or Chanumpa, and I heard them praying in Lakota. All the men were in white buckskins. There were no women as I recall. When they passed the pipe to me, I took it to my chest and held it as I prayed with the Lakota elders. I felt the answer that came was a "yes." Though clearly it was my decision, the prayers with the pipe helped me immensely. Then I felt their energy fade. I said thank you to the elders as they receded into the dark stary sky. I knew I was not alone making this decision.

This experience in the virtual teepee touched me deeply. Though I was certain I was making the right choice, I never told Timmy about the visit from the Lakota elders. I told Rick and Jeni about my vision, and they understood. Rick, being a minister, was also a mystic. Timmy was not a mystic, and not interested in spirituality. He was rather anti-religion of any kind due to his strict Dutch-Reform background he was raised in.

Rick tried to offer us counseling before we took the big step. Timmy flew into a rage about it, as he did not want Rick's advice nor interference. He was sure I was "the one," and that was that. In hindsight, I would have stopped the whole thing, right then and there, and asked Timmy to wait, but I was a romantic at heart and ignored this obvious warning sign. Perhaps it was part of my life lessons.

That was the end of October in 1976. We were married on Monday, November 1st at 9:30 in the morning by Rick and Jenny Prigmore, and an elder witness we called Gramps, on a Fort Lauderdale Beach. It felt as though it was meant to be.

The presidential election was raging, and a day later,

Timmy Carter won. I thought the name was ironic—and what he had wanted over my doubts. We called our parents and surprised them with the news. My mother almost fainted. My father's reaction was typical for him: "For Godsake, who'd ya marry?"

When Captain Skipper and Suzie returned, they brought Skipper's other two children from a previous marriage to Florida with them. He and Suzie had rescued them from his alcoholic and abusive ex-wife. Evidently the kids had called him in a panic the week before. The courts were not helping, and he decided to move them to Bimini to protect them from her rants and abuse and the court system that did not favor fathers.

After they told me the story, I told them I had gotten married and was going to go back to Michigan. I couldn't work for the charter, and the Captain would have to find a new cook. As it turned out, the Captain did not leave the harbor until the end of January due to bad weather, and he didn't hire anyone until he was sure he could go out to sea.

Timmy had already left before Skip and Suzie returned, and I followed him a few days later, as he had to find a place for us to live. So I felt that in the long run, our marriage was meant to be. At least we had karma we needed to clear!

When I arrived at the Detroit airport, Timmy picked me up in his old blue Ford truck. The truck was dented and had chipped paint, but I didn't care. We were happy to be together again and very much in love.

We moved into an apartment upstairs in an old farmhouse above the Reithmiller's who owned a Centennial farm. It was about a mile from Waterloo and only a half-hour from my sister Kisti's and brother-in-law Sidney's house in Eaton Rapids, Michigan. We eventually moved into the Mill and enjoyed country life, only a ten-minute drive to Chelsea, Michigan.

The old miller's house around the corner from the mill was haunted; so were several old farmhouses nearby. Since someone was living in the miller's house, I didn't pay attention to the ghost that eventually did visit me one day later in our marriage.

For the most part, Timmy and I were good together. However, I would later find out that he sometimes burst into rages from time to time, as he had with Rick, and that was difficult for me. I called him my "boy-man," as sometimes he acted quite adolescent for his age, and other times he was really a grown man in his actions. It took us about two years to really get to know each other. We were quite in love, and I felt more certain as time went on that I had made the right decision. I could manage his rage, and I soon found out what 'landmines' I should avoid when presenting things that were important to me. His talents were amazing; he played the guitar and sang, and we often had wonderful gatherings with live folk music in abundance. Our artistic interests dovetailed nicely. I often consulted with him on his designs and I inspired some of his furniture as well.

While Timmy pursued his custom furniture business, I worked at a bookstore for two years, and then started caretaking special needs kids. I also taught art history in the local junior college in Jackson, Michigan. Finally, I got a job as a curator at a small museum in Jackson, the Ella Sharp Museum. Timmy continued to struggle with his furniture business. I was the one bringing in a steady paycheck, and health insurance.

I loved my job and loved traveling back and forth on the winding Michigan roads. Many of our friends were mutual friends of Kisti and Sid's. Some were clients that Timmy had acquired in Ann Arbor who ordered furniture from him. Others were from the museum and the arts community, especially in Jackson. Kisti and I went to Unity Church in Jackson and in Lansing from time to time. I was on the dance council board, and in my spare time, made artwork and exhibited my art as far and wide as I could. As a curator, I formed a group of women artists, including Kisti, and we called ourselves the Red Dye #2 Artist Group. We had a good life.

However, as time wore on, I felt restless. I was not sure why, except that I felt something was missing in my life. That is when I met Jeanette Snyder, an astrologer.

Jeanette became my fairy godmother. She was in her

eighties, with sparkling violet eyes and a laugh that was so enchanting. Her smile made her eyes into triangles with purple-blue in the center, the color of Elizabeth Taylor's eyes. She was so wise I felt as though I could sit at her feet and soak in her wisdom all day. She wore purple and white, her house was purple and white, and even her miniature poodle was white and sported a purple collar. I would learn later that purple was the color of the sixth chakra, or third eye, the place of vision and insight.

Kisti discovered Jeanette at the Unity Church in Lansing, Michigan. Jeanette often had a flyer posted at Unity regarding her astrological services. On my first visit, after introducing us, Kisti went shopping and left me with Jeanette. I told Jeanette that I felt I may not be living out my destiny, and I wanted to be sure I was. I loved my husband and I had a good job. Why was I so restless?

She said the restlessness was due to my need to grow. It helped me to move me on, and not be contented with what I had currently. Not much of what she said I was to do in this life matched my current life at all. This scared me, because I wanted passionately to live my purpose. I think this urge came from my near death experience, and I knew life was short and I HAD to fulfill what I came to Earth to do. I will never forget her, as some of the things she taught me still echo through me today.

My visits were always mind-blowing. I felt as though she was telling me about my future, even though, quite often, I did not know what she was talking about.

Just before I met Jeanette for the first time, I had started dancing classes with the Jackson Area Dance Council. I took classes from a teacher named John, who drove the sixty miles from Ann Arbor to Jackson every week just to teach our advanced dance class. He was a gay man, who was a very good dancer, and had a dance company in Ann Arbor.

I did a workshop at Unity in Jackson, Michigan, and a woman who offered it, talked about our lives and how we could ask to find our path. She said, "If you want to do what you are here to do, ask God to show you what you are meant to do. Be aware that your life could radically change. But if you pray for what you are here to do, God will show you." So I did. I made the prayer to show me what I was here to do. Jeanette helped me too.

At one point during this time, I started having a spontaneous heart opening. Everything was about hearts. I made handmade paper-heart sculptures, some were large, others small, one was three feet tall, out of basket material. The three dimensional heart bounced while beating if anyone touched it. I made a feather sculpture of a heart bursting open. Feathers reminded me of the Native American world, so I used them profusely. My source for feathers, were geese around the many ponds and at the Mill Pond, as we often had dozens of geese coming in for a landing. Canadian geese lose their pinfeathers in the summer when raising their chicks. So we had plenty of them. Michigan is on a flyway for flocks of various birds from geese to sand hill cranes. They landed often in the cornfields behind our home.

The heart opening was an amazing experience. My heart felt like a flutter of petals opening continuously. I often thought of St. Theresa of Avila, though I didn't know much about her life. I had seen the Bernini sculpture of her in the Cornaro Chapel, in Santa Maria della Vittoria, in Rome as a freshman college student. Somehow, intuitively, I knew that I should talk with John about what I was experiencing.

When I told him about my heart opening, he smiled and said "Oh, that happened to me, too. Just enjoy it, honey!"

I was so grateful for his acknowledgement, as there were not too many people I could talk to about that experience in Jackson, or so I thought.

When I think of the sequence of events now, I see that my prayer to find my path, and my spontaneous heart opening led me right to Jeanette. I had to know my purpose, and while I loved art and curating, I was not sure this was my larger destiny.

The first memorable thing Jeanette said to me was, "You and I have the same Dharma/Karma, honey. That is, eventually you will be like me, the person sitting on the side of the road that others come to for advice. But you have to learn to go with the flow. Sometimes you will be busy with clients or people that come to see you, and other days, you can't get the pencil sharpened to write down anything for them on their charts! Not that you will be into astrology, but you will give advice and help others, as I am doing. You will do this later in your life, but first you have to live a little!" Then she winked at me.

Another thing she said to me was, " Your life lesson is patience! You don't pull up the flowers to check on the roots, now do you? You have to wait for them to establish themselves. So take your time."

I had no idea whether I would eventually be seeing clients, or if anything she told me would happen or not. I liked my work curating exhibits and educating the public at the museum in Jackson. I was not in any particular wisdom seat, but I did put exhibits together and bring ideas to others through the Arts Go to School program. That was a lot of fun. I was passing out art historical information to docents and kept the supplies and art pieces intact with educational information on the back of each picture. We had about 150 pictures and 20 objects from our collection that we made into hands-on touchable objects like spears, and stone grinding mallets, and baskets that we put into portable cases. Each object or picture had a tag that I made about ways to share it with the students, so the docents, who ranged from uneducated farmers wives, and blue-collar mothers, to educated businesswomen, could pick them up, read the back, and present to students.

Since then, as I reflect on what Jeanette said to me, I have learned to go with the flow. Today, I do sit by the "roadside" and wait for people to ask for advice and wisdom that I have to offer. All of those things that Jeanette predicted from my birth chart are true today, but back then, I thought she was a little crazy, as I did not see at all for myself what she was talking about. She had a sign on her wall that read: "We all begin like lumps of coal, and it takes a lot of heat and pressure to make us into the diamonds that we truly are." Every time I read that, I thought, "Boy, you can say that again!"

Her response to my trepidation of the future was, "I hear it, you're afraid. You are a bit of a worrywart you know; I can see that in your chart. Trust and let go. Your higher self will guide you; you have a lot of work to do here. Fear just attracts to you what you don't want. Love, love, love, it is all about love. Just follow your heart; it will give you the life lessons you need to have. You will have to surrender. Just ask God to show you what you are here to do."

I did listen to that wisdom. It became my prayer, day and night, "Please show me what I am here to do." That was about six years into my marriage to Timmy.

Looking back at Jeanette and her wisdom, I can still see her smiling, her bright twinkling eyes sparkling with the same Dharma/Karma as me. Her advice has lasted a lifetime.

The problem was, I had to hide all of this spiritual adventuring with Kisti from Timmy, because he had thrown the spiritual baby out with the bathwater and was dead-set against religion or spirituality of any kind. As our marriage continued, he got more set in his stance against God or faith. My influence did not soften him in the least. He had been born into a family of Dutch Reform Calvinists. (His mother was Mennonite originally.) His father was quite die-hard in his faith. He believed that you had to go to church, and believe the way he believed. We were sinners and we needed redeeming. That was his father's stance. Period. Timmy said repeatedly in a thousand ways, "NO WAY!"

Beginning as a Medium—Suicide of a Friend

During my marriage to Timmy, we had a lot of friends that we met in part through other friends and relatives. Timmy's brother Dewey was an emergency room doctor and made friends with Brian and his wife Mary, who was a colleague in the emergency room. We had been invited to a number of parties where Brian and Mary hosted gatherings on their small farm.

One fall day, we got a call from Dewey that Brian had committed suicide. Every one of our friends were as shocked as we were at his death. Our friend Brian had died of asphyxiation in his car in his garage. He left a five-year-old son and his wife, Dr. Mary.

This sudden death impacted me a great deal, as he had a pretty ideal life, or so I thought. Brian had been an engineer, but he retired early and developed a peach orchard he had planted. He was running the business out of his home. We did not know he was so depressed and had that inherently from his father and brother.

After the funeral service in Jackson, Timmy and I met there, then drove home separately, as he had come from our home at the Mill, and I had come from a meeting at my art studio with my art group, Red Dye #2.

Just as I was getting on the I-94 on-ramp after the funeral, I suddenly felt Brian, the deceased, in my car driving home with me in the rain. He seemed lost, sad, and confused.

"Brian, what are you doing here?" I asked him. I was angry with him. I had just watched his dear five-year-old son play with a skeleton-headed PEZ candy container under his coffin. His mother lifted him up to see his father inside, and he asked her, "Why won't Daddy wake up?" His son was too young to understand that his dad was not coming back. His mother was older, in her late forties, and their son had been a surprise in their later years. Brian was in his early fifties when he took his own life. I was crying a bucket of tears as I watched this scene at his wake.

"I, I feel lost, I don't know where I am," Brian said.

"You committed suicide, you died in your MG. You are on the other side, Brian."

"Oh," he replied. "I need help. You can help me. I know you can. I couldn't continue with the way life was. Depressed, I was so depressed. I couldn't face life anymore."

As he spoke, telling why he could not live anymore, I could see pictures of their life together, the arguments, and his concern for the effects of his depression on his family. His wife was absolutely committed to him and her son; she believed in that commitment from her Catholic background. She would never leave him. He had wanted a divorce because he didn't want to influence his son with his depression, not because he did not love him or his wife. He did not feel he was good for either of them. He felt unworthy. The more he spoke; I could see a line of suicides in his family—his father, an uncle, and a brother. The pictures flooded in. He did not want to burden his wife with his depression and its effect on her any longer.

"You are the only father he had, and now he has to live without one. How can you think he is better off?" I said, feeling furious with him.

"He is, believe me," Brian said solemnly. "He will have good men around him."

All the way down the freeway, I felt his angst, grief, and his depression.

"The trouble is, I don't know what to do now, " Brian said. "Nothing has changed. I am still depressed. I thought I would be relieved of it. But clearly I am not."

"Go to the light," I said bluntly. "You can't help your son unless you leave and come back. Just go to the light. Learn something about your own value, Brian."

Just then, as I was making my exit off the freeway to our home, not far from where he had lived with his family, I could see a light opening up above me through the rainy cloudscape around my car. Brian flew up and into the lighted tunnel. I sent a prayer for his healing as the light closed up after him, and the rain kept relentlessly pelting everything around me.

Outing Myself as a Medium - Another Kind of Wedding

Tim and I had been married for about six and a half years when we were invited to the wedding of his cousin in Grand Rapids, Michigan. I didn't know her well at all, though I had met her at an anniversary party for his parents a few months before, and at various family events over the years.

Tim's parents and cousins were members of the Dutch-Reform Church that followed the teachings of the Scottish theologian John Calvin. Tim told me that every Saturday from nine a.m. to noon the kids were forced to recite doctrine. Tim hated it vehemently. "Post-traumatic religious injury," I called it. We were returning to Grand Rapids for his cousin's wedding in that same synod. He was nervous and defensive even walking into another Calvinist church.

Inside this small church, Tim was jittery at best sitting in the pew waiting for the bride. He hated my interest in metaphysics and religion, especially after I had started attending a Unity Church in Jackson, and one in Lansing, where my sister went from time to time. Timmy made it clear he did not like me to attend even liberal Unity. I knew he could not control me, and I had to follow my own heart. So I lived a double life, quietly where I could; but sometimes I was not able to hide who I was.

When the music started to play, I turned and looked back to see the bride getting ready to come down the aisle. I saw her wipe away a tear. Then she stood up straight, and the song announcing the bride began.

As she floated past us, I could see a spirit behind her trying to let her know she was not alone. Her brother and her mother gave her away at the altar. Next to them was another spirit saying, "I'm here honey, I am here! Don't cry! I'm here!" The spirit was shouting into the bride's ear. Of course she could not hear him, but I could.

My wheels started spinning. Was this a forced marriage!? What was going on here? The spirit, who felt like someone she knew, kept trying to tell her, "I'm here, I'm here!" All through the wedding, I could see her love for her new husband and her pain of loss all mixed up like clouds over her head. I could not reconcile the mixture. As she managed a smile at her new husband, the spirit of someone—I guessed, her father, pressed on trying to communicate. "I AM HERE!"

Then I remembered Timmy's mother saying that the bride's father had terminal cancer. He had succumbed to the cancer just a few months before the wedding. Since I didn't know them except from family gatherings, the news about the father did not register for me until that moment when I saw her father trying to speak to her.

The reception, which was held in the church basement, opened out through the doors to beautiful crabapple trees blossoming along the path. The scent came into the reception as I asked my husband more information about his cousin, the bride, but he was clueless. He was drinking heavily and did not seem like a reliable source of information at that moment.

Finally, when the bride had greeted everyone and seemed to be somewhat alone, I went up to her quietly. After congratulating her and introducing myself again, I asked if she had lost someone recently.

"Yes, my father, he died a few months back, he was supposed to be here but he couldn't make it. He had cancer and it just went so fast."

I placed a hand on her shoulder to steady her. "Oh, I am so sorry to hear that," I said to her. "Well, I want you to know he was here, I saw him floating after you like a beacon of light. He was at the altar with you, trying to let you know that he was there with you. He kept his promise."

At that news, the bride burst out crying, and her husband came running to her rescue. "What just happened? What did she say to you?!" he demanded.

"No, Jason, it's alright. She just gave me the greatest wedding present I will ever receive. I'll tell you later." She threw her arms around me.

I gave the bride a hug and she managed a smile.

"He was here. I saw him," I whispered quietly in her ear.

"Thank you, thank you so much. You have no idea how much this means to me," the bride said emphatically.

"He loves you, he wanted you to know that he kept his promise to you. He is still here." We let go of each other and I joined my husband who was standing their looking rather aghast.

The crowd was thinning and we decided to leave too.

On our way out the door, Timmy demanded, "What the hell did you tell her?"

Under the crabapple trees, as the spring was showering us with petals, I said quietly, "You are not going to believe it, but if you have to know… I'll tell you when we get to the car."

I took the keys from him as he was too drunk to drive. We had a three-hour trip home.

When we got our seatbelts on, I told him the story of what had just happened. My husband, the rebel and atheist, was totally shocked.

"Jeeesus H. Keerist! Who the hell am I married to…!!!" he roared. He looked at me with such fear and trepidation that I thought he would jump out of his skin.

He rolled his eyes and banged the seat back with his back, slapping his arms over his chest in the car, and then turned his back to me and faced the door to get some sleep. He was also turning his back on me, which I felt like a slap.

I think the news that I could see spirits was overwhelming for him, especially since he was drunk. I hadn't told him, because it had never come up before. I hadn't said a thing to him about our friend Brian. He would have accused me of lying, or worse, that I was crazy and seeing things.

'Poor Tim,' I thought, 'he just doesn't get it … or me.' I knew I wasn't seeing things. I had been seeing spirits my whole life, and I was beginning to realize that I was living a double life: one with Timmy, and one with those who were more spiritually inclined and loved God. Timmy was angry with God, the church, everything having to do with spirituality or religion, and he was still reacting against his conservative punitive background. Nothing I tried to offer him seemed to influence his attitude or help him open up.

At that moment leaving the wedding, I didn't really care what he thought. I was just glad I could help the bride. She knew the truth I shared with her, and that was enough for me.

This was the first time I realized that I could help other people with my abilities, even though I had helped Grandpa and others here and there when it was appropriate. But, this was something else again. It seemed to change her life. Still, I did not think much of it. I was just grateful I could help her. It took several years before I would realize what I could do to help others with my gifts and talents. His cousin's reaction led me to believe that I was getting some kind of answer to my prayer.

At seven years of marriage, Tim and I were beginning to find large fractures in our relationship. I had tried very hard to get us into counseling for several years before this, but he always refused. After a particularly nasty argument, I insisted. I knew it was already too late, but I needed to try.

That was the same summer that the ghost came to visit me. One day I was sitting on the couch upstairs in our living room. The couch had it's back against the wall below a window that looked out to the Miller's house on the corner. I could see this ghost come through the window and sit next to me.

"Who are you?" I demanded.

"I live over there." he said, nodding to the little yellow house. "I'm the Miller."

"What do you want?" I asked.

"I really like children, I want you two to have children." He said in a sort of loving, creepy way.

"Well, I am not sure I want children. And I certainly don't want you influencing me. It is my decision! BE GONE!" I shouted. At that the ghost left and stayed over at the miller's house after that. I realized that all this baby talk I had been doing with friends and my sister, whether I wanted one or not, and whether Tim was a suitable father for a child, was being influenced by a ghost who wanted me to have kids! 'Enough of that,' I thought.

In the meantime, a little later in the summer, I decided to take the E.S.T. training (Erhard Seminars Training). Friends were going, and I got the feeling that it could help me; if it helped me, maybe it would help my marriage.

The training itself was a two-weekend workshop, where, in a large room with several hundred participants, you were asked to look more deeply into your cultural conditioning, your wounding, and your life history with relationships. I had never done that seriously before, so I thought I would try it.

Dave, who was my dentist, and a friend who had come to our parties, decided to attend the workshop, too. Both Timmy and I really liked Dave. He came by every other week or so to drop off his daughter, Amy, at our house when exchanging her with his ex-wife. They had done this exchange since their daughter was four years old; she was almost ten at this time. So Amy and I got to know each other well. I was really like an auntie to her, and I loved her like a daughter.

Dave and I decided to drive the hour and a half to Detroit together. In our minds, we were two friends traveling to Detroit together to attend this training. On the drive in, we began to share things with each other about our past that I could not share with Timmy. By the second weekend, I felt that I had met a man I could talk with who understood me, and my metaphysical interests. No more double life. While we stayed in integrity, and did not become entangled during the training, the Universe was definitely showing me there were other choices.

A month after the E.S.T. training, after a disastrous counseling session where Timmy walked out, I decided to leave him and go stay with my sister for a while. The next week, we had one more try at counseling. It did not work at all.

Now in my early thirties, I found myself getting divorced within months after the E.S.T. training experience. Later on, I discovered that many couples split after E.S.T. training unless they went through that experience together and were willing to process their feelings together.

Leaving Timmy and divorcing him was like the Apollo rocket letting go of its jet propulsion unit and flying off into space with just a capsule, continuing and reaching for the stars. That was me, I was finally free.

After a brief stay at Kisti's, I moved to Hatsy's (Hatty's) house in Stockbridge. Papa, Pappy or Dr. Sidney, Hatsy's husband, had passed away the year before. So she was happy to have someone live with her. I found a sanctuary at Hatsy's.

She had a studio I could use to paint and draw, and there were cross-country ski trails crisscrossing her land. We called her house Hatsy's Finishing School, as many young women, some granddaugters, others divorced nieces, or relatives like me, who spent time with Hatsy, were influenced by her conversation, wonderful cooking, and cultural interests.

Two months after Tim and I divorced, Dave and I got together. As I was driving with David one day, he asked me what I wanted. I said I needed to be supported so I could paint and draw and get a body of work together for shows. He agreed with this, and said he wanted to support me. The next spring, after quitting my job at the museum, I got a job at the library doing the graphic design and substituting at all the branches throughout the county. I also started painting a series of black and white charcoal paintings. By the following summer, I was showing my artwork at statewide art fairs and exhibits.

Dad and his friend John made a booth for art shows and a whole set up to hang my artwork. I was so happy, I was finally able to devote more time and energy to my artwork, which had also been a big frustration for me with Tim. Working at the library was my back-up, and it gave me money for framing, travel, and to help pay the bills.

David was also very connected to nature, and we often took long walks on his 150-acre farm. We so enjoyed being together. We skied through the woods, took saunas in his sauna, and jumped in the icy river afterwards. I wanted this relationship to work. I especially did not want to be alone. He was the answer to my prayers.

Nine months after moving into Hatsy's, I moved into Dave's house. However, what I didn't know was that I wasn't supposed to get into another relationship right after a divorce. Bad idea! I did not realize I was jumping from one frying pan into another. I got myself into therapy after the divorce, but it didn't help much. Nine months later, Dave had started building the studio of my dreams. I had about fifteen drawings ready to exhibit. It felt like the right time for a discussion about having children.

Shortly after building me the art studio—not more than a month after it was finished, we had the big talk about children. It was September. He did not want more children, as he already had a daughter and an extremely difficult relationship with his ex-wife. He also told me he was not as "into transformation" as I was. I wanted a child, and realized that my aversion previously was based on being married to Timmy. I wanted transformation as part of my life. That was the beginning of the end of our relationship.

He asked me to leave his home by the end of January. Needless to say, I had become very attached to him and my new studio and his 150 acre farm land. Besides feeling as though I had found "the one" in him, I was devasted. He was everything I had wanted in a man—smart, tall, dark, and handsome, and financially stable. He worked as a dentist, and was supporting me to some extent. He was also creative and liked building tables and cabinets. He really wanted that studio he had built me for his woodworking shop, and he withdrew from our relationship like a freight train in reverse, slow but relentless. The problem was that we kept dating even after I moved out. I realized this was my second biggest mistake.

I came out of this second relationship broken beyond recognition. Not because he was a batterer, he wasn't. But emotionally I came out battered, because I confused love and possession, love and ownership. I wanted to become a part of another, instead of standing on my own two feet. After all, my mother was part of my father, as he was the breadwinner and she raised us kids. They were a team, two halves of a whole, as was her mother and her mother's mother.

But I was a child of the 60s and a young adult in the 70s, so the times were totally different than the life she grew up in during the twenties and thirties, which included the depression between the two World Wars. My generation had the Vietnam War, and protests, and women's liberation. Women in my generation had to say an emphatic No!—to the long history of women—as objects or extensions of men. We were required by our own spirits to be our own persons, a whole person inside:

breadwinner and caretaker of ourselves, and families. Men had to shift, too. Their journey drew them into more nurturing, and connection with their feminine nature as well as their "doing" masculine nature. Even though I agreed philosophically with this theory, I resisted the actuality of it like mad. I was terrified to be alone on my own, even though I considered myself a feminist. I had to develop myself as a whole person, not a half of the other. This was why I had to be on my own.

On the night of my birthday just before I moved out of Dave's, January 3, 1986, I decided to take myself out to the woods for a ritual cleansing. David had a sauna on his land that we used frequently. After I knew that we were breaking up, and I was going to have to move on, I found myself on the birth night of my double golden birthday (33) going out to the sauna at two o'clock in the morning; it was about a half-mile walk from the house.

I was so full of confusion. Besides a move, I was uncertain that I would stay in Michigan. I was thinking about applying for schools, and did not know where I would be going, East coast or West, whether to focus on art of something else.

The sauna was an old log cabin that Dave had built himself next to a creek that ran through his property. After I built a fire and heated the rocks, I stripped down and laid down in the sauna, praying for direction. I splashed cold water on the rocks so the steam would rise and engulf me. After getting the Sauna heated up, I walked with my boots on through the snow to the nearby river. I had to break the ice to get through to the water with the bucket. I would douse myself with icy water, and then dive back into the sauna. The last time I came out, I did not pour cold water over me; instead I put on my boots, wrapped myself in my jacket and my grandmother's crocheted blanket, and walked into the woods. The air temperature was about eighteen to twenty degrees. But with the heat from my body and my blanket I was warm. The labor of love my grandma made me was purple and blue and maroon in zigzag stripes and fringe on the ends. I must have looked like a shadow as I walked out into woods. The moon was nearly full, so it reflected on the snow on this cold Michigan winter morning. I did not need a flashlight. I walked along the field and into the woods on a trail road big enough to drive a truck down. Finding a spot at a fork in the road that I knew in the woods, I wanted to sit and meditate at the crossroads. I put my jacket under me and kept the blanket around me. After a long time, maybe an hour, the sun was barely coloring the sky with a thin line of pale blue light along the horizon. I knew the coming year would be full of change, and full of challenge. So I stayed there listening, listening to the world dawning on my birthday.

Suddenly I heard a rustling in the bushes and three deer rose not twelve feet from where I was sitting. They stood up sleepily and stretched, then walked right past me, not smelling my scent because I had sweat it off in the sauna. Their musty scent wafted to my nostrils, and I could hear them breathing. I could have reached my hand out and touched them, but I sat still and let them pass. They walked right down the same trail I had come up, and one of the bucks had a five-point rack on its head. As I watched them, they walked into the brightening horizon into the cornfield. I felt a great peace. Whatever would happen this next year, would be fine. I was ready for the changes. I got up and followed the deer.

Several years later, I wrote this poem about my experience. It seemed to me the beginning of my new life.

Deerise

Four a.m.
    snow-covered Michigan morning
        sauna steam
    releases all scent
        from my body
            keeps me warm
    at my birth time the 3rd day of January, my 33rd year.
I walk out into snow-covered woods
    as a purple shadow
        as a long moon lit trail

                              bare trees arch over
          shadow fingers interlock

Wearing a lightning bolt blanket?
        crocheted by my grandmother
                smelling cold winter clear?
                        her arms still around me in her labor

I sit at the end of the road... in a crossroads
Moon a bright disk
        steam rises
                laying my coat down under me   boots on
settling in   sitting for my dive into self
        a soft gaze out sitting in shadow   waiting
waiting   listening to night
an hour passes
                    then a stirring near by
three deer rise behind me
            sleepy   waking slow
                    legs close enough to touch
                            to smell their musty fur
they saunter down the same trail I had come up
            a five-point rack buds on one in silhouette
                with the dawn sun
                    only a blue glow on one horizon lip
a threesome
        become shadow
            a wild must
                    gait along
saunter down,
            a moon-blue trail
trees arching over
                    I rise[1]
        By the end of January of 1985, I moved in with a friend, Marcia, who had been divorced after a marriage of thirty years.

---

1 'Deerise' was first published in Poems for the Lost Deer, published by Blue Bone Books, Santa Cruz, CA, 2014, page 6.

She had a room to rent, and I was a disaster and needed a place to stay and recuperate. The room I rented was small, but I had access to the large house and the lake below the house. I remember laying down on the bed in my new room for the first time and looking into the wall of mirrors on one side of the room. I honestly had no idea who that woman was in the mirror. I realized I did not know myself at all.

The library work helped a lot after leaving the museum. Because I was a nervous wreck, another friend said to me one day, "You are a mess! Why don't you take this massage class I just finished, you would love it! You get certified, and you can do massage instead of the library." Her command resonated with me deeply.

So I did.

On the second day of that class, Bob Brown, our instructor from Santa Rosa, California, was very clear: "Six out of eight of you are highly intuitive, and you need to develop your skills. We are going to rush you through the massage curriculum so you can begin to use what God gave you to use." Finally, I felt I was on track.

The next day we start to experiment with our intuitive skills after we had learned the format of his massage technique. That was the beginning of my massage career and the awareness that I could use my intuitive gifts to help others. It absolutely changed my life. My prayers were being answered. However, I had no idea at what cost when I had prayed for guidance a few years before: "Show me what you want me to do." I was being shown without a doubt. When one prays such a prayer, you cannot assume your life will stay the same.

I later took Past Life Regression training with Bob Brown. I also took several classes at the Unity churches in Lansing and Jackson on various healing topics. It was a rough landing, but soon I was working in my Chiropractor's office as a massage therapist. I loved the work, though I still worked at the library to pay my bills.

Slowly I was piecing the broken parts of myself together. My personal and spiritual progress became the most important thing in my life. I had been in three different places for nine months each. Now I moved out on my own to a small apartment on a farm in Parma, Michigan, on the property where I had taken the massage training. As a result, my life would change again.

Dad and Mom 1944

Kemper Hall Graduation class 1971

Robin in Kemper Hall bedroom window 1970

Mom and Dad in Pt. Lobos, CA 1993

Sisters, Cousins, and Aunt Priscilla, 1959

Sisters, Cousins, Grandma Heerens in a hammock, 1953

Chapter Three
Hiking Slowly Up the Mountain

Slowly I began to learn that if I was going to help others, I had to heal myself. I also realized that I had to open up to this spiritual life if I wanted to find more of my purpose. Part of my purpose would be spiritual, but I didn't know how to start. I began to realize that I had unexplored beliefs about religion, spirituality, myself, my family, roles, and the world at large.

Because I was brought up and confirmed in the Lutheran Church, and then joined the Unity Church informally, I was basically a Christian, but I had issues with dogma of any kind. Tim and I had agreed on releasing dogma in any religion.

I hated people telling me that you couldn't have a direct connection with God. I knew this wasn't true. I did have a direct connection, and I wasn't unusual—many people did. I got messages from God all the time if I listened. I was seeking something more authentic that was not filtered through a human mind, especially male minds and the patriarchal dogma that excluded the feminine. Nature was not included in most churches. The divine lived in nature too. This I knew in every fiber of my being.

What about women, why couldn't they be priests, or ministers, or rabbis? I had no idea what something more "authentic" might look like. I did know what was true for me, and I was beginning to develop my inner resonance with that truth. This was my "inner ding" as Louise Hay[2] often said.

For example, I didn't like the idea of Father, Son, and Holy Ghost. The Unity Church spoke of a truer trinity that was

---
[2] Louise Hay, Author of *Heal your Body*, and several other books, she started Hay House Publishing.

Father, Mother, and Child, rather than "Holy Ghost." Who was the Holy Ghost anyway? That term really confused me. No one taught me adequately about the Mystery. Lutherans were not interested in the Mystery or mystical revelations as Catholics were. I wanted to know more about Mystery and how it played out in my life. I wanted nature as part of my spirituality. Nature is what got me realigned when I felt confused, so I knew God was in nature, too.

After my divorce from Timmy, and the disastrous rebound relationship after him with Dave, I got into some groups that would help me make sense of what had just happened. I needed help. The ending of my relationship with Dave got me into many relational addiction groups, including Adult Children of Alcoholics (A.C.A.), AA (even though my parents did not drink, my grandfather Lysne did at one time) and Relationship Anonymous (R.A.), and other such 12-step groups, four meetings a week for months. I felt I was in recovery from failed relationships and relationship addiction. I learned that relationship addiction was where you put yourself last and everyone else first, especially a partner. It was also about requiring a relationship in your life even if you were being shown it was not for you, and you needed to know yourself better.

In my new tiny apartment, it was perfect to just be alone and do some self-reflection. I had never lived alone, so this was as good a time as any to find out what that would be like. I took a yoga class and started to discover who "I" was.

Everything I thought I knew was turned upside down. I started searching for answers—Who is God really, outside of any dogma? I was also angry. I wanted to understand what or who this God was that tossed my life into ruins and what the hell was I supposed to do now! I shook my fist at the sky, "Tell me the true order of things, who or what is GOD anyway?!!!"

A week or so after my rant, I was at my favorite coffee shop in Ann Arbor, Michigan. On the bulletin board I saw a notice that said in large letters: "Do you want to know God?" I laughed out loud, and copied down the information. It was a direct answer to the very question I had asked the week before.

It seemed the answers were coming faster now. I was definitely on the right track.

The next week I returned to Ann Arbor, and found myself in the backyard of a beautiful stone house where I met Brenda Morgan. She was a tall stately blonde woman. She talked about Michael Illehu (Michael Silverman), her spiritual teacher. She invited us to sit with him in meditative appointments that she was willing to schedule for us. She was a Ph.D. psychologist and seemed as though she was honestly and clearly making an offer if those of us in attendance wanted to know God.

She was not at all attached to whether we would accept an appointment or not. I trusted her instantly. We could pay what we could. She suggested a fee of $50, which even at that time was very low for therapy. She talked about her own transformation, and told us that Michael's presence had changed her life after the deaths of her husband, father, and brother all in one year. Wow, I thought, she had really gone through a series of tragedies much worse than mine. I signed up.

The next week I found myself at the house of Michael Silverman. Michael meditated with me individually, and with others like me, at his house in Ann Arbor during that fall of 1986. He was about 5'10" with very long dark hair. He had an accent that sounded like he was from Brooklyn, New York. He was a kind man, with smiling eyes. He invited me to sit with him in meditation. I sat with Michael for nine sessions over a period of about twelve weeks. That was the most life changing adventure I could have ever received at the time and the most confusing. My mind was a total mess.

Beliefs were tossed out the window faster than I could chuck them. I felt I did not know anything about God, spirituality, or what I believed anymore. I was experiencing something in Michael totally different than what I had been told growing up. At least he was offering something clear, immediately present, and very simple. It was clear that Michael knew something about the Divine that I did not.

He and I sat in an empty bedroom with flowered wallpaper that had no furniture. Running through my head was the thought that if my parents could see me now they'd think I was crazy. They would have said, "What are you doing with a man you barely know sitting in his empty bedroom!"

In one session, he said, "Now watch me, keep your eyes open."

Open-eyed meditation was new to me. He wanted me to gaze at him. Michael was there sitting against the wallpaper, then he became transparent and I could see through him! He was smiling the whole time. Then it happened again. 'A real Cheshire Cat?' I thought. I rubbed my eyes, but he was there one moment and not there the next, all the time grinning. I was absolutely astounded.

Who was this guy? Most certainly a spiritual teacher, a magician, maybe a yogi, I knew he was some kind of Avatar. But I did not know what an Avatar was at the time. I had not heard of true enlightenment. Until this time, I had only read about God as someone outside of myself. I knew little about Indian Swamis.

In college I had taken meditation from a Transcendental Meditation (TM) teacher inspired by Maharishi Mahesh Yogi. But I had never done more with the group than basic meditation practice.

My chiropractor, Ron Chalfant, was my yoga teacher. I had taken Yoga from him for four years. Ron and I and other students had gone to a dinner to honor our teacher, the famous yoga master Iyengar, when he came to visit his students in the states. Still, I didn't really understand anything about enlightenment or the devotee/guru relationship.

I had meditated for the better part of ten years. I thought I knew what meditation was. I had never heard of darshan, or "direct transmission." Transcendental Meditation did not teach that in beginning meditation.

Sitting with Michael, I learned that I was sitting with an enlightened teacher, who radiated divine love towards me in direct transmission. This was darshan. The experience is awesome and different with every teacher. Sitting in the presence of unconditional love, I felt transformed. All my stuff came roaring up after each session. I did not know at the time that the more light that is directed into your unconscious self, the more stuff comes up to be cleared and released.

Every time I saw Michael something in me changed. I let go of the sense of betrayal and disappointment in myself with two failed relationships. I stopped blaming myself for growing beyond my relationships. He called me on my part of things, and I could not wiggle free from his gaze. Yet, he was not manipulating me. I was "pinned by his truth."

There was absolutely no physical attraction, only a sense of unconditional love emanating from him. I could not sexualize the relationship. He was Michael, a being. I was Robin, another being. He knew me better than I knew myself. How could this be? Somehow he could see into my subconscious. He could see things in me that I had not yet discovered for myself. EEK! It was very scary. But it was also compelling. I had to keep seeing him.

It was a feeling that I could not really describe. It was not a feeling, more like a warm ray of light that passed over me with his gaze. If this was love, then what was loving a man or anyone else about? What about sex? I thought loving had to do with touching and being sexual. How could I ever find my desire of true happiness by myself in meditation?

This was not what my family taught me. Relationships were all there was in my family. You HAD to be paired or you were not quite whole or right. Something was wrong with you if you did not want a relationship. Here I was single, with another single man, and there was NO attraction, except that I was compelled to keep learning a lot. Michael was my teacher. That was all I could understand.

My parents could not have prepared me for this. I was utterly confused. I had a feeling I was going beyond anything I had known before. Would I leave my family behind? I had heard of people leaving their families to become devotees. My fears were raging through me. I had no idea what was happening! No doubt, I was being transformed into my true self.

Another thing he said during one of the darshans was, "You do not understand that if someone came in here with a chainsaw and cut off my leg, I would have to go to the hospital, I would have to get it taken care of, but I would still be happy. I am permanently happy. You are not happy, and if that was done to you, you would go into 'the victim.' You would say 'Why me?'"

"That is what I have that you need—permanent Happiness. But you need someone who can really teach you. Clearly you do not have an understanding of the Guru tradition."

He was right, I had no idea what the hell he was talking about. When he moved into his new house, he asked if I wanted to see it. I said no, thinking I was being "spiritual." I wanted to get down to "business," to show him how spiritual I was. The truth is I did want to see it. But I discovered that he was offering to share himself with me. "That had hurt," he shared in our final session the next week. He also scolded me a bit. After he called me on what I did not understand, he then very compassionately suggested I go to California and meet Da Free John. "Go to Da, you have so much to learn about the Guru-Devotee relationship and what is appropriate." It seemed that he was quite disgusted with my lackluster performance and ignorant behavior. I agreed that I would try to understand better with Brenda's help.

After that last meeting, I never saw him again. Though I heard about him all the time from Brenda. She gave me a night-shirt of his that I still have. I wore it all the time in order to absorb into me what he was—his essence. As it turned out, the others who meditated with him were also dismissed around the same time. Well, at least I wasn't alone. We were all failing at sitting with a true teacher. I felt slightly better knowing I wasn't the only one.

Brenda began to distribute Michael's writing to those of us interested in his teachings. I read his materials voraciously, and I also stayed in touch with Brenda as best I could. We received stacks and stacks of his writings and I could not always comprehend what he taught, but I felt something was sinking in.

Many of us "rejected" by Michael began to take Brenda's group therapy sessions once a week for a year. Brenda and I became friends in the process. Since I lived about an hour from her house, in the winter when the roads were icy, I stayed overnight at her house on her living room floor. I also got to know Brenda's eight-year-old daughter Sarah. She was delightful.

I learned a lot from Brenda including what working on my "stuff" was all about. My stuff was the unconscious conditioned responses and assumptions that I made all the time, as well as my ego patterns. Those patterns became clear in the group setting. I also learned I had issues defining a sense of self. I had been so crushed by both Timmy and David that I felt very damaged when it came to relationships. During that year I began to let go and understand more about the spiritual world of Guru-devotee relationships and Michael's teachings. I was so hurt by failed relationships that I felt it would probably take many more years before I healed completely. And it did.

I found a new lover, Yo, and we enjoyed our time together. He was a fellow artist I had known peripherally in my art-soaked world. I helped him with an exhibit on the feminine he was working on. With the help from a grant from the Michigan Arts Council he was exploring the feminine. He told me I was his "feminine exploration" and I helped him with it in our interactions. He taught me a lot about Japanese culture. To this day, I am fascinated with Japanese art and design. It was a great pairing and very healing for me.

I asked the Universe when I started to get to know Yo, "Please, don't let us hurt each other." Yo and I spent many wonderful times together, making food and making love, going out to dinner, visiting museums, and making art. He was a dear soul, and we remained friends after I broke it off to go to grad school. Neither of us hurt the other at all, as far as I know.

When I broke it off to return to school, I told him that I saw him with a lovely and feisty Chinese woman, who he would marry. Ten years later, when I returned to Michigan for my first book tour, I saw him again and the two of them seemed very happy. She was indeed Chinese, and also a wonderful artist.

At the end of the summer in 1987, Brenda and I and a few others from the group decided to go to a Woman's Retreat in Ontario, Canada. She was going to go ahead of me, and I would follow in my pickup truck a day later. I would be returning with her and give her a ride back after the weekend. I also knew it would be the last time I would see her for a while, as Michael, Brenda, and Sarah were moving from Ann Arbor to New Jersey. I would leave for school in California a few weeks after the retreat.

I was still in love with Dave, but clearly he wasn't in love with me. He had moved on and found a new woman who got pregnant right after they got together. They were getting married. At least that was the news from the grapevine. It seemed such an odd turn of events for both of us. He was having a child with someone else, the very reason he left our relationship. I was free to pursue my interests besides relationship.

Even so, I decided to make a final dentist appointment with him. He had been my dentist for several years before we fell in love. Right before I left for the retreat, I went to get one last checkup from him. We tried to be friends, but it wasn't working. It was so clear that he was done with me and I felt so hurt that I left his office very angry and upset, mostly with myself. As I walked out, I asked God, "Where the hell are good men!? Here he is gloating how 'over me' he is. I am PISSED OFF! That bastard!" I fumed all the way to Detroit—a two-hour drive. My anger was something new I was discovering.

I had to work all day before my appointment, and left Dave's office at four o'clock, with a long drive ahead of me. I made it through rush hour in Detroit. A good four hours later from Detroit, I was driving to Toronto in the dark in the middle of nowhere. I had been on the road for six hours total. I was exhausted, especially emotionally, though I was pushing to get as far as I could before I stopped somewhere to sleep. There were not as many motels as there were in the States, and I kept looking for them. I thought I would look for a rest stop or a truck stop. The retreat center was farther away than I thought; I was only halfway there.

That is when I fell asleep in my Toyota pick-up truck for just a moment. My truck made a slow-motion spin, then slowly, as my wheels got caught in the gravel on the shoulder of the four-lane freeway, it fell over on its side. I was suddenly looking down the freeway off the road, lights pointing westward the way I had come, suspended by my seat belt. Everything in my truck had been tossed into utter chaos.

I was feeling rather helpless and shaken up. I noticed that many cars and trucks were stopping in either direction. There was a huge grassy median about fifty feet wide between the westbound and eastbound lanes that went into a gully. My truck was rocking back and forth on its side on the embankment, ready to roll over with me in it. I was afraid to breathe or move. My truck and I could roll down into the gully, wrecking my vehicle and breaking my neck or worse.

Within two minutes, eight men were surrounding my truck holding it up and trying to help me out of it. Some of them held up one side, while I crawled out of the driver's door. Once I was out, they righted my truck. A tow truck was on the scene in less than ten minutes. Two of these good men, a trucker and an off-duty police officer, had called in the tow truck on their radios. It seemed clear that some men were protecting me from the other men. There was a possibility that some of them might have harmed a woman by herself.

I thanked everyone profusely and the men disappeared back into their vehicles and left one by one. Then the policeman who had assessed the accident kindly said, "You are in Canada, and it is safe to just pull off the freeway and park off the road if you want to. Crawl in the back of your truck and sleep if you need to. No one will bother you." He didn't give me a ticket.

'Okay, God, I thought, 'I got it, there are some good men here.' I tried not to chuckle.

After examining my truck, the man with the tow truck filled my tires, and I got in and turned my truck around to face east again. I shook off the shock of the accident as best I could, and pulled off the highway at the next exit. A quarter of a mile down the road, I found a farm lane and drove into a field road off the highway. I crawled into the back of my pick-up, locked up my truck, and fell asleep. Nothing was wrong with the truck, except a small dent on one side where it had rolled on its side.

In the morning, after a quick breakfast in a small nearby cafe, I drove several more hours to the Woman's retreat. It was held on a farm owned by an elderly woman who was a retired dancer. She had been a ballerina for the Canadian National Ballet. The farm could have been anywhere in Michigan, with a long gravel drive moving between fields of long grasses with trees of every northern variety—elm, oak, walnut, beech and birch. This farm had a house and several barns; some of the low sheds had been converted into places for outdoor workshops.

Brenda and I found one another pretty quickly. She was worried about me, and I was still quite shaken up. She showed me around and introduced me to people. We attended several group gatherings together. Women were doing psychic readings, healing work, massage, and tarot readings. I felt at home and in an element I belonged in, but it was still so new to me. I was not clear what was really my direction, except massage. I exchanged and worked on people as they asked me to.

That night we attended a sweat lodge. I recalled my first lodge, years before when I had been invited to South Dakota by my Kemper Hall friend, Mary Ann Godfrey. I did not know what was really going on in the lodge with Mary Ann because it was my first experience in a sacred lodge.

This time in Canada, I was wide-awake to what the lodge was all about. I loved every minute of it. Willa Mankiller, leader of the Cherokee nation, was supposed to be there. Her daughter came instead and led the lodges, as Willa Mankiller had just become the leader of the Cherokee people two years before. She was very busy, and we heard she was also quite ill.

The lodge at this women's retreat ran all night. I will never forget the spirits in that lodge, nor the women I met. All of us, of all races, were into metaphysical things together and I was learning so much. Perhaps I was just remembering who I was and why I came here.

After the retreat, Brenda and I returned to Michigan before going our separate ways. It was a bittersweet event, as I also felt a tug when she left. She was my friend and spiritual teacher, and I was going to have to leave her behind. She had helped me more than I could say. As she and I departed each other, I sent a prayer to God to help me become my authentic Divine Self.

All I knew for certain was that I still wanted to make art, and suddenly poems were coming out as twins with my paintings. As I was preparing to leave Michigan, I had several one-person art shows with all the work I had done at Dave's. They would be hanging in galleries while I was on the road. I went to both openings. My sister agreed to pick up the artwork after I left for California and store it in her barn.

Lysne, my niece, Kisti and Sid's oldest daughter, was eighteen by then. We left for California together. I was going to graduate school and wanted to meet the spiritual teacher Da Free John. Lysne was going to visit friends. Before I left, I bought a book of Da's and took one look at his picture and really fell in love with him. It was not the same as falling in love with Timmy or Dave. It was something deeper. I knew I had to meet him. I wanted to sit at his feet and learn something that, at that time, I did not know. I had to learn about unconditional love from an enlightened master teacher. Da was going to help me understand the Guru-devotee relationship and help me become closer to my higher self.

Moving to California and Grad School

In 1986, the year before I left for California, I had applied to grad school at Pratt Institute in Brooklyn. To my surprise, I got in and was supposed to start in the fall. Then I attended a seminar by Matt Fox, a Dominican priest that was shaking the Vatican up with his book, *Original Blessing*. The seminar was held in Rockford, Illinois, and at my parent's invitation, in the spring of 1987. We attended the event together where I met several people that were offering workshops and helping to present the day-long experience with Matt Fox. I was excited to discover that Matt Fox was offering a graduate program at Holy Names College called the Institute in Culture and Creation Spirituality, in Oakland, CA, that seemed to be custom tailored to me. It included the study of various spiritual earth-based traditions, the arts, and the study of environmental cosmology.

At the end of that summer of 1987, after learning that I was accepted, off I went to California, not really sure if I could do it financially. No one was reachable in the office during August, so I had to go on faith that I would be covered financially when I got to the school, otherwise, I would have to look for an apartment in Berkeley or Oakland, California. I packed my truck with both options in mind.

My niece Lysne and I drove across country together in my Toyota pickup truck. She wanted to show me Moab, Utah, and the red rocks. Two years before with her high school class, she had visited these amazing formations. We hiked up red rocks to the arches and sat together in the silence of the bountiful red rocks and blue sky. It was a moment I cherish to this day.

As we crossed the line from Nevada to California, we stopped and I took a picture of the sign that read: "Welcome to California." I felt lightning bolts racing up and down my arms and legs. I knew I had made the right decision after so many bad ones. The next day after dropping Lysne off at a friend's in Marysville outside Sacramento, I drove the last few hours by myself to the San Francisco Bay Area.

I was terrified. I gripped the steering wheel all the way. Stopping at an overlook as I entered the Bay Area, I got a good look at the terrain. There was an illustration of how mudslides occur in heavy rains. Welcome to California! I thought—mudslides, earthquakes, and fires. Oh my!

I rolled down the freeways all the way to Ashby Avenue, Hwy. 13, and into the hillside campus, white knuckling it all the way from Marysville. When I parked and got on campus, I found the registration office. When I went inside, I met a nun who was working there, and I learned from her at Holy Names that I had gotten a scholarship, financial aide for the rest of the tuition, and my dorm room was waiting. Whee! What a relief. I almost cried I was so excited. I would be secure for the next year!

The first person I met was Paul Bibbo. We bonded immediately. He was also an artist and had gone to Pratt! We always had a lot to talk about, it seemed, between art, cosmology and creation spirituality that Matt Fox taught us. The second person I met was Mary Ellen Hill. 'Ah, a sister!' I thought. Both of them are still dear friends to this day.

Graduate school was another life changing year. Mathew Fox's Institute in Culture and Creation Spirituality focused on three branches, Spirituality, Cosmology, and Psychology woven together with the Arts. Ecology was also a big component. There was a Geo-Justice emphasis, a Psychology emphasis, and Theological emphasis. It was there that I met my Native American teacher, Buck Ghost Horse, who offered Sweat Lodges and classes on Native American spirituality outside as well as inside the school. Many of my new friends became life-long friends through Matt's courses.

While attending school, I had my first vision quest with Buck, and attended many Sacred Sweat Lodges. During that time, I was also traveling over the Richmond Bridge to Marin County to Da Free John's Ashram once a week to attend Sunday services in San Rafael. It was quite a contrast, but I was a sponge for learning anything I could in the spiritual realms, so it felt right to go there.

During Thanksgiving holiday, I joined a group of thirty-four classmates, mostly from Europe and the East Coast. We rented a group of houses on Lake Tahoe in a Presbyterian camp for the weekend. After a wonderful day of ritual and feasting with my friends on Thanksgiving night, I decided to take some time alone and to sit by the still lake. While sitting on the rocks looking at the lake, full of gratitude, stars bright and the lake reflecting them so brightly in the fresh cold air, I felt the stars fall right through me into the lake.

The old Native American story of how lake lilies are made from stars as a gift from Star Woman, or Divine Mother, came to me, and for a moment I felt one with everything around me—the stars, the water, the mountains, and the rock and my being merged with all of nature. There was no separation with the world, I experienced that we are all One with Divine Mother Earth.

Meeting a Master - Da Free John

In California, I was definitely not in the Midwest anymore. There were several massage schools around the Bay Area. I decided to get as much training as I could with other classes on metaphysics and psychic healing, massage, and other modalities. At the time, in 1987, this was not available in the Midwest. I knew of one massage school just opening up in Detroit, Michigan after I had taken my massage course in Michigan the year before from a California teacher!

I had started to work with energies and entities around me and around others. I was not using the gifts I knew I had to my fullest capacity, but I was exchanging sessions with a medium and learning little by little as I went. My ability to perceive spirits was being used, and it was interesting to observe them around others. I rarely engaged them or "sent them to the light." I just watched them and acknowledged them when it felt right to do so.

Da was not always in attendance at the San Rafael Ashram, as he lived part-time in Fiji and part time in Lake County, California. But there was a meditation room, and his picture on altar was there. It felt as though he was present in his photos even when he was not physically present. I also realized that Matt Fox's program did not offer anything about the Guru tradition, nor Eastern Philosophy, though Jesus could be considered a Guru as the word Guru means teacher, guide or master teacher.

After I finished Matt's program, I received my masters, and a grant from Mathew Fox to explore whether a summer camp was feasible following school for young children. I moved to Orinda, California, a 15-minute drive from Holy

Names College, and temporarily worked on the grant. I also kept attending Da's Marin County ashram.

After the grant was finished, I moved temporarily into a friend's house, then across the Bay to Marin County to be closer to Da's ashram and to start a practice in an area with people who could readily afford massage. I worked initially in two spas, one in Oakland, and another in San Francisco.

I also started to go up to Lake County, where Da Free John's retreat center was located, and where members from the Ashram would spend the weekend retreat,to meditate and sit with him in darshan (direct transmission) when he was present. I had never sat in the presence of an enlightened being before, except Michael, but this was quite a different experience. Michael's transmissions were gentle and easy and you hardly knew what was going on. Still the effects afterwards were radical; the transforming came in small but potent with realizations over the next few days.

When you sat with Da, he was able to send waves of light from his heart out to everyone. You could feel it like lightning bolts surging through us all. People jumped up as he slowly turned his gaze from one side of the room to the other.

Many of us responded with kriyas, which are bodily tremors and prostrations that a devotee spontaneously experiences beyond one's control. His gaze was so powerful I found my body waving like a flag at his loving beam as I sat in my chair. My body would sway back and forth in response to his gaze, my arms up over my head waving. I witnessed two hundred people in a large room responding to his gaze in a similar fashion as he looked slowly around the room.

Da could inspire kriyas within the line of his sight through dozens of people at the same time. I was overwhelmed with love. Sitting in the back of the room, I met his wives (he had four of them) who were so beautiful and kind. All were glowing like light bulbs with their radiance. They all were devoted to him. He was, needless to say, quite controversial.

He became among his followers known as a crazy wisdom master. His four wives and several children from the wives all lived together and traveled together. He had gone through several periods of his teachings. A period of time he named 'Garbage and the Goddess,' for example, was a crazy time when everyone partied wildly. When I met him, he was in a more austere phase of his teachings. He would go through several phases over his life as he brought his devotees along with him for their growth towards Self-Realization.

On the way to one of the retreats, I drove up a back road through a valley that felt awful to me. I was halfway through it before I realized that something was really off. As I slowed down and tuned into the spirits around the car, I could see two conflicting factions of Native American and settler ghosts in an all-out battle on one side of the valley.

Driving slowly past the scene, I said to them psychically, "Hey you are all dead, time to move on. Stop your fighting, it is over now!" I began to pray for them as they turned to me. I remember saying to myself, "Please wake up and stop fighting. Please God, send them to the light." Slowly they "woke up" out of the battle that had been going on for a hundred years and some of them left, following the bright light that opened overhead.

With more and more prayers, the spirits began to leave as the heavens opened, and soon the fighting stopped. I kept praying for them all the way to the ashram. I felt that most of them were gone by the time I got to my destination.

When I arrived at the Lake Retreat, Da gave a talk. He said to tell everyone to avoid the route I had taken, because there were ghosts there that were quite nasty and fighting. I thought to myself, 'not anymore.'

I was at Da's ashram attending his retreat for a second time and doing service for two years of learning when I began to understand the Guru-Devotee relationship and the process of becoming enlightened. Michael was right, I knew nothing before this, and nothing in Christian services had prepared me for what I was learning from the community and from Da's books.

Devotees basically are under the Ray of Light of the master teacher, or Guru, and they learn from the light of that

Ray as well as from written teachings. Actually, Jesus was another "Ray" and I recognized that, but Da Free John was a living teacher, like Michael. It was more direct to me, and the transmissions were astounding, mind blowing and unforgettable. Christ Consciousness was in Da and Michael as that consciousness came in as Jesus.

At Grad school, my teacher in the Native American Lakota tradition was Buck Ghost Horse. A year after school, he and his wife moved to Washington state, and wanted to give us a woman's ceremony at his home in Snohomish, Washington a year or two after he moved away. I was part of his Tiosbye, or extended family, and we met a few times a month while Buck was with us in the San Francisco Bay Area. After they left we continued meeting. Many of those people are still friends today.

A few years after school, I felt I had to make a choice between following Da or following Buck. But I was conflicted. Buck had told us that if we were supposed to go to the ceremony we would have a dream. We were instructed to listen to our dreams. He was impartial as to whether we were to go or not. He was guided to invite us, and it was up to us whether we would accept the invitation.

One night I had a dream. Da was on one side of the road and I was facing him looking straight at him. As soon as I saw him, I knelt down and bowed my head and exclaimed, "Master!" He said softly, "Do you know who I am?" I said, "Yes!" He said, "Then Get UP!"

At that, I stood up and we faced each other looking into each other's eyes. As the scene turned 180 degrees, I was now on one side of the road and he was on the other. I was suddenly wearing a blue dress that I recognized was for the ceremony. There were beads around the sleeves and neckline and the dress had a waistline, which was not traditional, but it was my dress for the woman's ceremony anyway.

When I woke up, I heard Da say to me, "I will go with you wherever you go!" If I needed to go to the ceremonies of the Lakota, then so be it. I made my dress to be worn in the ceremony and traveled to Washington to attend the first Woman's

Ceremony with twenty or so other women, many of whom were dear friends. Some I had gone to Graduate school with at Holy Names College, and others I had met while connecting with Buck at his talks and ceremonies.

I felt Da's presence often as I attended these ceremonies. He was quite a force in my life for some time. I tried to read his books over the years. They are still some of the most brilliant writing I have ever read and not easy to comprehend from a logical point of view. There is no linear thinking in them. They are intuitive and meant to be received intuitively.

For years after the Woman's Ceremony, I meditated with Da's picture and did "pujas" – a ritual washing of his picture, and I also became a pipe carrier and attended many different kinds of Native American Ceremonies. I was again living a double life, but this time in the realm of spirituality, one Earth-based and one Sky-based. I felt that the Earth-based rituals of the Native American tradition grounded me, and the "sky" based rituals of Da's writing and work were a balance to the earthiness of the Lakota tradition that Buck taught us.

Da is still with me, even though I have been following the teachings of Paramhansa Yogananda since 2014. Yogananda, who was the first East Indian teachers to spread his teachings to the West, created the Self-Realization Fellowship (SRF) in Southern California in the 1920's. After Yogananda's death in 1952, some of his disciples split from SRF and one of his disciples, Swami Kryiananda started Ananda, which also became a worldwide spiritual community. That is my community today, and will remain my community for the rest of my life.

Brenda Morgan

Michael Silverman

Da Free John / Adi Da

Section Two:
Native American Wisdom- Discovering Earth-based Traditions

Chapter Four
Beginning Native American Path

The Woman's Ceremony

 Buck recognized that most of us women had been injured during relationships or in our childhoods in one way or the other. His guides had asked him to begin a ceremony for us. Once I had my dream, I chose to go, and knew that the ceremony would change something for me. Buck had a long list of things we needed to bring, an ear of corn, a stick painted blue, a dress we made for the occasion, a pendant we made ourselves, 405 prayer ties[3], camping equipment, food, the list went on and on.

 My truck's transmission had given out on the way up in the middle of the central Sacramento Valley, and I had to leave my truck in Williams, California, where my transmission would be replaced. After calling friends to ask if they would pick me up on the way, they met me at the gas station where I was

---

3 Prayer ties are a square cloth about 2" x 2" that have tobacco in it, with prayers. The cloth is then tied on a string that then adds another pray tie. When you are about to do a ceremony, you often make 405 to prepare for the ceremony.

stranded. I was aware that I was already in the ceremony. This unexpected stop was part of it. I was changing vehicles both literally and symbolically—going from Da to Buck. I would be carried by friends to my destination; 'Just a little God joke,' I thought.

We arrived in Snohomish after a very long drive from the San Francisco Bay Area. We arrived on Buck and Donna's land, about five acres outside Snohomish. We got our things together and set up our tents. It was a wooded piece of land and had a manufactured home on it, with a couple of large teepees, several fire pits, and an area for a lodge. We would be beginning with a sacred sweat lodge, then talks, ceremonial circles, and finally, on two different occasions, we would be given face paintings with different symbols painted on our faces.

Buck acknowledged our pain before the first sacred lodge of the ceremony. He gathered us to give us an overview of sorts, though we did not really know what the ceremony would entail in its entirety. We were to tell our stories and release the wounds we had. Buck did not run the first lodge; a woman student of his, Adriana, did. He wanted us to feel safe with other women and open up.

We wailed and cried our pain out. Most of us had experienced rape, abuse, divorce, abortions, or some sort of put down of our selves as women growing to adulthood. After the lodge, we dressed in our ceremonial dresses, and one by one, we entered a teepee where Buck and several assistants were standing around him.

We were given a talk, and a face painting layer, with the strength of the culture resting on the women; this ceremony was to help us understand who we were as keepers of this amazing tradition. He painted our faces, first with blue on one side, then white on the other. Dots of white, or 'hail medicine,' were painted on our faces in the third round to end the cycles of suffering. He explained that the Hail Medicine was a very powerful tool to end our grief and help us release the past. He talked about other ceremonies, and how women were considered sacred in the Lakota tradition. Closing, we had another lodge and felt really freed up from our pasts.

I had never heard a man say that women were sacred before. It shocked me. But I was so grateful that he did. The corn and stick were "planted" in two rows on the way into the lodge. We planted them before the first lodge and burned them at that last one. The entire ceremony lasted two days. To honor Buck's memory and the sacredness of the ceremony for all of us women, I will not share any more of the details.

At the end, I felt new. So did the other women. We were to keep it secret, because other people, especially Native Lakota activists, could attack us and Buck for giving this ceremony to white women. In truth, we represented many races, Scandinavian, Irish, Native American, Eastern European, Latino, African American, and East Indian, etc.

Over a two-year period, I participated in the Women's Ceremony and two vision quests under Buck's guidance. A year after the Woman's Ceremony at the last vision quest I did with Buck, he said to me, "You have your own power now, you don't need me anymore. Go on, go your own way." I was surprised, but I knew there were others who needed him who were coming out of addiction, or were veterans with wounds from the war and he wanted to spend his time with the ones more broken. I felt healed by his help along with that of Da, Michael, and Brenda.

That same year, my dear friends from Illinois, Jeff and Therese, who I went to graduate school with, invited me to Sundance in South Dakota. The Native Dances spoke to me; they were familiar, as though I was remembering them, not just participating in them. I learned so much from the people. It would be the first of many Sundances and Ogitchidaah dances I would attend over the next twenty-five years that took place from Northern Wisconsin and Canada to South Dakota, Washington State, and California.

My First Native American Dance

At home, I had established my massage practice and could take time off when I needed to. After my dream, in which Da Free John told me he would go wherever I needed to go, and after attending the Women's Ceremony, I found myself in South Dakota with a group of friends from graduate school.

I was in a camp in the Black Hills with about 500 people made up of mostly Lakota and Oglala Native Americans and their supporters and friends of various races. My friends had already arrived. Many of the people were from all over the world, though mostly from the reservations. I was surprised to see a contingent of Hollywood starlets. One of the main leaders of that group was a stuntman and actor. He was quite handsome and had several women who worked with him, as well as his wife and kids. Lakota people call him a Heyoka. I did not know what that term meant, but I was about to find out.

As mentioned before, I was there on the invitation of friends Jeff and Therese, who were there at the invitation of other friends that were supporting several dancers. While I did not know the dancers personally, at the end of the dance I felt like we all knew each other deeply, even though we never spoke to each other.

My friends Jeff and Therese brought their two children, their new baby Bretta, and their daughter Margaret who attended school with us during the year in California. Margaret was five then and seven now and Bretta was about nine months old at the point of the ceremony. Paul Bibbo flew in from New York. Paul and I were godparents to Bretta, and we were very close to Margaret growing up. We always enjoyed seeing them every summer at some point. We had our own little family at the Sundance.

The purpose of me writing about Sundance at all is only to share my experience, and not to give the details as those memories are privately held in our hearts. I learned quickly that no photos, poems, or stories were allowed from or about the dance. What I intend to do here is give you a general idea of the dance without talking about details of the ceremony. Sundance and Lakota culture has so profoundly shaped me that to bypass this part would not do justice to my story, nor to the Lakota people who gave me so much. If anything, I want to acknowledge the Native American ceremonies and traditions, and Earth-based ceremonies in general, as highly influential in my mind and heart, as I deeply and humbly respect them.

To describe Sundance is like trying to describe your first glimpse of Notre Dame Cathedral in Paris without the building. That is, it is a feeling that transcends architectural structures. Unlike Western buildings made for prayer, we did the dances outside within an arbor of tree branches that were made to shelter the supporters from the sun while they prayed for the dancers who were in the sun.

People who dance and those who support give unselfishly ways to support a dance that takes everyone's participation. There is so much to do in a Sundance or any traditional dance: splitting wood, gathering sage, building the arbor, making the prayer ties, gathering chokecherry—the list goes on. We all pitched in. The ceremonies are a lot of work. Yet, it was an honor and a great privilege to be a part of them everywhere I have gone.

When you Sundance, you take responsibility for this world, you say to the Creator, "The buck stops here, with me, and I will shoulder this life with honor and humility. I am willing to be fully responsible. With my prayers I surrender to your will. Bring it on."

Imagine two big shaded semi-circular arbors 6-8 feet tall surrounding the dance grounds like big arms with an opening at the east, and in the west a shaded arbor room, the place where the dancers rested between dance rounds. The west arbor was covered with pine boughs and tarps, connecting the two semi-circles of arbor like a hinge. The east gate opening, was where the spirits of the Earth entered the dance and no one was allowed to cross that area, nor camp there either. Anyone who might venture to camp there, probably would have been up all night if they had slept at all, with spirits running through their tent! But anyone seen crossing the East gate, would have been called out on a loud speaker so no one dared cross it.

The purpose of the dance is to unify the consciousness of the people towards peace, love and harmony. Originally, this unification was done for the purpose of war, creating one mind as the warriors went into battle. But the dance went underground in the 1880s because Native American Ceremonies of any kind were outlawed until 1972. After the 1880s, the dance was done in secret, and it was changed to a dance for peace. Mostly a male initiation, women began dancing to support the men. Today both women and men dance, but it is still considered a male initiation. Women are also there to pray for the people, their families, all people, including the various races of man, trouble spots around the world, animals, and the Earth herself.

But you would never catch a traditional Sundancer speaking this way. Suffice it to say that a Sundance is like Christmas, New Years, and a four-day sacred family reunion all rolled into one without any alcohol or drugs. At the same time it is very private. Every Sundancer is praying for others who they only know. You never asked a Sundancer who they are dancing for, it was private between them and the Creator. Sometimes they would volunteer that information, but you honored their privacy otherwise.

What I want to express here is how different these ceremonies are from anything we might experience in Western European culture. One feels as though when we enter the Sundance space we enter into another dimension, and then have to return to the outer world and it takes several days to reintegrate to western civilization. This is not always easy to do, especially when you fall in love with the ceremonies and the feeling of oneness that exists there. It is a hard transition for everyone, no matter one's race.

The leader of this particular dance was a man named Norbert Running. His sons and several adopted sons were also involved in the leadership. At this dance there were at least 20 leaders and probably 150 dancers. Add supporters at the various camps and we were probably a group of 500-600 people, maybe more.

Always there is a lot going on in a Sundance, and your job as a supporter was to watch and pray for all the dancers and help when you can with prayers and food for the people supporting after the rounds. You had to eat and drink, because you were helping the dancers by eating for them, as all the dancers fasted from food and water during the four days of the dance and four days before the dance started too. Before the dance started, for some dancers, they could drink liquids but not water; and in other Sundances, they were allowed to eat and drink anything they wanted (except alcohol) until the last lodge before the dance started. It differed from Sundance to Sundance.

All the male dancers help to carry the Sundance tree. Female dancers also assisted if there were not enough men to carry the tree into the grounds from the place where it was cut. If it is too far, then the tree is carried only from the gate of the Sundance grounds to the arbor. Flat bed trucks are used to manage the tree from the cut site to the gate. Because there was a whopping big hill that went way down into a gully and then up again to the top of the next mesa where this dance took place, the dancers were to drive the tree in as far as possible and then, navigating the hill, while walking it down then up again to the Sundance Grounds. Every body was needed.

I was not there to witness the tree ceremony, as I had arrived after the tree was already up. But I had heard that it was very tricky getting this one to the arbor because of the gully. All the men, Sundancers or not, were asked to help and also the women dancers.

Imagine a central round arbor with a live tree in the middle that was cut and brought in ceremonially. That is what the grounds looked like once the tree was in place. There are four days of purification where everyone attending the dance does at least one sweat lodge ceremony a day, in four large lodges. All the dancers do two sweat lodges a day, morning and night. When I arrived, I had to get into a lodge immediately, because the dance had already started with the cutting and installation of the tree and I was going to witness the first day of the dance the next morning.

The dance began at dawn in a beautiful procession, as the dancers filed in one at a time. They were in their regalia, Sundance skirts for the men with bare chests, and dresses for the women, all handmade in the four direction colors, red (south), yellow (east), blue or black (west), and white (north), dancing rhythmically to the beat of the mother drum. All the dancers wore sage crowns, wristlets and ankle bracelets to protect them and honor themselves in the dance. Everyone's vision of what they are to bring into the dance with them, staffs, masks, or headdresses, are unique depending on their vision and dreams before the dance.

The crowns also shaded their eyes when the sun was highest and brightest at mid-day. Most dancers were barefooted, but some had moccasins on to protect their feet if they were diabetic or had other ailments. It was often 50 degrees in the morning before the sun came up and 100-105 degrees by midday!

The dancers danced in rounds that lasted from an hour to three hours, depending on what was happening out there. As attendees, rather than dancers, our job was to primarily support the dancers in prayer. All the dancers were praying for others whether family, friends or relatives. We also supported each other and the dancers by gathering sage, helping them make their crowns and wristlets, and preparing food for the camp. It is quite common to see spirits during the dance, as they come in at various times. But this usually happens after we have been in prayer for several days. By the third day, people often witness spirits, and experience synchronicities with nature that are quite phenomenal. This can include eagles soaring overhead when certain dancers are dancing, or wild animals such as deer or coyotes dancing in plain sight on the next hill with certain medicine men or women. This often happened when the medicine people would set altars for that particular animal such as black-tailed deer, or hawks, or other animals.

On the last night of the first dance I attended, I wanted

to sweat one more time, as did several other women. Usually, only the dancers pour water for the lodges during the dance. The dance was technically over, except for the giveaway, which happened at the end of the dance on the fifth day at this particular Sundance. All the dancers were exhausted and no one wanted to pour water for us.

A group of women and I were standing around waiting for a leader to come and pour the water over the hot rocks that were in a camp fire outside for the lodge. After inquiring at several camps, finally the stuntman from Hollywood showed up. He was the Heyoka, that is, he brings in joy of life and the reality of death to the dance. They are the clowns, or the jesters in Western mythology. They usually wear black and white, spots, stripes or opposite colors like red and blue in the Sundance and carry comical objects into the dance to make people laugh.

They do things comically and with great flair, dancing backwards and bringing their clowning in to help with healing; smoking when smoking is banned at the dance, and splashing water on the dancers when they are not supposed to touch water for four days, unless a Heyoka douses them, which usually doesn't happen to dancers as much as the audience.

At the end of the dance, after dancing in the hot sun for four day, this man volunteered to give us a Heyoka lodge. Men generally ran men's lodges, and women, women's lodges, but a Heyoka can do what he wants. He seemed not to be tired at all. I couldn't wait.

He sat at the opposite side from where the regular leaders usually sit, he sang the songs backwards, and prayed to Heyoka Tungashiela, the backwards ones. It was one of the most remarkable lodges I had ever attended up until that time, because every prayer and every song was sung backwards, from start to finish! Lodges are fundamentally prayer ceremonies. So we all prayed for our families, our friends, and safe travels back to our homes. There were several women who spoke other languages as their native tongues—a French, Spanish, and German woman, there was a Lakota women too. It was amazing that we could unite in one circle.

After the lodge that night, I had an amazing dream. I saw a modern yet ancient stone house on a street where I was visiting. Sweat Lodges are often referred to as a sacred stone lodge or stone house. This one looked like a square stone two-story house from the front, but this Heyoka, the same one who poured the lodge for us, invited me to come to the back on a stone trail. The house was "L" shaped, and when we reached the back, the house was all glass. I think the "L" shape of the house was for laughter, Love, or Light, as the Heyokas bring in Joy. I could see several leaders of the Sundance I had just attended and medicine men and women inside that I did not know.

Inviting me into it, he said, "Welcome sister." I was thrilled to be a part of the community. "Come on in, you are one of us," he said. Then I woke up.

At first I thought he meant that I was a Heyoka, but later, I realized what that dream meant to me. I was to bring in those things too, joy of connecting with loved ones, and the reality of death to those who came to me. As a medium in training, this made sense to me. Entering the stone house of Love, I was connecting with others like myself who could see spirits and were seers. Death is a "doorway" that we go through to get healing. It was a prophetic dream, one of my future life as a healer, medium, and psychic. I was not yet practicing my mediumistic work at this point, only doing massage and some energy healing like Reiki. Perhaps I am a Heyoka in Western Culture, as I am unconventional, no question about that!

I later learned that white people are often referred to as "Wasechu," which for years I thought meant white people. However, years later, after my seventh or eighth dance, a Lakota girl said that it translates as, "those who take," a way of life that is not regarded as in line with Lakota values.

It had nothing to do with the color of their skin, but more to do with one's actions. In Lakota values, generosity is the heart of God. "Taking" is considered selfish, as everyone in a tribal setting has to share to survive.

One thing that stands out above all else over the twenty-six years that I attended and danced in many Sundances and

Ogitchidaah ceremonies of the Annishnabe (Ojibway) people in Northern Wisconsin, was that I learned more about Christ Consciousness than in any Christian church I had ever been in. I saw more self-sacrifice in an authentic way, more prayer, bodily prayer, prayer that rattled from one's whole being, and we were held by that prayer as we danced for four days with no food or water during sun rise to sun down dancing. I saw miracles everyday and the spirits of nature dancing with us, everyone sees them, and feels them all around everywhere. I also feel a deep connection with the Earth.

As often as I could at home, I went to Point Reyes National Seashore, or to a park at the top of the mountain during the time I was living in San Rafael. As I took my morning walk up to the park on top of the mountain, I surprised five deer as they grazed there. None of them moved. I showed them my ears with my palms cupped like theirs, and they went back to grazing. I walked past them a few feet away, and they continued grazing.

In another encounter, I wrote this poem. Later I would write a whole book about this relationship with the deer, called *Poems for the Lost Deer* (Blue Bone Books, Santa Cruz, CA., 2014)

>I tucked a tuft into my hat.
>Laying down strands of hair in exchange
>
>An old Indian song rose up in my throat:
>
>Pelamayeo,   Palamayeo?
>Thank you, Thank you Creator,
>Wakan Tanka, Toka Heya, Che wa kealo.
>
>Tufts of their fur lay at my feet.
>Seven white deer appear
>grazing on a hillside.
>
>An apparition? Their presence answers
>their gaze at me, going back to grazing,

just after asking for a sign

Is writing my path?

After fasting for two days,
walking those hills
Rounding the corner of a yellow trail...

Since this time in the early 1990's, I have completed running my own sacred lodge for fourteen years offering a healing lodge to hundreds of people, including friends in the two Native traditions that I participated in, the Lakota Sundance, and the Annishnabe Ogitchidaah. Always the spirits come in to help and to heal. Always, I am extremely grateful.

After many years in Lakota Sundances, I also visited and became a part of Afro-Brazilian traditions called Umbanda—a mediumistic tradition popular in Brazil. It is through Umbanda that I learned how to be a medium professionally and learned about channeling spirits of light. Umbanda is also a healing ceremony, which is why I was so attracted to the tradition. There is more on Umbanda in a later chapter.

Chapter Five

Beginning my Work
Gold Miner's Ghosts

One day, a year after my first Sundance, my friend Christine invited me to go to a hot springs. I had been in California for a few years. Like most transplants from the Midwest, I had gone to Calistoga almost immediately after my arrival, but this was Wilbur Hot Springs, set deep in gold mining country, near Williams, California. At the time, Wilbur was still getting rebuilt, and was starting to grow its clientele.

Wilbur is an historic place. It is where the Patwin, Pomo, Wintun and Colusi—Native American inhabitants of Northern California's Coast Range mountains—had lived before the hotel was built. They used the healing waters of Wilbur Springs for healing for centuries. The Victorian Hotel was built in the 1880's and it had been a destination spot for relaxation on and off over the last century and a half.[4]

As we drove down the dirt road, kicking up dust behind us, we could not see from where we had come. Cows dotted the road, and at one point we had to drive very slowly through a herd that was not that interested in whether we wanted to get through or not.

Five miles on a dirt road, and through a cattle gate, we finally arrived at the hotel. We saw a three story Victorian hotel

---

[4] In March 2014 the historic hotel burned to the cement first floor. The infrastructure and the hot springs were still intact and people still visit. The owner, Dr. Richard L. Miller, has done much rebuilding and the hotel is experiencing a renaissance.

He sold the hotel a few years ago, and it continues to be a destination.

complete with a large cupola on top where one room had a panoramic view of the surrounding hills. Across the road are the hot springs.

    We stayed in the group room on the second floor of the hotel. In a large room for sleeping were many different people who stayed each with their own wardrobe and bed arranged for each bed to be somewhat private. The toilet was down the hall and a common sink was in a separate alcove. This was a much cheaper alternative to visiting the hot springs, as the rooms could be pricey. But to stay anywhere at Wilbur was well worth it.

    Across the driveway from the hotel were the hot spring baths. They are amazing, large baths that look like troughs 3-4 feet wide and 12-15 feet long and 3 feet deep. The waters are different temperatures from one pool to another. The three pools were under the roof of the well-crafted bathhouse, which is made of timbers in Japanese architectural style. One end of the bathhouse was open to view the swimming pool and paths to the sauna on the opposite side, while the other side of the bathhouse had long windows covered in the winter with plexiglas to keep the cold winds from blowing through from the surrounding hills. Those windows looked out on a cold plunge tub and wooden Adirondack chairs looking upstream. There was a swimming pool outside the bathhouse down a few steps and decks with a private tub around the corner under the highest deck.

    At the time we were there in the early 90s, the whole place was still quite rustic. They were renovating a little at a time. My friend told me of the days several years earlier when people came to do work-trade clean up during the day and tubing in the afternoon, with long walks through the cattle pastures when they could fit them in.

    Wilbur is adjacent to a thousand acres of gold mining territory, which had not been purchased yet by the owner of the hotel. When I visited on that trip with Christine, cattle were roaming on it in a lovely valley surrounded by dry brown hills. The valley took a wide dogleg turn after you passed the geyser.

The geyser had an old house that was falling apart in front of it on the road. In one corner of the wide valley about a mile from the lodge, the road divided and one lane went down into the valley, while the other road continued up a slight hill to the left. Up that road to the left, that was somewhat hidden by salt bush and trees, a gold mine shaft was still there.

Christine took me to a gold mining shafts with tin sheets flapping in the wind to the left of the valley. A tunnel at the end of the shaft was blocked off. Opposite the gold mine on the other side of the dirt road was a fence around a property with a chimney still standing and no house. Only the gate of the old metal fence remained, most of which had fallen down or was gone altogether. A border of plants, mostly very old rose bushes, outlined the edge of the property. It was clear to me that there had been a large house there at one time.

It was early morning as we wanted to avoid the heat that would develop in the valley later in the day. "This place is haunted!" Christine said of the gold mine and the surrounding property. "I thought you might like to tune in with me and see what we see."

"Sure!" I replied, "Let's see what develops."

As soon as we sat in a lotus position in the middle of nowhere, with the tin sheets of the mineshafts creaking behind us, Christine and I began to focus on this gate and the absent house where the chimney still stood on this piece of property. She did not say a thing about what she perceived.

Soon I began to see a whole boarding house with a woman getting people up, moving as if they had just awoken in the early morning. She was cooking biscuits. All the boarders were men and they worked in the mine. All of this was in ghost form. The ghosts were acting as if they were still alive living in the boarding house. I could hear the pans banging and the stove lids being clanked into their circular opening in the woodstove. I could even smell the biscuits!

When I asked the spirits of the land what happened to the boarding house, I perceived a fire that started with the stove chimney that grew red-hot and set the timbers on fire. The fire burned the whole place down in an instant, with the high winds rising in the early morning. It had been a dry fall day and no one survived. Everyone perished in minutes. The miners and the couple that ran the house died before they knew what hit them.

When I told Christine the story, she agreed with what I shared with her and saw it, too. Then she told me she wasn't sure what to do with the property, or whether it was her place to do anything with the miners' ghosts. As we discussed it, I asked my guidance what we should do. I was guided to pray for those who had died. We decided to pray them over to the other side. Clearly, they were stuck in this reality with no way over.

So I projected my spirit to the house, and "woke up" the woman cooking by saying to her,

"I am sorry about the fire. Did you know you all perished that day?"

That was news to her! She looked startled, and then as the rest of the house miners woke up to the fact of their death, a veil was lifted from the whole house. I asked for them to find the light, and they all left, moving closer and closer to a bright yellow portal that seemed to open just for them. One by one, they began to leave by floating up to the hole that was made for them by the angels to the other side. I could see their spirits floating into the light.

Christine and I were both startled and felt a sense of peace as the spirits rose out of sight. When it was over, the wind picked up and rattled the bushes with a slight wild rose scent in the air. The gate creaked as the wind blew it open. We felt the winds of change around us.

We turned around from where we sat and checked the mineshaft and other areas around the mine for ghosts. Neither of us felt any spirits there as we had at the burned down boarding house. We walked back to the lodge and dodged the cattle and cow pies on our way back to the hot springs. Both of us walked in the silence of the moment feeling grateful to be of such service.

Little did I know this would be the first in a long line of house clearings that I would do professionally in the future to help people release ghosts and various spirits that were stuck between worlds in their houses all over California.

Medium with a Massage Practice

During the time I lived in Marin County, first in San Anselmo, and then in San Rafael, I found that people who I gave massage to were often wanting the other services I offered, such as energy clearing, or color healing, or mediumistic work like clearing entities from them. I also cleared curses from them if they had any in or around them. I found that I could do it, and didn't know how I knew. I would look for devices, mechanisms, or controls implanted in their fields. They usually came complaining of a pain, or a feeling of being manipulated. Then I would look at their fields and bingo, there was the control attached where they were hurting.

It often took me some time to clear the energies that were attached to them from me. Very often the entities were seeking their life force from anger, fear or saddness. It took me a few times to clear these entities within a few hours. I also used sage to clear my field and that really helped.

In my spare time I began writing my first book, *Dancing Up the Moon*, a book on ritual that started as my graduate thesis, and I wrote poetry, making trips south to Monterey to study with the poet David Whyte. He was an extraordinary bard, who taught a year-long course on writing and speaking poems. I had first met him in grad school while assisting speakers as part of my work-study. I got on his mailing list and for six years, I followed him around selling his books and listening to him read poetry. He awakened my own poet within me.

One day while coming home from Monterey after a poetry group, I felt a strong compulsion to drive to the ocean along Sand City. It was as if an unseen force other than myself was driving my car. I found an access road and drove to a parking lot. Getting out of my car, I was drawn to walk up a sand dune and over the top to face the ocean. When I scurried down the other side about halfway to the shore, it was as though I was forced to sit down by invisible hands that pressed down on my shoulders. No one else was on this beach.

I meditated for a few minutes, and then gazed out at the sea. Suddenly, a dolphin came right up out of the sea about ten yards from the shore. It was as though he was looking at me and communing in a language I did not know but could readily understand. It kept its head out of water and I could see it sculling with its tail to stay above the water. I could not tell you what he told me, but it was as though it was a connection I needed to make for some larger plan.

When its communication was over, it dove, then resurfaced again facing me; then it dove and resurfaced again, and finally dove under the water and disappeared. I felt blessed and grateful, and part of some plan I had not been aware of until that moment. This plan was much greater than me. It felt like this was about rebalancing humanity in some way through nature, and in healing work. When the dolphin disappeared into the waves, people began walking and coming onto dunes, and I left the beach. It was as though our meeting was over, and it was time to go home to San Anselmo.

During this time, I also traded sessions with people who did other modalities other than what I offered at the time, Swedish/Esalen massage, or energetic healing. One of those people was Sally Aderton. Sally was a medium, and she practiced throughout Marin County and across the country.

Sally would channel her guides for me and then I would give her a massage, usually in two different sessions within the same week or two. One time when Sally was channeling for me, she brought in WuLan. He was a Tibetan Buddhist guide who she had had a relationship with in a past life. I had too, apparently. At first I thought, 'Okay she is giving me an opportunity to talk with my guides.' Then after a while, I was thinking, 'Wait a minute, why am I not talking to my guides directly?'

Wulan through Sally said to me, "You can do this, too, Robin dear, if you want to." Meaning, I could also channel.

"No thanks," I said to Wulan. "If you bring me a teacher who really knows what they are doing, I might consider it."

I did start channeling WuLan right away through automatic writing, a technique my Grandfather Lysne had talked about when I was a child. Automatic writing surrenders your arm to the entity and you let your hand go and let the entity write the answers through your body. It is very effective. That is how I began to talk with WuLan, and later with other Angels and Guides. The difference between Angels and Guides is that generally, Guides have been in a body, while Angels generally haven't, though a few have briefly to learn about the Earth.

Eventually, I did find a teacher, several actually. One was Lily Cornforth, a color-healing teacher from England, and her student, Richard White who lived in Marin County. I learned from Richard over the course of a year. At the end of that year, Lily came over from England and tested us. She was a lovely elderly woman, very dedicated to color healing and bringing it to the world. I passed her testing very well.

Another one of these teachers was Richard Maldonado. I met him in a sweat lodge in Marin County near Santa Rosa. He sat behind the lodge leader with his light glowing in the dark like a light bulb. Every month that the lodge was being held, I bugged him for nearly two years to teach me what he knew. Finally, one day after a lodge, he invited me to his house to talk about my work and what I wanted to learn. But before I could say, "Teacher" he said, "I am your consultant, not your teacher. Got it?!" He felt I knew enough. I just did not yet have all the techniques consolidated into a way of working within my practice.

So he helped me over the course of a year, pulling together energetic seeing with color and sound healing, chakra clearing, Reiki, and rebuilding charkas, and what I knew of entities, releasing negative energies—all in weekly meetings that lasted from one to three hours. He did not charge me very much, about $40 a session. He was fun, and funny, and I felt blessed to be hanging out with him. We shared the same outrageous sense of humor. Then one day he said, "Enough, you know what you are doing, get yourself out there!"

However, before I could fully become a professional medium, I first had some more lessons to learn. Those lessons took place within my own family.

Martha Lysne Heerens 1940's

Jo and Walther Lysne 1970's

Family Photo 1956 or 57: Right to left: Aunt Trudy, Dad, Mom, Grandpa and Grandma Heerens, Great Aunt, Uncle Ralph laying above, cousin Wanda, Great Aunt, Sisters Jill, Sara, Robin, Sisters Nancy, Kisti, cousin Karen.

Chapter Six
"April is the cruelest Month"
William Shakespeare from Hamlet

Mom's Story

If you think that grief is any easier for a medium than it is for anyone else, think again. Grief is grief, and even though a medium can experience other realms of existence beyond this one, it doesn't make it easier to let go of those you love in this world.

Besides the loss of all four grandparents by this time in the late 1980's, my first experience of this was with my mother. She was diagnosed with pancreatic cancer in 1995, eight years after I had left Michigan for California. Naturally, when anyone hears of a loved one's impending death, there is tremendous upset. It was no different for me. At this time, there was no cure and we all knew the disease was fatal. My mom was just seventy-three when she received this diagnosis.

The night before I got the news, I had enjoyed a glass of wine with friends and had a great time celebrating my first book release. I was too tired to listen to the messages on my answering machine when I got home as I usually did; for some reason I just couldn't take in another thing and it was very late. So in the morning after meditating, I listened to the first message. It was my sister Jill, who said with a great deal of stress in her voice, "Robby call Mom. It is urgent. Just call Mom." Then she abruptly hung up.

When I called Mom in the morning, she answered the phone, and sounded tired and somewhat defeated. After she stuttered around the issue, she finally said, "Robby, I had a CAT scan yesterday after coming home with your father early from our trip. We went right to the hospital, and didn't stop at home as I was having symptoms for the last week when we drove across country. Honey, my liver looks like Swiss cheese. I have pancreatic cancer. I could see the look on the other doctors' faces through the glass as they looked at my scan."

There was not much they could do. With liver involvement and metastasis, she was certainly not going to survive long—at most, from what I understood about the disease, maybe a few months.

After crying and talking about what had happened on the trip and how they had decided to come back to Rockford early because of her symptoms, we told each other we loved one another, and hung up the phone. My head was spinning. I felt shaken to the core.

It was just a month before this diagnosis when my first book had come out. Flowers from my publisher were dropping their petals on the windowsill as I talked to my mom on the phone. I was preparing for a book tour that my publisher set up. I was going to leave the end of May and take the summer to visit many places already established on my way. It was the first part of April. What was I to do now?

I did what I often did in those days; I took my sacred pipe, or Chanumpa, and walked up the trail to the woods. The trail was just at the end of the road, about five driveways away from the house where I was renting the downstairs. The couple, who I rented from were dear friends. We were like family.

Once on the mountain, I felt the sun breaking through the clouds, and I was up high enough to get some perspective. Mount Tamalpais rose to the south, and I was on the northern slope where a beautiful field opened up to trails and wild flowers. As I sat down in the grass I felt my confusion.

Book tour or not, I had to know what I should do with Mom. I had a frequent flyer ticket and maybe I could go back for Easter weekend, which was coming up that very next weekend.

Once my Chanumpa was loaded with special tobacco and tree bark, and I sang the songs preparing me for prayer, I faced the west, as was the custom, lit the pipe and asked for an answer. I asked the Creator what I should do. "Please show me a sign if I should go back to Rockford or not." I felt a hand above me come down on my pipe turning it deliberately to the East. My whole body had to turn around with it. Time to go home! The message could not be clearer.

That afternoon, I had an appointment with a friend, Anna, in Fairfax who did readings. We traded sessions. I gave her a massage and she did psychic readings for me.

When I got to her place, my head was spinning again. "Please help me Anna, I don't know what I should do, if or when I should go, or for how long."

After clearing my energy field with long breaths, and some sage, she said, "You are very hard to read today Robin. Your emotional turmoil is making it hard for me to get anything. Take some deep breaths and settle down."

I did this, struggling to center myself, and Anna intuitively tuned into my energy field. Then she gave me feedback on what she found. She directed me in some more breath-work to calm me enough to release the pent-up volcano that I had not been able to tap into myself. After a good cry, and some time talking about my feelings with her, she said, "I think I can tap in a little better now. Are you ready?"

"Go for it," I said without hesitation.

"You asked me about going back to Illinois. Yes this seems appropriate this weekend and also for an extended time during the rest of your mother's life. I see two paths before her. One that is short, a few months. It is the more unconscious way, short and very painful, much to be resolved in the next life. The other path is longer, maybe a year or more, and it seems that there would be more healing for her and the whole family with less physical pain for her as well. She has a window of choice right now. She can set her intention and chose what she wants to do. She needs to know this. It is why you are going back this weekend--to give her this information."

When we finished, I thanked Anna and left to do the innumerable errands that had to be done before I left for the weekend. In the next two days, I got my flight arranged, called my folks to tell them I would be home for Easter weekend, packed, and rescheduled clients.

When I called my parents the Thursday before I was to leave for Rockford, my sister Jill was visiting from her home in Iowa having dinner with them. Sully Johns, a few doors down from my parent's house, had just died not an hour before my call. Jill and Mom had just returned from being with Dotty, our family friend, and Sully's wife.

The wheel of life was definitely turning. Moving back became more likely for me because now my friend Jake, Sully's son and fellow Sundancer, was grieving with Dotty. His mom was also a personal friend. It seemed I was being called back. It was one more strand of interwoven events. I needed this trip to test the waters and see if it was something my parents wanted as well. My book and clients would have to wait. When I got home, I started writing in my journal to process the events of the week and wrote this poem.

Deluge

> Spring has come with a vengeance.
> The pelting rains have not stopped
> since I arrived. The earth and sky
> are weeping for my Mother.

I got the last seat available on a flight from San Francisco to Chicago via Kansas City, Pittsburgh, and South Bend, Indiana. This was not my favorite flight path, but a free flight was a free flight. I wanted to kiss the tarmac when I arrived at O'Hare. After the hour and fifteen-minute bus ride to Rockford, my parents greeted me at the Clock Tower Inn where the bus stopped.

As the bus pulled into the Inn, I caught a glimpse of my parents through the bus window. They looked stunned and vulnerable, as they huddled together. It was Easter weekend. I hadn't been home for Easter in years. This year it seemed more poignant than ever to be there for this holiday.

As the bus pulled to a stop, I was flooded with compassion for my parents, and realized that I wanted nothing more than to spend this time with them after such a shock. Mom had been diagnosed on the same day as the Oklahoma City bombing. It was a "get your house in order" kind of diagnosis. At least she had time to say goodbye to everyone, unlike the people in Oklahoma City.

After hugs and collecting my luggage, my parents and I drove a few miles to their home with little conversation, punctuated with awkward and sometimes bottomless silences. Mom was visibly tired and somewhat shaky as I settled into the familiar surroundings of my parent's house.

"I'll get dinner in a few minutes, I just need to lay down for a little while," Mom said as she laid down on the couch that divided the living room from the dining area.

"There is no rush, Mom," I reassured her.

Jill had gone home a few days before. It was Good Friday. I would leave on Tuesday with a similar flight pattern home. I was grateful to have a few days with them alone.

As I watched my mother lay down on the couch, I wondered when the time would be right to share with her what I had learned from Anna. During the conversation with Anna, I had listened carefully as she spoke to feel into Anna's words to see if they were true for me too. They seemed accurate to my own inner resonance, once I was able to calm down enough to locate that quiet sense of "yes" inside me, I knew I had to share this message with Mom.

Illinois was so different than life in Marin County, California. The social cultures were opposite. I lived with other single people in a town that seemed to be mostly single people. A few couples I knew were married or living with others, struggling with their relationships. But the predominant spirit was independence. Rockford was made up of mostly couples, a family town, a good place to raise children, but single people were a bit strange to them. Single wasn't done much in Rockford.

Being back for such a short time, it was hard to fully

grasp the contrast between the West coast and the North Central Midwest. But I wondered how it would be to live there again, even for a few months. I often felt like a fish out of water in my hometown after almost ten years in California.

Just as my sisters and I had experienced for much of our childhood, Mom cooked dinner and we helped wherever we could, setting the table, getting the water on, making the salad. That night, Mom made her famous curried shrimp. She sent Dad to the store with a long list of other things we needed.

I always loved this time with my Mom. I realized for the first time, as we fell into familiar rhythms of conversation, that these familiar rhythms would not go on forever. It was time to bond with Mom in the kitchen like we always had.

"You know how to make this Robby? Come here let me show you," Mom said.

She added lemon juice and then the sour cream. I didn't have the heart to tell her I was not eating dairy; but my eating habits would soon adapt to the Midwest. Living so close to Wisconsin farms, dairy and meat were almost unavoidable.

My mother was always a fabulous cook. She made the most of mealtime, where a beautiful table complemented the elegant feast. She had passed on her cooking skills and her aesthetics to all of us girls. I always felt I was apprenticing her, even then in my early forties.

Our dinner conversation was tender. I learned details of Sully's death and of the other local folks who had passed on recently. Dotty had called Mom after calling the ambulance. She arrived before the paramedics with Jill. I heard about the ambulance, how Dottie and family were in shock after such a sudden death. We also spoke of mother's CAT scan where her liver "looked like Swiss cheese."

"Mom, there are people I knew at Commonweal Cancer Help Program, where I worked as a massage therapist, with liver cancer who lived two years or more after their diagnosis. I know pancreatic moves faster generally, but who knows how long you have?"

Her eyes were soft and hopeful. "Well, however long I

have, I intend to make the most of the time I have left."

I thought then of Anna's words. It didn't seem to be the time to tell her what I had been told by my wise friend. Tomorrow, we'll talk, I thought to myself.

The next day there was a time that presented itself. My father was on errands around town and Mom and I had some time alone together. Dad would not have been receptive to this information at that point in his life. He was too much of a scientist, so I wanted her alone.

"Mom, I wanted to share some information with you that I got from a psychic friend. I want you to know before I say anything that you will want to listen with discernment about what she has told me. See if it feels true for you. Don't take it in if it doesn't feel right."

"O.K. Robby, you know I usually make up my own mind anyway," Mom said with a grin, sitting across from me on the couch.

Mom and I were well aware of the psychic dimensions of the universe, as we both shared the ability to see or sense energy. Often when I was growing up, we saw the same phenomena. Energy or spirits or angels or ghosts hovered around the ceiling of the Lutheran church we attended. Sometimes they stood behind the minister. Her father, sister, and mother were also highly intuitive. One of my sisters, Kisti, was also somewhat sensitive. Astral travel, psychic readings, and spiritual channeling were often topics for conversation during visits to her parents-in-law, and my Lysne grandparent's home.

"Well, you know I exchange healing sessions with a number of people out there in California. One friend is Anna. Wednesday, I had a session from her after hearing about your diagnosis. She really did a mini-reading for both of us. She said that it seems that you have a window of choice right now. She said that while this diagnosis isn't a great one, that you can choose a longer course, or a short one. The shorter way will have less opportunity for healing; while quick, it will be more painful. The other way will give you time to work things through with Dad and the rest of us for optimal healing. But it is your choice."

I went on to add, "I have witnessed this at Commonweal too. People often go there as a retreat to take some time out after their diagnosis to decide how they are going to approach this disease, what it means to them, what their lives will mean from here on out. It is almost as if they decide, in some cases, whether they will leave now or later. It seems that you have the same kind of window, Mom."

"That is odd, Robby, the doctors have sent my biopsy slides to Mayo's.[5] They are uncertain what kind of cancer this is, if it is a fast-growing cell or a slow-growing one. It never occurred to me that I might have a choice about the progression. Your friend seems to be picking up on something here."

"All you have to do Mom is set your intention. It is nobody's choice but yours. It is your body, your life."

"The other thing I wanted to ask you is if you want me to come home. I would be happy to come back from California if you need me to."

We both started to cry. "You would do that for me?" Mom wailed.

"Yes, and I would do it for me, too. It is so hard being so far away. I think I would feel better if I could come home and walk with you and Dad through this."

I felt a sense of fear and elation as I said those words. I knew it wouldn't be easy for me to make the transition. But I was so out of touch in California, so far away from the unfolding events of the next few days, weeks or months.

Dad came home and we started to get dinner ready. While we were eating, Mom told Dad that I was thinking about coming home.

"Only if it works for you Rob. We don't want you to make an emotional decision. Think about whether it will work for you professionally. But you know we would love to have you."

I was touched by his candor. They always wanted what was right for each of us first, their needs second. By his state-

---
[5] Mayo Clinic, in Rochester, Minnesota

ment, I also knew he wanted me to come home.

"Well, I am doing a book tour across the country in May and June—of course, all depending on how you are. I have things scheduled into July. But Chicago is a more central location than California to reach Midwestern locales and the East coast. Rockford could be a great central departure place!"

As we talked it became clear that it was a good idea to move back to Rockford temporarily, just an hour and a quarter from O'Hare Airport, even in the middle of launching my first book. Eventually if I decided to stay in the Midwest, I would move to Chicago or somewhere else. Maybe I would eventually go back to California. But I wasn't sure. I wanted to see more clearly the next steps before I made any permanent plans or final decisions.

Everything would depend on Mom and how she was. She didn't seem bad right now, but it seemed uncertain at best. Of course, no one can predict the course of someone's life or the date of death. I shuddered at the thought and I knew how unprepared I was for such an event.

That weekend went by so quickly. On Easter Sunday we went to their Unity church. Sully's funeral was also that weekend. It was so good to see so many old friends. I was especially glad to be there with Dotty, Jake, and my Mom and Dad. Going to a funeral after receiving such a diagnosis was not easy for either of my parents, especially when it was a neighbor so close to home. It wasn't easy for me either, but somehow, it was better to share the difficulty together than alone. At that point they did not want anyone in the community to know about her fatal diagnosis.

On the flight home I reviewed the choice I was making. In some way it seemed not a choice at all, but what was required at this time of my life, and at this time of my parents' lives too.

I reflected on the plane home how my parents never played favorites with each of their five daughters. This I appreciated a great deal.

Mom was close to all of us in her own way. With me, she talked about metaphysical things and how things were going with my life and theirs. Dad was open, too, but Mom was the one who communicated with us about things that were important to us, namely our relationship with God, and how we were discovering our own path.

When I returned to California, I set about planning and making decisions about what to put into storage and what to take with me. My head was spinning as I walked through the door of my apartment.

What I learned from this interaction with Mom and sharing with her about her choices, was that there seems to be a direct connection between suffering and healing karma. At least for her, a longer life was the reward for doing the healing work in relationships, and life would be less painful in the long run. The shorter course would be more painful with less healing and with more karma down the road in the next life. This was a revelation that took a long time to understand as I watched my mother go through her last year.

Leaving and Arriving: The First Book Tour

Making Dinner
I almost threw out the strawberry jam that Mom made.
Preserves too sweet for me, but not for her.
Tonight, enshrine each jar.

Wind howling, dead branches crack outside.
Inside I turn up the heat, mix curry with her jelly
pour it over sizzling chicken, taste spice,
Mom's indelible sweetness is too sweet for me.

When I arrived home to California from Easter weekend with my parents, I made myself a fine dinner. It was comfort food after such a long trip, yet way too sweet. I threw some garlic powder on top, just to make it more palatable for me.

The next day my adopted family told me I had to move because the neighbors were complaining, and the police had visited with a zoning ordinance in hand. We were having trouble with the neighbors who complained about my landlords having a renter. I had been there less than two months.

"But we're family!" I protested. My friends agreed.

The only problem was I wasn't family according to the neighborhood rules. Only single-family homes were allowed unless a relative moved in, like your mother, or a child showed up on your doorstep. We solved that problem by adoption. We did a ritual and everything. According to us, we were family.

However, the neighbors didn't see it that way, and I have to admit I could see why. I am tall and lanky, rather Norwegian looking with fair hair and tall stature. My friends are short and tiny framed, rather Eastern European looking. One has a New York accent mine is definitely Midwestern. The genetics were definitely not a match.

As we were discussing the matter in my little apartment, the phone rang. It was another friend and client, Barbara.

"Robin, my radar tells me that you need some help. What can I do for you?" After a short silence, I burst out laughing.

"I can't believe you are calling! Well, I need a place to live."

"No problem, you can have my Marin house. How long do you need it?"

"Just until I leave for Rockford, no longer than a month. Can you help me out for that long?"

"That's fine. There is a couple leaving this week by Friday morning, I'll meet you with the key on Friday afternoon, one o'clock. How's that?"

"Can I bring my cat?"

"I'll have to talk with my husband. He's allergic, but I think for that short a time, it won't be a problem."

That was grace at work. I love serendipity. I began packing immediately.

After moving most of my stuff into storage and then staying at Barbara and Lincoln's house for a month, I said my goodbyes to my friends, and loaded my cat and what little I had to take on my road trip for a temporary move across country. Minka was not used to cars, she hated them. I tried my best to acclimate her that month, but nothing seemed to work.

By the time I left on my trip home, and made it to Mt. Shasta, Minka was not doing well. The next morning at a motel, as I was getting ready for the second leg of my trip, I said to her, "Okay, Minka, you stay here in your harness, and I will get things packed and ready to go." I could hear her say to me, "NOOO WAY!"

My cat slipped out of her harness and ran away, which was devastating. I really wanted Minka to make it home with me. But there was nothing I could do except give the hotel manager a description of her with my phone numbers in California and Illinois. I had a schedule to keep and I did not want to blow this opportunity by not meeting the obligations of my first book tour. My first stop was Eugene.

After two weeks of traveling across country and offering workshops, book signings, and radio interviews, I arrived at my parents' home exhausted but ready to begin my new life for the time being, in Rockford. I came in with a lot of expectations and was surprised with a full-on family dinner for my youngest sister's birthday. It did not go well. I felt sad and angry that no one acknowledged my book release. There was not a whisper of congratulations and I was too tired to care about trying to hide my disappointment. It was the first time I had seen everyone since it was published. My parents were the only ones that voiced any congratulations, which they had done privately.

I also had a full schedule in Madison and Chicago with book signings, workshops, and a sermon on Sunday in Rockford at a Unitarian church. The whole family came to listen to the sermon. I was so excited but at the same time just wanted to get through it without any fallout. There was a great deal of tension due to us all being cramped into the two rooms downstairs to sleep in. I needed my space and considered going to a motel. But with little money and big family expectations, I decided to comply. I was quite inexperienced in taking care of myself emotionally with my family all around me. I had never done a book tour before and I was not prepared for how exhausting it could be. This was my first foray in throwing myself completely out of balance.

I learned a hard lesson that first weekend back home. That I must take care of my energy first, before I get so far out of balance that I can't seem to get centered again. The way for me to do that is to be alone, not with sisters, brother-in-laws, grandkids and the whole family sleeping in two large rooms.

After my sisters left, I was able to get more sleep to recover from the long trip and the exhausting schedule. I finally had more opportunity to write and be with myself so I could hear my spirit guides. At this stage of my development, I could listen to them often and hear them clearly when I asked for information. That is when I realized I was on a different mission than the one I had thought I was on.

The first two instructions from my guides were clear: be with your own healing around this journey, and let your mom have her process. My guides always expect me to make my own decisions, as they are guides, not generals. But this time was different. The third instruction was not a suggestion.

I was ordered (which they had never done before): ROBIN Dear: Do NOT help your mother heal except to make her more comfortable. You are not to interfere with another's process, even your own mother."

My mother was destined to die from this disease. It would not help her soul growth to relieve her of the disease. If I had tried to "heal" her, it would have wasted my energy and eventually harmed her because her disease was part of her growth as a soul. I was to make her more comfortable, not heal her. Period! Needless to say, this was very hard for me to implement. It required me to be very much in the moment when I was around her massaging her sore muscles.

I was used to healing people with massage and energy work that I had learned from many various teachers in California. I got great responses and was quite busy as a result in California. I loved watching people rise entirely new after an energy balancing and massage. But now I was in a new place where I had to start over with a new practice, and instead of massage, I decided to focus just on the energy healing.

I attended a massage therapists meeting and met several people who then began to send me clients. It was my guidance at work. Suddenly I had a rather full practice.

I realized that my guides were correct. Mom and Dad had their own process to go through as a couple, and they had things to work through together. I was not a part of it.

Some neighbors needed someone to house-sit while they left for Arizona. So I moved to a two story condo a few doors down the street from my parents, a month after I arrived. I had my own place to process and finish my book tour, and be with my parents as I joined them for dinner almost every night. Friends from Sundance, who lived in Rockford and attended the same dance, helped me move in to the new place. Mom was doing quite well at this stage. It was October, and I was finally finished flying back and forth to New York, California, and driving into Madison, Milwaukee, and Chicago. We spent a nice Christmas Holiday together, realizing that it might be the last one with Mom.

By January, my parents were planning a trip to Brownsville, Texas to visit my sister Kisti. They often took trips in the winter—their "perigrinations," as they liked to call them, to warmer states.

After a few weeks traveling through Florida, they arrived in Texas, and my mother began to have severe pain. I flew down and joined them. My sister Kisti and I talked to Mom, and tried to help her. Dad arranged flights for them back home the next day. She needed Chemo or radiation, as a fast growing tumor was pushing hard on the nerves in her neck. It came up suddenly, which was a big concern. This was January, I knew it would be a tough spring.

Through the winter Mom felt pretty awful from the radiation the doctors had given her for the tumor in her neck. Radiation shrunk the tumor, but it had burned her esophagus and she couldn't swallow much of anything. It hurt too much. She lost a lot of weight and was staying home all the time now.

She slept most of the day in little catnaps, up and down all through the night too.

Still, she was able to rally the troops for Easter, and had us host an all-out Easter dinner for some friends and our family. It took four of us plus Dad to come close to offering a Martha Heerens Feast, with a beautiful table, and splendid lamb roast, potatoes, salad, gravy, and vegetables, with pie for dessert. In the past when she was feeling well, she had presented dinners like this effortlessly for twenty or more relatives.

Right after Easter, Mom called me into her bedroom. "Robby, I need some new shoes. Will you get me some? Here is my credit card. Go to Target, or Walmart, nothing fancy. Size 8."

Her command was so direct and deliberate. She wanted new shoes even though she was not wearing anything but slippers. "Sure Mom, whatever you need," was the only answer I could muster. I got her the shoes—just some simple sandals—nothing fancy.

The second week of May, a few weeks after Easter, I got a bad cold and I was feeling really terrible. I had just moved back into my parents' house the first part of May when the neighbors came back from their winter stay in Arizona. Because I did not want to make Mom's complications worse, I called my sisters and asked if I could come recover at their place over night. They were fine with a visit. I talked to Dad, then Mom.

"I will only be gone 'till Saturday. I don't want to get Mom sicker from this cold. Pop you might want to get some coverage in here. Call Hospice, or see if Dotty or someone can bring a meal or two."

I rationalized that Hospice was already notified and had been over to see Mom. But my parents had decided not to use their services. My logical statement about leaving for a day was understood intellectually by them, but not emotionally. Energetically, I felt I had to leave to break contact with Mom for even a short amount of time. I felt that she was drawing energy from me, which is part of the reason I was getting sick. She was so energetically dependent, it did not feel right to stay, and I did not want to be blamed for killing her with my cold, her immune system was so weak.

So the next day, a Friday, I drove to Iowa City and stayed with Nan and Ralph. They had a room ready and I crashed in bed until late the next morning. We called Dad to check on Mom. She was not better at all, though Dad disguised his feelings about it. I felt a little better the next day after sleeping for fourteen hours straight, and late Saturday afternoon I drove back the three hours to Rockford. When I walked in that evening, less than twenty-four hours after driving to Iowa, Mom was already in bed. Dad reported that she had not gotten out of bed the day before.

The next morning, a Sunday, Mom hardly moved. She seemed to be in and out of consciousness. I talked to her, but she could only squeeze my hand that someone was there. She could not talk or respond much, except when she was in pain.

My sisters Jill and Nan followed me home Sunday afternoon, on the road they had travelled every weekend that entire year. They were in shock at how much Mom had deteriorated in one week.

"We are calling Kisti and Sara, now!" Nan announced. "It seems to be getting close."

By Monday evening, all four of my sisters were there. It was good to see them, and I was still quite sick with a bad head cold. My sisters took over Mom's care, except for what Dad did, giving her morphine and helping to relieve the pain she had more frequently now. He also took care of her at night.

Neighbors and friends that we hadn't seen for years brought food over for us. We called some of her closest friends, like Mae Gustafson, who came on Tuesday. They spoke alone together, and out of respect, because Mae had known Mom since nurses training, over fifty years before, we gladly left them to themselves. When Mae left, she came out of the room looking so sad. Then, in typical Mae fashion, she straightened her shoulders, said her good-byes to us warmly, and walked directly out of the house.

The door seemed to be spinning open with visitors; brothers-in-law, nieces and nephews, friends and relatives were in and out of the house. Friends called to offer places to stay for family coming into town. My sisters moved into various friends' homes, and got settled off site, as the house was always so full of people.

On Wednesday afternoon, May 15, 1996, Mom started to cheyne-stoke her breath, which is common at the end of life. We already had a vigil going from the moment my sisters came home on Sunday; someone was with her at all times. The whole family was around her bed all the time now. I took out my pen and paper to capture these last precious moments.

Los Angeles del Muerte

My sisters, Las Angeles,
bathe my Mother's arms and legs

wipe the dried tears from her eyes
dress her in her favorite satin gown.

My father hovers near the door, then checks her
pulse and breathing, pats her hand, her cheek.

They are getting her ready for the journey,
not far away nor a winding path.

Yet she inhales dust from the road
which gathers in her throat with every breath.

On the other side her mother, our Abuela,
sings to her with a host of others like her.

Their wings brush the arches of my sister's wings,
my father's. It is only a matter of time.

At six-thirty in the evening, several people came and went. My friend Sherrie, who had been like a sister through the whole ordeal, came by with a dish. She wanted to see Mom.

I brought her into the bedroom. I was aware that some of my sisters were wondering who in the hell this person was, even though they had all met her before.

Sherrie took one look at my mom laying there unconscious and barely breathing and began to cry softly. She put her arms around me and cried. We hugged each other. My sisters were dialing all the nieces and nephews, and they were saying goodbye one at a time. I wished they would let her die in peace, I thought, although I knew that Mom would love to talk to her grandchildren one last time too, if she could talk now. As she hears Keegan, my nephew say goodbye, I touch my Mom's feet, and they are icy cold. Nan yelled for Dad in the next room, and I can see Mom's spirit, getting ready to go, beginning to lift off.

I see her mother, our Grandma Lysne, there on the other side ready to catch her. A host of angels are all singing that song that Mom had been hearing for weeks. I hear it now too. Grandma, her mother, is telling me she's got her. My sisters are shouting their goodbyes.

Mom is going fast and getting reborn at the same time. Her spirit exits out her head, and she is off in a tunnel of cloudlike love. Grandma is catching her on the other side and looking so radiant. Sherrie holds onto me tight with both arms around my waist, as though to tether me to the Earth. My sisters are all around, each a strong oak tree themselves. Dad holds her hand, feels her pulse, pronounces her dead. Mom changes color and her eyes relax, the same distance apart, both opened a little. Dad passes his hand over her eyes to close her lids. It is over.

Immediately a wash of relief and grief passes over me, for her to be out of pain, for her loss, for the rest I so desperately need now, that we all need. Now we were all in the postmortem time: the time after.

Some of my sisters exhibit hostility towards Sherrie. I hugged and turned to her at the same time, "You better go. Thanks for being here, Sher." She kissed me and dried her tears, and left. She was there for a reason that I did not know, and I was so glad to have her there. I felt she tethered me to the

Earth, and kept me in my body. In spirit, I felt Mom being taken away somewhere. It seemed right and good. She was going to be fine.

    We washed her and dressed her body in the outfit she had told Dad she wanted to wear. It was a black outfit that had hand-painted feathers floating down the chest. Her new socks and sandals, which I had bought a few days before, were ready for her now and we slipped them onto her feet. My niece pinned a broach on her that she had made for her Grand Mom. I felt her to be in good hands on both sides of the veil.

Birth into Light

It was a little like dawn but coming from the inside out
first a tiny but potent hydrogen blast

Then the slow motion acceleration
well beyond the boundaries of previous limits.

The initial tear was excruciating ripping at fear tissue
held tightly together for centuries.

But then the realization that this is
being reborn ripping away the old womb world into the new.

It is so hard to die, but the staging comes in tiny dress rehearsals, then there is only you

in your new egg self, glowing from the inside out
brilliant, bright and golden.

    Over the next few days, we made decisions together about her ashes, the memorial, took walks, and waited for the next Sunday to come when the funeral was scheduled to take place in a church by the river. Mom was cremated and her ashes were to be placed under a new tree that we selected in Klehm

Arboretum, not far from the first home in Rockford where my parents had lived. But that wouldn't be for a while, not until the fall, when it would be a better time to plant a tree.

In the meantime, flowers, cards, and money came flooding in. My cold got better, and by the time of the memorial, I was able to be there without sneezing. My sisters got pictures out and make posters in preparations for the front lobby of the church. My sister Nan, brother-in-law Ralph, Cousin Michelle, and I all shared some writing at the funeral, along with three different ministers who spoke. We sing "On Eagles Wings", a hymn that we sang at Mom's Mother's funeral. There are so many people in the church some had to stand in the back lobby. Everyone loved Martha.

The reception was downstairs in the large hall where we had catered food. It was good to see all my family together, along with all of my Sundance community, not to mention all the extended friends and family who brought food and gathered around us at this major life transition. I was so grateful for everyone.

Mom was the first to die in our immediate family; it seemed she broke a good luck chain with her death. Now we were all vulnerable. "All bets are off," we said to each other.

On Saturday before the memorial, I moved into another new house sit with the help of my Sundance community of friends. I was so glad to be in my own place again, where silence and a meditative state can be exercised. My guidance was back, and my guides informed me that Mom is fine and do not try to contact her right now as she is in transition. This was another lesson: Don't contact the dead right away. Give them time to cross over to the other world. I am fine with letting her be. After the funeral, and after everyone returns home, for the first time in months, I have time to think about what I will do next. I cannot decide if I should stay in Rockford or move back to California.

Nothing else is planned, but I do have a few clients ahead of me. Then I get the idea to travel with some of the grant money I had received for writing. The grants are unrestricted, and therefore I could use the money how I saw fit. I also got a huge "retainer fee" from a generous client. All in all, it was enough to get me to Norway and back and to get home to California when the time was right. I wanted to be sure my Dad was okay first.

Traveling seemed a good idea, one that helps give some order to the chaos I had been experiencing. I brought my guides in to discuss my plans. There has been a revival of relationship with a man I used to know in San Francisco, and I ask about him and my travel plans.

WuLan came through in an automatic writing session.

"Good morning Robin, you have moved into your new house. It will be important to draw and paint some pictures in this new house, what do you want it filled with?

"Love, sweet Love, Wulan! Hello, dear heart. Yes, I am in my new house. It feels very good, and I am pregnant with the grace of life. I am contented and feel as though this were the best life I could live, right now."

"Are you complete with your grief, and lack of faith?"

"Yes, I think so."

"Your faith was tried and it has been stronger than we thought. So we are very pleased. We know how difficult it is to be in this plane of the Earth, and we understand that we are here to serve you while we can. There will be a changing of the guard for you as there are new guides for you coming in. This will help you realign to California. You have been steeped in the Midwest too long. Time to go to your home in the West.

"When you go back you will feel the difference. It will feel like coming home. When you recognize this, it will be time to set up a new life there. Look where you want to live. Draw and paint your home over the next few days. Be with who you are in this home. Manifest it!

"Contact those people who you love and care for. Look to Susan, and Paul and others. Of course, Mary Ellen.

"Hold them close. Move back for yourself, not for a marriage and potential pregnancy."

"Will you still be here, Wulan?"

"Yes, and soon you will see the changes in your own life. It is your faith that has made you whole."

"It seems that California was to be the choice. But I want to be sure. I planned to go to Europe to the places my Mother's family was from, Norway, and Scotland. I needed to go alone, before I made a move. Will Dad be okay? It seems as though I should stay for the summer."

"He will be fine. Do not worry about a thing." Love, Wulan.

Dad and I decided to take a workshop in Iowa at the Iowa's Writers Workshop the first week in June, just two weeks after Mom's death. I still felt as though I was walking in an altered state with the awareness that nothing is the same, yet, everything is the same.

Dad and I drove to Iowa City, and stayed at Jill and Dave's house while they were away. I am ecstatic to be taking a poetry workshop and wondering about my father who took a college workshop for the first time in fifty-five years. He is much enjoying his freedom, and wanting it now, wanting to explore life alone, even though every day was hard at the same time without Mom.

We drove into town to class together. He has finished writing his first essay in a memoir class about Mom and how they met. Dad was beginning the first few pages of a book he later called, *Love and Synchronicity*. I was glad he was writing and processing his life. I was in a poetry class with Timothy Lui and fellow poets, which always feels like a long cool drink of water for me after a hot dry journey. Right now, it was a good time to be with Dad, and heal.

Trip Home from Rockford via Norway

In late July, 1996, I took another trip to California to interview people for one of the books I had begun to write. In California, Alyssa (my therapist) and I completed our final therapy session, and we agreed to have one final lunch together when I arrived back in California to live. I met with friends, interviewed people who were making a difference by inventing programs that were innovative and exceptional. The last interview for my new book was with a man who I connected with very well. Surprisingly enough he called me, and he continued to call when I returned to Rockford. Perhaps he was it, perhaps not. I didn't know, and considering my own desire for a mate and family, my hopes were high. But I was also feeling very cautious as I had met and married in the past in a blaze of feelings without evaluating what kind of person the man was who I married to the first time around. I had learned the hard way and did not want to repeat my mistakes again.

In mid-August I was on my way to Norway to see the land of my ancestors. I wanted to see where my great-grandfathers and grandmothers had come from. Since I am half-Norwegian, I could visit both my grandfathers' families there. In Scotland, where my grandmother Jo Collins Lysne's family descended from, I could see the land of my mother's family on both sides. If I had time I would visit Denmark where my other grandmother's relatives were from, although it would be harder to find any relatives there, as her name, Larsen, was very common.

This trip was just what I needed before settling down somewhere. Arriving in Oslo, then traveling to Kragerø, I stayed with my Father's cousin Svein and his wife Ragnhild. They introduced me to their children and grandchildren. They toured me through the land in southern Norway where I saw medicine wheels, the same as Native American ones, at boat launches of Vikings. They took me to the house my great-grandmother and great-grandfather lived on Kragerø. My Great-grandmother was born in Kragerø, a small island attached to the mainland by a bridge. I was so thrilled, and even met a shirt-tail relative whose father was my great-grandfather's brother. He had a picture of the brothers Toraldsen on the wall. My great-grandfather had changed his name from Alfred Taraldsen Severin (our American family was told it was Thoraldsen or son of Thor) to Heerens (Belongs to God) on the boat over the Atlantic, after a religious experience on his boat trip. I could pick out my great-grandfather from the pictures. It was the same photograph my Grandpa Heerens had on his bedroom wall in Evanston before he and Grandma died. Svein translated for us our discussion with the cousin/man we met as he nor I spoke the other's language.

After leaving Svein and Ragnhild, I took the train to Oslo, then on to Lillihammer to stay with my sisters friends, then on to Bergen. Eventually, I was able to meet relatives on my mother's side in Laerdal at the end of the Sognefjord. We had not connected with our family in four generations. What a delight to meet the Lysne family in Laerdal. I learned a great deal about my family history that I did not know from the birth records. I saw where my grandfathers had come from on both sides of the family. This felt so important to me. I discovered many long-lost relatives including my great, great, great grandmother, Randine,[6] a midwife in Laerdal, Norway in the 1820s and 30s. All through the rest of the trip I wondered, what would it be like to be Randine? Eventually I wrote two books about her.

The ferryboat ride from Bergen to England was amazing over the North Sea. The sea was calm and the passengers were very friendly. I landed in Newcastle, which contrasted from Bergen's clean and relatively safe harbor, with New Castle's dark dingy buildings and people more depressed and less friendly than in Norway. It seemed economically much more strained in New Castle than in Bergen.

After spending a few days getting a rental car and trying to plan the last leg of my trip, I headed up the coast into Scotland. The land had a dark, sweet sadness to it that reminded me of my grandmother and mother. When I asked people about it they nodded in agreement and said "Ahh, yes, it's the Clearing." I had no idea what they meant. I had never studied Scottish history and did not know about "The Clearing."

---

[6] Two novels are part of the Legendary Ancestral Women's Series: Book One: *The Legend of Randine: Entering the Sisterhood, 2021*; and Book Two: *The Legend of Randine: The Laerdal Letters, 2022*. A narrative non-fiction book is the third series book: *Kisti's Royal Garden, 2023*. Both by Blue Bone Books.

I took a trip to Findhorn and interviewed several people there who had lived in the community for years. They told me of some of the history of the place. These would become interviews for my next book, added to the ones in California.[7]

Driving down to Cambridge I met my friend Madeline. She was an Irish nun who I went to graduate school with in California. She supervised a retreat center for her convent. When I told her about the land in Scotland, she explained that the English had cleared the land of Scotts, to make way for sheep, which were cheaper to keep on the land than the people who had always been there, hence "The Clearing." Of course, this is the event that prompted Rob Roy and other Scottish heroes to fight back. "The Clearing" had taken place over 300 years before, and it was still with the people today and imbedded in the land as this melancholic sadness. 'No wonder Blue Girl is still with me,' I thought.

"Blue Girl" was a part of me inside that I felt to be perpetually melancholy. Nothing I did could change her or make her feel better. She was just sad, a tragic romantic. I did not quite know what to do with her. I just acknowledged her and gave her a place to live in my heart. Eventually I would know more how to be with her and become her and not be sad. But at this time of my life, it was clear that I did not know how to do this yet.

Madeline and I visited Cambridge and had tea in an English teahouse near campus. It was wonderful to see her again.

After visiting Stonehenge and few other monuments from ancient times, I flew home. This time I was sure my home was not in Rockford, my time was over in my hometown. After the two trips, one to California and then to Norway, it was clear to me that I needed to go back to California.

When I returned, my father made it clear that he was also ready to have me leave. After dinner one night he said, "I

---
[7] The book I was researching never was completed. Instead, I integrated the information into a new book that Conari Press asked me to write on my arrival back to California, called; *Living A Sacred Life; 365 Meditations and Celebrations.*

don't want you hanging around for my sake, go on and live your life." It seemed I needed to move on.

Once in a while, I would check in on Mom, Grandma and Grandpa, but not often. I would not contact her directly, but "viewed" her activity psychically with a remote perspective on the other side, as though I were looking through a picture window a good distance from where she was. I did this very occasionally. This seemed to be a way I could check on her without disturbing her. She did not seem to notice that I was looking in on her. I did not call her back or try to speak to her at all. I was just checking to see how she was and what her progress was as she moved within the other realm where she lived now.

I laid out my plans to return to California. But I kept feeling quite exhausted, and I could not understand why. Yes, this trip was wonderful, but by mid-September after resting and seeing clients, I should have been back on my feet. This was not the case. I could not seem to get out of bed before ten or eleven o'clock and I was in bed by 9:30 p.m. almost every night, which was not my usual late-night pattern.

Before I left, I decided to visit a psychic for a reading to see if he could tell me why I was losing energy. It felt like I had a psychic drain stuck in my side and could not hold my own. He said I was still bonded to my mother and felt the need to take care of her. That did not sound right to me, as I was not communicating with her regularly at all, just checking to see how she was "remotely." Besides, my guides had told me not to, and I had obeyed them. The checking-in was just to see where she was occasionally, and I was not trying to take care of her or communicate in any way. He did an exercise with me where we cut the cords and did a little ritual to release whatever ties I still had with her that may be subconscious.

But what was not released was some other connection that I could not put my finger on. After visiting the psychic, I felt better, and had more energy for a few days, but after about a week I felt drained again.

It's the transition, I kept thinking, the unresolved grief perhaps, it's leaving Rockford and moving back to California, it is all happening rather quickly.

By the first of October, I was nearly packed and felt the sadness of leaving my friends who I had made over the past year and a half. Some I had known through Sundance in South Dakota and in graduate school ten years before. They were wonderful, and I had helped me so much. I could not have lived in and transitioned so well to Rockford without them. Several of them got together to offer me a going away party and ritual. It was so beautiful. Dad came too. I was touched by his sharing and love for me.

The man I had met in California for an interview with one of my future books was willing to come out and drive me cross-country, which was a nice surprise. I was feeling a little scared about it, primarily because I did not know him well at all, except in the interview and in phone calls we were making, but he would be meeting my family and friends and if he was willing to go through that fire, I figured I was going to be fine.

At the same time, I seemed to be rushing into this relationship, and while I felt a lot of caring for him, I knew from hard experience the fickleness of new love, and I was rather skeptical. (This was way before internet dating.) I kept trying to be the voice of reality for both of us with moderate success.

When he started talking about marriage, I put my foot down, and I finally told him the week before he came, that I would not talk of the "M" word until after we had spent considerable time together; at least a few months! I would be happy to stay at his place, if that worked for him, or until I figured out what to do next. But I was not promising him a thing. We agreed to travel together back to California, and that was that. There was no commitment.

A week later he landed in Chicago. I picked him up at his hotel, and he and I spent some time together—first with his older brother chaperoning at Chicago Pier—then us alone. I was getting some red flags from him early on, but thought, "well at least I'll get back to California if it doesn't work out." He was excited to make the trip.

The next day or so we were busy packing my truck and

getting the clam-shell on top. My father was patient with us both and helped us prepare to leave. His name was Jerald, and he was a chef and had prepared a feast for my friends the night before. We were still satiated from dinner as we pulled out of Rockford together. There were more warnings of his odd behavior over the course of our long drive home to California. I made a mental note of them and kept going as if we were going to overcome some of these obstacles in the future.

After saying goodbyes on the way through Iowa with two sisters and families then on to Denver to visit a third sister, we stopped to visit my old friend from Michigan, Brenda Morgan, who was now living in Boulder, Colorado. She was a wonderful, very insightful friend and spiritual teacher that I had had in Michigan along with Michael Silverman, the enlightened teacher she studied with. She gave us a place to stay as I had some catching up to do after not seeing her for ten years.

Jerald exploded at her house the next morning at breakfast, saying that this whole trip was focused on me, and he had had enough. He let go of a lot of stored up emotions.

I was embarrassed, shocked, and felt again as I had with my first husband, whittled down for having a self and expressing it. We had talked of the plan of the trip well in advance and he had agreed to it. I could not understand what he was complaining about. He seemed like a very small child stomping his feet because he wasn't getting enough attention!

"I am the one moving across country, leaving friends and family and I am saying good bye to them. I thought you were really quite the star in Rockford. What is the real problem here?" I shot back.

Brenda was a psychic and a psychotherapist. She spent some time talking to him. I felt as though he was being very childish. But I was still too exhausted to get angry or really react to his outburst.

Brenda gave me a reading after she spoke to Jerald. It felt good to be with her again. She affirmed that what I was doing was the right thing, and helped me see that this relationship was karmic. He was repaying me for some old karmic debt. That was the extent of our agreement. I owed him nothing beyond that, and it was a lesson for me about what I truly wanted in a relationship.

"Brenda I am so tired, I feel like my energy is leaking and I don't know why."

We agreed that it was my Mom, and the relationship with Jerald and the move. The combination perhaps, but something was still not right.

Jerald and I piled back into the car. He was still huffy and not speaking to me. His silence was a little absurd to me. I felt that it would be damn difficult to build a relationship on this kind of dissent. But it was also a relief not to talk, as I was tired of his argumentative state, and I wanted to just get on with the trip.

After we got over the Rockies, at a rest stop, he had his final outburst, and once again I felt diminished for being me. Brenda had helped me see that he was emotionally a small child of about three, a brilliant artistic genius, and a sad man who had not let go of the past. His combined personality characteristics were volatile. I felt like I had to handle him like I was his mother, definitely not what I wanted in a relationship. So I handled him the best I could, and we continued on our way.

Despite my skepticism, I wanted to take him to Utah, to the Aches National Park near Moab that I had seen with my niece when I first traveled to California ten years before. He had never crossed the country and really wanted to see the land.

By sunset we landed in Moab. He loved it and being a visual artistic type of person, he appreciated the red rocks and the strangeness of the landscape. We were able to see the arches the next morning. Sunrise set the red rocks surrounding Moab on fire. The red rocks seem to accentuate and change color with the red and orange sky. Blue shadows were everywhere as the sun lowered at night.

Since we were finally near a phone, he was able to make several calls to work and to his home phone. His paycheck had bounced, and he was bouncing checks in California like crazy.

He was off again on another diatribe. It was my fault somehow, and this definitely put a damper on our trip needless to say. I paid for the rest of the gas, and dinner, and motels. Honestly, I wanted to pack him into a diaper and send him home on a plane.

The rest of the trip was fairly uneventful. By the end of the week we had arrived at his home in Pt. Richmond. He lived in a two-flat apartment building.

After moving in temporarily, and visiting my storage unit across the Bay, and unloading what I could of it, Jerald and I settled in. I was there about three weeks, and at the end of that time, I felt worse than I had at the end of eight years of my first marriage. I was done with this. He hardly spoke to me, never told me where he was going or what he was up to. I found out he was being sued by one former lover, and had another suit from a former employer. He was very secretive about what he was doing, and I felt like he was sitting on a can of worms, or a powder keg, perhaps he was involved in drugs, I wasn't sure, but I knew I did not want to be around when it all came tumbling down.

At the beginning of the third week, I received a visit from my mother's spirit unbidden. I was just waking up. Jerald was already gone. I felt Mom's presence and 'saw her' sitting on the end of the bed. Then I heard Mom's voice say to me, "Honey, just leave. This isn't working. You do not need this aggravation. Just go."

When I got up that morning, I called a friend in Santa Cruz. I was calling for Sally Aderton at a number she had given me, but Roseline, an old friend from Marin, answered the phone instead. I had no idea they even knew each other.

"I'm calling for Sally or Susan. Oh my God, is this Roseline?!!"

"Robin? Oh my God!! What is happening, girlfriend? I can't believe it is you."

I was calling for Susan who worked part time for Sally doing secretarial things. Susan was also a business partner to Roseline who was operating a new business from Roseline's house. The last time I had seen Roseline she was in Marin and then had moved south to Santa Cruz, a two-hour drive, about two years before.

"Well, Roseline I need a place to stay, I am living with this man, I don't feel good about it, and it is time to go. Do you know anyone with a room to rent?"

"Well I can't believe this. Robin, I have a roommate that just left, or is in the process of leaving today, and I have a room here. You want to come see it?"

"Yes. Today works after 2? Fine, Give me directions."

That afternoon I arrived at Roseline's house in Aptos, about two hours south of Pt. Richmond. She was near a golf course, and there were trees and broad lawns, and a neighborhood with medium-sized two to three bedroom houses, very near the ocean. I felt at home coming to this area south of Santa Cruz. She invited me for supper. It was such a relief to be there.

She lived with her son, Segar. She and Susan sold new age products and vitamins, and got the word out in the usual Roseline style: "I found the most amazing thing, you have to see it!!!" she often said.

"Well, I was exhausted, I told her, I felt as though this relationship is ending, and I am sick about that too. I felt like such a fool."

"Robin, honey, you just got to move on, life is too short!" she smiled from ear to ear.

"Let me look around." I got a paper on my way out of town. I was frustrated. This would be easy but would it be right for me? She was glad to have me stay.

That night, one more time, Jerald did not come home until late. I think he had been drinking, or perhaps he really was at the kitchen working late—who knows. I didn't care anymore. It was over.

If I could only get over my exhaustion, I could tackle any situation. But something was not right. Just before I left his house, I got a call from my publisher. They wanted me to do another book for them. Was I game? Absolutely, I was ready to write again full tilt! I made a date with them to discuss the idea, and set my intention on moving forward to Aptos, south of Santa Cruz.

Jerald was nowhere to be found. I decided not to go through a big explanation; I would leave him a note, and just go.

"Step out the back, Jack, make a new plan Stan, don't need to be coy Roy, just listen to me…" That song, written by Paul Simon kept going through my brain. Brenda, Mom, and Rosline were right, just let go.

I called Roseline immediately and decided to move there. I moved over the next few days, sorting my things, getting ready to put things in storage again, and deciding what I would need to take with me to Roseline's house.

Before I left I got a call from my father. In his matter of fact style, he described to me Mom's burial which he wanted to do alone.

"It was real quick, the workers lifted the tree ball up, I threw the ashes in, and they put the tree in the hole. I shoveled one scoop of Earth, they did the rest. That was it."

We had decided we would plant a tree in Klehm Arboretum in her honor. Her ashes went under the tree. Kelm Arboretum was a sanctuary of tree varieties near their house on Cole Avenue where they had lived when they first moved to Rockford, some fifty-three years before. Eventually the Arboretum would place a plaque there, not far from the children's garden. It was a fitting living memorial to our mother who loved the outdoors and had five daughters and nine grandchildren.

It was no easy task for my father to bury my mom's ashes alone. Not only because of the finality of the act, but because we both knew my sisters wanted to be there too, as did I. But Dad did what he needed to do for himself, and I was glad he did.

He and Mom had begun together, just the two of them, and he wanted to complete their relationship that way too. I was grateful he could follow what he needed to do for himself. I told him of my impending move. He did not sound too surprised.

"Well, you have to do what is right for you, Robby. Let me know where you end up."

I loved his faith in me. He knew I would land on my feet. I told him about Roseline's and said I would call him when I got settled.

Arches National Park, Moab, Utah

Mom-Martha Lysne Heerens

Dad standing by Mom's Tree

Chapter Seven
Landing in Santa Cruz and Cutting the Ties that Bind

When I finally made it to Roseline's in Aptos, I was so relieved. I was exhausted from moving, but I couldn't shake an overall exhaustion that went much deeper. I was tired, deeply tired. Something had to shift. The next thing I knew I was laying on my bed, crying for the added loss and relocation. Roseline popped her head into my room.

"Mind if I come in?" When she saw me crying, she came in and gave me a hug. "Come on Robin, get over that guy, it seems he wasn't much anyway. Celebrate! You got out and it is over, yeah!"

She was right. But I was overwhelmed. "Oh, I almost forgot! I have to tell you that I have some people coming next week. I hope you don't mind," she continued looking somewhat guilty.

"Who's coming?" I asked not addressing the fact that I minded.

"We are hosting—are you ready for this—a Maori Medicine Woman, named Erena." She said Erena as though she was a movie starlet. E-R-E-N-A-A-A! Roseline was so excited, her broad, infectious smile stretched from ear to ear.

"Now I know I am truly back in California." I smiled. "Who is this woman?"

"I don't know, this friend is sponsoring her, but she is a Maori Medicine woman who is coming to do sessions and a workshop at Mount Madonna. Here is her picture and the flyer. As I looked at the picture, I immediately knew I had to see Erena. There was a fierce happiness to her round brown face. Her tattooed chin and lips were in the traditional Maori pattern of a warrior.

The next week I found myself face to face with the Mother Earth herself! This wonderful large, round, dark woman with a traditional "maku" tattoo embraced me immediately when I saw her. She carried a staff from a 1,000 year old Swedish yew tree from her husband's country. As fierce as she first appeared, she had a loving smile that filled the room. Her assistant, an Italian woman, was also very loving and warm. She was by contrast to Erena, very thin, and spoke little English. They were an odd pair for sure, but I knew they could help me somehow.

When I arrived in the room for my session, two steps from my own bedroom, after the initial hug, Erena looked at me deeply and asked me gently why I was there.

"Something is draining my energy. I don't know what it is. My mother died in May, I have moved across country, which could be part of the exhaustion, but something else is happening and I don't know why. Can you help me?"

She looked at me and around me as she surveyed my energy field. I knew she could see my spirit as well as my physical body. I felt her eyes penetrate my skin and she was looking deeply into my soul.

"Do you know you are very close to death?" She stated flatly.

"No I don't!" I replied with a shock.

"You are, and if we don't do a ceremony right now to release your Mother's spirit, you will join her very soon."

"Let's do it. I knew you could help me." I said with total clarity and relief.

She closed her eyes and prepared herself by going into the deep recesses of her soul and the Earth itself, to center herself. When she opened her eyes again, she placed her hand on my forehead and pushed me straight back onto a futon that was on the floor. I lay spread eagle, while her assistant threw cold water on me, and arranged my arms near my body, so she could get closer to me.

Erena began to chant very loudly in Maori. Her assistant knelt next to me, and shook a large rattle over my body. I felt the presence of my Mother, then something I have never felt from my mild mannered Mom before: her rage. As Erena stood in the way to protect me, she shouted at her in Maori very loudly. I could feel them battling on a psychic level. We witnessed together all the rage that my Mother denied herself during her life and illness. It was pretty raw and ugly.

"She says you were not there at her death as you promised you would be."

"I was there at her feet. I was there for days before, weeks before, months before every day! She was unconscious, we were all there, my Dad and four sisters and my friend Sherrie. I only left a for day so she wouldn't die from my cold."

"She is drawing your spirit out of you, your inner child wants to go with her, your Mother wants you to heal the tear in the Pleiades."

"What?! What tear in the Pleiades? Tell her thanks for the compliment, but that is not my plan."

"She is complimenting you on one hand, recognizing your healing capability, and taking your right to live at the same time. She cannot do that!"

Erena says in a loud voice. "Stop. GO, Be gone!" Erena waves her staff and shouts at her. I can feel my Mother and then my Grandmother trying to come after me circumventing Erena. Internally, I throw my arms around my body and my inner child and say silently to her, "I am your Mother, stay here, it is safe, I love you, I will take care of you!"

Immediately, I feel a part of me spring back in a flash. Tears of joy and relief flood me. I feel the tiny arms of my inner child around my neck. She is holding on for dear life.

Erena stands at the foot of the futon and shakes her staff, chanting, "Go Mama, Go, time to leave your daughter alone. Do not come back here, do not take her spirit, do not take her again, she has work to do here. Be gone NOW!"

As she said those words, I felt my mother and grandmother let go. It was over, they were sent away. I could sense a host of other spirits escorting her somewhere else. For the second time that year, I was relieved when she was gone; the first time for her release from pain and suffering, and the second for the renewal of my own spirit.

"I did not like her." Erena said in a quiet voice shaking her head. "She never allowed herself to express her rage and anger. That is what ate her pancreas and her liver. It killed her, but now she is free to find out more of who she really is. It is so important that she do so. She will not bother you again. But you have to affirm your willingness to be here and not contact her either. Channel your inner child's desire to join your Mother, and put it into something, like a piece of art work or write a poem. Then return it to your Mother's grave. Take your prayers and karma and leave it there. She is banished from you for now this will seal it. Do not pick this up again." Erena instructed firmly.

I shook my head in agreement. "Don't worry, I won't."

Erena bent over to sit down next to me on the futon as I sat up drying my eyes. She had something to say to me, so I listened intently. She sat close and patted my hand while she spoke.

"My mother also tried to draw me out during her illness and death. We had quite a battle. But I was not as good a daughter as you, I did not want to go and take care of her. I wanted to stay with my husband in Sweden. She was very angry at me, and kept after me for the longest time. I finally did this ceremony with some other Maoris and we got her to let go. It was a big battle of wills."

"I have never experienced this Erena, I have experienced spirits trying to enter people, but not trying to draw them out of their bodies!"

"It is more common than you think. It is why people often die in pairs or groups in families. A person's will to live is weakened after a loss, and if they agree, they go. You have always had a desire to be back in spirit. This was a test of your death wish. Now you have to clearly decide to stay. You have work to do here."

"Yes, I have struggled with my death wish for a long time. But I thought I was over it."

"It is your child that wanted her Mommy. You need to mother that child, and release this karma now with your mother. You have done your work for your mother and for yourself. It's over now."

I felt a great release as Erena said those words. It's really over. I don't have to watch my mother suffer, nor watch her suppress her feelings, nor hide mine from her mockery. I can really release her, and now she has finally released me.

"Your Mother wanted you to come and heal the tear in the Pleiades. Can you imagine? This is a backhanded compliment for sure. She also wanted you to join her. Then she wanted to punish you for what she perceived as your absence near her death."

I got sick Erena, right before she died. I was trying to protect her from suffering anymore than she already was. I also had to separate from her so that she would let go. She was draining me dry. Seriously, I was gone for one night!"

We hugged each other and I thanked her for her help. The next morning I felt like my energy was back completely. I felt Erena's protection around me, and my own. I had to attend her workshop that weekend. I also started writing my new book, *Sacred Living*.

During the rest of that week, I had several occasions to talk with Susan and Roseline, and we discussed relationships at length. One night we sat around the fireplace in the living room.

"I never want to go through what I just did with Jerald. I really want to know what it was that makes a great relationship, do either of you know?"

Roseline and Susan, who were both single, looked at me. Susan, who does spiritual channeling looked at me in a strange way, as though she was getting a message that we could not hear.

"Michael wants to speak." Her voice deepened and her presence shifted, and Archangel Michael, who was a presence that Susan channeled frequently, boomed through with the best advice I have heard in years.

"Robin, you must have Love, Trust and Respect, if you do not have these in a relationship, it will not work. Love, trust and respect, these are the keys."

Archangel Michael was right on target. Whether it was Susan or Michael it was the most profound sense I had ever heard. Susan's presence returned as quickly as Michael had come.

Susan and Roseline and I discussed the information. Respect, that was a key, I had to have respect for the man I would be with, and he had to respect me too. That had been missing in a lot of relationships. Trust was an issue also. Often I had the love without these other two. I wrote it down, and made a commitment to myself that I would not venture into a relationship that did not have all three. Love, trust and respect. This was a point with no compromise. Later I added communication. A good relationship had to have great communication too! Love, trust, respect, and great communication, these were the keys.

Adventures on Mt. Madonna

Before Dawn
The Gods are melting
into each other;
Kwan Yin and White Buffalo Calf Woman,
Buddha and Jesus,
Amachi and Liberachi,
the eagle and the pigeon,
mouse and rat,
St. Gregory and St. Germain,
Mother Mary and Mother Theresa,
Madonna and Judith,
Moses and John the Baptist,

Shango, the African God of Lightning
and Pan, the God of Earthly delights,
the Mountain and the rain clouds,
rivers and the sea,
sand and rocks,
surf and sand,
stars and sky,
sun and earth,
earth and moon,
moon and woman,
sun and man,
man and woman,
moon and sun,
hand and mouth,
eyes and ears,
mind and body,
fire and water,
you and me.

Mt. Madonna is a long way from Illinois, not only physically, but spiritually. I had been in Santa Cruz for a little over three weeks and here I was in a Maori Medicine Workshop on top of Mt. Madonna, a Hindu-based spiritual retreat center, the ashram and retreat Center of Baba Hari Das. Mt. Madonna was covered with redwoods and looked over the city of Watsonville below, which was largely populated with Mexican emigrants, most of whom were Catholic.

Mt. Madonna hosted a variety of people from every spiritual tradition. Erena was one more leader that would present her work. Eclectic is the word for the central coast of California.

We were to stay two nights, ending with a sweat lodge on the last day. We had been instructed to bring different colored clothes. Afterward in the drumming circle, Erena laid out her plan for the weekend. As we were getting ready to sleep after we completed our first drumming circle and Erena's talk, there were about twenty-five of us, and we were to sleep in a huge wheel with our heads in the center of the room for optimal dreaming. I saw this interesting man across the room, and decided to see if he was open to have me sleep near him. I walked over to him across the room.

"Hi, do you snore?" I asked him as I approached him.

"I beg your pardon." He said in a Spanish accent.

"Do you snore?" I said again.

"Yes," he said plainly, "I have been told I do, although I never hear it."

Erena was a few bodies away, and hearing our conversation, started to laugh hysterically. "Ha! I not only snore, I grind my teeth and talk in my sleep!" she chortled. Everyone started to laugh.

Not finding her comments amusing, I picked up my sleeping bag and blankets and went directly across the room from them. I could not tolerate snoring, teeth grinding or talking in one's sleep. However, I did discover that the man's name was Alfonzo. It was a nice name I thought. It meant 'the noble and ready one.'

The next day, Alfonzo and I did an exercise together that Erena had planned for the group of us. She asked that we sit across from each other in pairs and look into each other's eyes and perceive the other. Then, tell each other what we saw. We did the exercise twice, the first time, I was with Sally Aderton, who happened to be in the workshop also.

The second time, when Alfonzo and I sat across from each other, I felt myself falling into his dark Latin eyes. I saw a bear and a buffalo, and I felt his eternal depth. I liked this man, and I knew somehow, that if nothing else we would be great friends.

I told him what I saw, and he looked startled.

"What color are they," he said flatly.

"White," I said.

He opened his hand and in his fists were two stone fetishes, a white bear and a white buffalo. Then he said to me,

"You carry your pain on the left. I see it in your face, this is like me." Now it was my turn to be stunned.

Later that night over dinner, the group processed various world issues together and what could be done about them.

One issue, that was very close in Santa Cruz County, were all the gang violence in Watsonville. Recently, several young people had been murdered in a very short time span in gang related incidents.

Erena gathered us together to announce our evening plan. We were to go to Watsonville a few miles away, and Alfonzo was to throw his fetishes into the fountain in the center of Watsonville, with the intention of healing the inner city strife between gangs there. When Erena pronounced the idea, I broke into a howl of laughter, I couldn't help it, the idea was so ridiculous it made perfect sense. I was not afraid and Alfonzo wasn't either. This was our collective adventure for the evening!

Most people were shocked and reacted with disbelief, fear and resistance. Some refused to go because of the recent gang violence that had erupted there. Eventually all but one decided to travel together into the heart of gang territory.

Halfway down the mountain, we stopped at a huge grandfather tree that had to be thirty feet around. Erena sang some traditional Maori songs as we stood in a semi-circle together under the tree.

She smudged us with a sage stick. The stick was smoking very nicely and billowed sage over each member of the group. When she came to Alfonzo, she was able to sage him off just fine, but when she came to me the sage stick went out as if it had been doused by water. A spark flew off on to the ground, and she gathered it up gingerly with a bit of Earth under it and handed it to me. It was still glowing in the pinch of earth that rested in my hand, and she instructed me to blow on it.

"Here's your medicine, Medicine Woman."

She looked at me, raised an eyebrow and tilted her head to Alfonzo. I knew what she meant. After she completed the circle, I handed the spark to Alfonzo, and pressed our two hands together, saying nothing.

The next day at a sweat lodge, a most remarkable one, that Erena created with the help of Lionel, the medicine lodge leader. Alfonzo and I connected at the sweat lodge. Before the fire, we talked about whether it would work for us to come together and begin dating, obviously there was something going on here between the two of us. We talked about the next steps. We spoke in quiet phrases and low tones so no one else could hear us.

Inside the lodge at one point as Alfonzo and I sat next to each other on the bare earth. Erena said emphatically to everyone, "Hold onto each other this moment is sacred!" That was it, Alfonzo and I grasped hands, and arms and came out of the lodge feeling we had started something very important for both of us as we held each other in the lodge.

Over the next few weeks Alfonzo and I got to know each other very slowly. We decided to start as friends, and see what happened.

Over the holidays, I had flown back to spend Christmas with my family, this time with a huge absence felt from my Mom's loss. I said nothing of her attachment to me to my family, but I missed her physical presence none-the-less like everyone else. Dad and I visited her tree, and I tied a poem/prayer on the tree as Erena had instructed. Alfonzo went to Hawaii over the holidays with his sister. Both of us had completed something on our trips. I was less nervous this time seeing him.

A few weeks later, Alfonzo and I had our second date. We drove to Marin County for a Creative Arts Salon gathering at another friends' home. It is a place where people gathered to share poetry, and music and art together. Before we arrived, we stopped at the Marin Headlands for a break to eat and look at the stars. It was wonderful to be with him again.

On the way home we continued our conversation we had started on the phone a few days before. We spoke about relationship, about romantic love and about where we each were in this cosmic dance that we were seemingly beginning. It was quite an extraordinary conversation, the most significant I have ever had with a man that I was interested in, up to that point.

What I realized in the middle of our discussion, was that because of who we both are, our experience, and our lives and how they have developed - because of our mistakes as well as our knowledge, we have a rare and wonderful opportunity to go deeply with integrity, to define commitment together, if we choose this. We have a chance to create a truly healthy relationship.

The reason this relationship can be healthy is that neither of us are willing to abandon ourselves for the other. We are absolutely committed to our own process first. What I began to understand deeply with Alfonzo was that we are in a position to heal ourselves through relating, to discover how to do that. We could learn how to have a healthy relationship with another and to be together with integrity. Besides my writing this seems very important right now, extraordinarily important. We decided to give ourselves 4-5 months, and see how we liked being friends first.

Both Alfonzo and I were aware that our primary female and male partners are inside ourselves, that this is where we are truly at home. The changes that were necessary could come from inside out, and because we are aware of this, there was a possibility that there would be less projection, where one person "runs their movie over the other."

Slowly we moved into a relationship, until we were ready to relax into commitment. Until we were ready to be together in a committed way, we were not willing to be sexual. This was a great agreement for both of us because it meant that although I wanted a committed relationship initially more than him, neither of us were willing to leave ourselves behind in order to have half a marriage. We both needed to show up one-hundred percent in the relationship, and bring our whole selves.

I knew he was a man with whom I could form a "we" in the best or healthiest sense of the word. I felt grateful for the opportunity to explore the possibilities. I felt blessed by his presence, but more importantly I had done enough self-healing to be blessed by my own presence whether I am in a relationship or not!

It reminded me of the hole in the Pleiades. The Lakota story is of the seven maidens, who were picking berries in the woods when a bear started to chase them. They got to a clearing where they huddled together and started to pray. As they prayed, the Earth heard them and as they prayed the land rose up, creating devil's tower in eastern Wyoming. The bear was so angry that it kept clawing it's way up the side, and made some deep gouges in the mound. The maidens kept praying. Soon the Gods heard them, and called them forth into the stars, creating the Pleiades.

The tear came from the rage of the male bear, and the fear of the maidens had of male rage. The tear is between the stars, between the maidens in the very fabric of their star cluster and the bear constellations. The injury those women suffered through the bear's raging and disregard of their being, somehow, this can heal between us, at least in this relationship. Perhaps these virgins, these maidens, like my Mother, were not owning their own rage, their own earthliness and the bear could not own it's fear of not being in control of change. In their lack of ownership of their rage-full bear, it came out of the woodwork and forced them to retreat to the stars, to the heavens for comfort, safety and survival.

If Alfonzo and I can acknowledge and control our anger, maybe we can maintain respect, trust and love. We have these three. We also had good communication, which I felt was the fourth leg of this four-legged support for good relationships.

Thank you Universe!

As the relationship with Alfonzo grew, I wrote my new book, and settled into a life in Santa Cruz. My book was done by March, edits by April, with gallies ready by June and by Mid-May he and I were living together. I couldn't have been happier.

A few months after Erena's session and finishing my second book, my Mother's spirit returned to check in. This time she came with respect and with a sense of regret for what she had done. She apologized for her attacking me. I made it clear that she would not be welcome at all if she interferes with my life again. She agreed to my conditions of her visits. She wanted me to know that those of us working on emotional healing in bodies are very brave indeed. From her perspective on the other side, she wanted me to know this and share it with others.

Now when she occasionally comes to say hi and check in, she sometimes reports what she is learning. She especially likes to visit when I am cooking, which I welcome. Sometimes she helps with ingredients and suggests sumptuous combinations of herbs. We are relating differently now. We come together with respect for our autonomy, and a deeper understanding of what we each are willing to offer the other, from our own free will. She has taught me a profound lesson; that learning continues even after death.

After my Mother apologized to me and we started communicating again, I shared with her that Alfonzo and I were working on healing the relationship between men and women. Through our love this tear would be resolved if it was meant to be at least between us. I was not responsible for the tear between men and women collectively, that had been there for centuries. Each couple would have to heal it for themselves, within themselves, if it would heal completely.

But through my conversations with my Mother's spirit, I realized more profoundly that what we do here on Earth ripples out to the entire galaxy. The healing we do on ourselves becomes critically important for the whole of universal consciousness. Through my Mother I realized that she is continuing to heal on the other side too. After Erena's work on me, Mom realized that she only knew the light side of herself on Earth and had not recognized her own darkness, which she could see more clearly over there.

During her illness I noticed that Dad and I often suddenly felt so angry at her when she came into the room when she was ignoring her feelings. She denied her discomfort, pain, and feelings unless they were happy ones. In denying her anger she denied consequently, her own power. If she didn't have those things being our mother, we couldn't either as daugters. I realized that what had happened with her was that I was somehow suppose to teach her about the importance of all her feelings. But I could not get through to her with this understanding when she was alive.

One day, when she was alive, she had asked me what it was that bothered me about her, when we were talking about other things. I told her then that anger was something I needed to own in myself, and that I saw that she had it too. Her answer then was; "But I don't have anger." Consequently, we did finish our karmic agreement after her death. She finally did own her anger.

I could not deny my feelings anymore than I could deny my hair or the color of my eyes. The more I contacted my true nature, the more joy I felt. But the other parts were instructive and healing, and part of my lessons too. I needed to own all of myself!

I was grateful to understand that the learning never stops as Mom was learning about it on the other side. I felt at peace. I still missed her physically. But I was glad she was out of pain, and this phase of the learning was over for her. She was often present to me, sometimes at critical junctures, like when Alfonzo and I got married.

Within a year of our coming together, and our workshop with Erena, Alfonzo got a job in Watsonville counseling kids that were in gangs directly across the street from the fountain where he had placed his white fetishes.

He proposed to me in front of Erena at a story telling conference in July that same year, 1997. Two weeks later I became pregnant. I was running out of money and looking for work. I was experiencing morning sickness a lot, although my tiredness this time was from being pregnant. I was also getting to know our daughter. We named her Mari Luna del Sol, Sea and Moon of the Sun. Her kicking, especially during drum music, was fierce and energetic. She loved music and she loved being with other people.

We were ecstatic to have her. We also had Alfonzo's two sons from a previous marriage, Chris (16 going on 17) and Matt (19 almost 20) who were now living with us. I had this large family of my own within a year of my mother's death! Wulan had been right, my life was changing and fast!

Alfonzo and I Begin our Life Together

Feast

You and I are in our hacienda, seats at opposite ends of the long planks. We toast each other and our friends. Nothing exists for me but your eyes - the center of the fireball, of the earth, the navel in the ocean, clouds gathering the blessing of rain, and I am drawn in, and leap above the table and float with you on the same pink cloud.

We are one heart, speaking poems that do not rhythm and bring bouquet after bouquet to each other clasped in a hand of death. For to love this completely is to die over and over. And it is ecstatic, it is what I want. So then let the ripping begin, that ecstatic ripping of fear tissue, which grew in place, got locked in place by hours of driving on the same old roads with the wrong partners.

For we have found each other, and our path is unraveling splendidly. It is a new road, there is no road really. At least, you are that for me, and I know you would say it your way, in Spanish perhaps, with your rich chocolate voice granting and opening me, and I am that for you too. The brightness between us is so bright that we read poems with sunglasses on. And we swirl, in our ancient-new solar system, a pink cloud supporting us, supporting each other. One heart—a sacred heart—an ocean heart with rose petals and magnolia blossoms falling around us, gifting those that we love.

Children were something I had always wanted and now I was finally with the right man and **boom**, we had a small tribe! The only problem was that I was forty-four, going on forty-five by the time my daughter would be born. The rate of Downs Syndrome or worse infant mortality was very high. However, I was in communion with her often. I wrote her letters and shared with her about life that she was coming into, how I was feeling to have her within me. I felt she was fine.

I was so grateful to be pregnant, but my finances were in a big mess. I was coming to the end of several grants as well as a small book advance for my second book, which was now in the final stages of being produced. My money was quickly running out. Alfonzo and I had moved in together in May with the boys. While I had worked with several clients, and done some work advertising my services as an intuitive counselor, it was very important that I begin the process of finding some additional work. By the fall I was getting a bit desperate, and looking for anything I could find. Because Alfonzo had the kids to support we initially decided to keep our finances separate.

Morning sickness was a factor for the first few months. I could not seem to get out of bed before ten. Everything was spinning. I was in no shape to help anyone else. By the end of October I just wanted a job. I felt it was a good time to find something due to the holidays, at least I could find something in retail. My publisher let me know that this new book, *Sacred Living*, would not have a book tour, it was just going to be released and on their list. That made it better for me, as I could not imagine another book tour.

By October, I was feeling Mari Luna kicking, we had hired midwives, and I was seeing them regularly. First it was once a month, then after three months it was once every three weeks, then two weeks, then as we got closer it was once a week. It was odd and wonderful to feel new life kicking in me. I had all the fears and hopes of any woman my age, or any woman perhaps giving birth for the first time. I also had regular communication with Mari Luna. She was, after all, living within me. As she grew and developed, it was clear to me that there was a very special person growing in me. I felt so blessed and so grateful.

I got a job as a clerk in a kitchen supply store to bring in extra money for the holidays and to meet my expenses. The place was extraordinarily busy. It was not a great place for me because I was on my feet all day. But it was a paycheck, and at least I could bring in some money before the baby was born. I got support hose, sat when the boss was not looking and tried not to worry about the bills, which seemed to be mounting even with a job.

Finally at the end of my holiday job, I talked with Alfonzo and told him I needed support through the baby's birth, and I could not pay the bills myself. He agreed, and I became a dependent person for the first time since I was initially living with my parents as a teenager. It was awful. I hated being dependent on anyone. I wanted more than ever to be contributing, but I had to accept that I was contributing something else.

Alfonzo and I had many discussions about it, and by the time I was five months pregnant, he sat me down, after I was frustrated at work one day, near the end of my time at the store. I was so tired from working and grateful to be home. He spoke to me about the value of what I was doing. He was glad for the birth, even though I wanted the baby more than he. He wanted me to focus on my health and the baby, forget about the money, and do what was good for me to do. I felt glad to have a husband that respected women and childbirth. I had just never gone through it before, so I did not know what to expect. I was so surprised how much rest I needed, and how much space away from other people I needed too, much more than usual. My psychic sponge was tuned higher than normal, and I was frustrated by the limitations of being pregnant. My independent nature had to fly out the window.

After a long discussion one night, Alfonzo helped me to see I had a new job. Thank God he had been through this before. Being a mother was a full time job and supporting this baby into the world was up to me more than him, at least initially. He was fine with me working, but there was something more important here and he helped me to see it.

After our conversation, I surrendered to my state. Alfonzo was right. I had to embraced Mari Luna as my responsibility, as my job for the next five years initially, and longer if necessary. Then it was clear that I had to let go of the career thing entirely, and just be a budding Mom. I embraced motherhood totally at five months pregnant. I was so glad I had.

We woke up one morning and said to each other, today is the day! We were married officially on December 29, 1997 at the Unity Church with the ministers of that church and our friend Bill. We kept it secret because we wanted to gather our family together after the baby was born to celebrate with a big wedding later in the summer. Plans for that day were already underway.

A few days later, it was my 45 birthday on the third of January. When I awoke that morning, I was having a vision/dream. Several Saints dressed in black were standing around me. There were at least eight of them, four on each side, Mother Mary, Quan Yin, Isis, White Buffalo Calf Woman, Sister Sophia, Theresa of Avila, St Catherine, and an East Indian woman who I do not know but who knew me. Mother Mary spoke to me, as they formed a circle around me, "We are your midwives, we are here for you." Under the black cloaks they wore, were brilliant shades of blue, magenta and the white deerskins of White Buffalo Calf Woman. They were very solemn, and serious.

"OK, Hi, I am glad you are with me. A little early though, but thank you." I thought. As I received their message and they received my message the vision faded.

That afternoon, on my birthday, Alfonzo and I went to a place where we could take a salt-water bath in a flotation tank. Each person entered a private room with a shower. The room was a womb-like fiberglass container that has a space-aged door. After a shower you entered your own tub and soaked at body temperature for an hour or so. I had always wanted to come and experience this, so my birthday felt like a good day. We checked out the viability of this experience for safety in pregnancy, and there was no danger at all.

I was happy to be with the waters and the salt. It was like going in a warm ocean. Inside the tank, I had quite a profound experience. Floating in the water, I was soon floating in the heavens, and I was happy to be there. Just floating in the stars. Mari was there too, and we were connected with a thin cord that attached us and then to a far away star or solar system.

'This is where you are from. You are star people," a voice

said while we were floating together in space. The voice seemed to be a body of stars, perhaps Star Woman, whom I knew from Native American Ceremonies. Alfonzo and I had called Mari to the Earth, she was here to help the planet. I was so grateful for her presence and my part in her life.

Then I was brought back into my body and I felt a sense of purpose of being a mom like I had not previously had, 'Oh this little one will make a difference.' I thought. We finished our baths and went out to dinner. I told Alfonzo everything about my visions that day.

I started having cramps on Tuesday night, January 5th, 1998 two nights later. Though it felt more like a bladder infection, there was a definite tightening of my lower abdomen. For some of that day, I had been having this pain. Sometimes it was for a few minutes, other times it was not, short bursts, and constant awareness that something was not right. I had to pee a lot. I called the midwife.

By her tone, the midwife seemed to indicate that there was something going on. "Come in tomorrow for your regular appointment." She stated. Coincidently, I was already scheduled at 9 a.m., January 6th, 1998.

After I got off the phone, I sat on the stairs and looked at Alfonzo sitting at his desk.

"Alfonzo, do you feel that we are losing the baby?" He looked at me with his piercing black eyes, and said to me after a long while of silence, "No, it doesn't feel like it."

"It doesn't feel like it from here either." I replied. But then again, I wouldn't know what that was like.

That night I started to feel pain, I didn't sleep well. I got up to pee a bunch of times, I had a little bleeding, but not much.

That morning Alfonzo got dressed as usual and went to work. I got up and went to the midwives office thinking that I had one hell of a bladder infection. On the morning of the 6th I stopped to get a urinalysis, as Kate my midwife had asked me to do on the way to her office. But there was no order there, or they couldn't find it, and I couldn't remember why they wanted me to get a pee test anyway. Bladder infection. Have to get a doctor's order. Right.

That morning when I arrived at Kate and Roxanne's Midwifery office, I felt my only purpose there was to get this bladder infection checked. I weighed myself as usual, and peed, and did the litmus test the way I had done all those times before visiting their office. Then I went into the room and laid back on the bed, and bared my round tummy. The two midwives alternated appointments with each of their clients, this time I was with Roxanne.

"Any bleeding?"

"A little, but not a lot at all, like at the end of my period."

Then she put the fetal monitor on me, and couldn't get a heartbeat.

"When did you last feel her kicking?"

"A few days ago, when we were at First Night, we went to see Dondaro, the musical group, and she usually loves that band. But this time she was not too active. I thought she might be sleepy, so I didn't think much of it."

"I am not getting much of a heart beat. Let me try Kate's machine. Sometimes the batteries don't work well on these things."

I could hear her talking in the next room. Her voice was strained, and she was trying to hold it together. It was as though she was really saying 'EEK Kate, we are losing another one! Not again!!!'

I was floating a little out of my body, and decided to pray hard. Rox came back in. The cold jelly she put on my belly made me jump, but there was no heartbeat with my baby. She was still. The odd thing was I felt Mariluna's presence as I had since conception. She was clearly around me, in me, as she had always been the last five and a half months.

"The only way to know for sure is to get you to an ultrasound, lets call the Emergency Room (ER) and see who's on call." Rox said, She called and got Dr. Salvay.

"We got a good one," she reported. Then she sat by me and took my hand.

"Robin, this may be premature, but my teacher has said that in India, when a woman is pregnant it is a great gift. No matter how long, no matter what the circumstances. It is a gift.

"In this country we think if something happens during pregnancy that it is the mother's fault, what is wrong with her, what did she do, why? But there, in India, they focus on the blessing of pregnancy. In any case, it maybe something to hang onto."

As things turned out, it helped me a great deal.

"Dr. Salvay can't see you for an hour or so, so I want you to come in this other room and rest until we can go." I laid in another room of an adjoining acupuncture office, while Rox cleared her schedule. She called my husband at work, and asked him to meet us at the doctor's office, instead of the ER, that way it was more private and less chaotic.

She got a sandwich that we split, but I couldn't eat anything much, even one with smoked salmon, which I loved. It did not taste that good, nothing did.

Then we went over to Dr. Salvay's office.

"He is great," she said, "He is a little rough around the edges, but he is a great doctor." She kept saying on the way over.

I greeted Alfonzo in the parking lot. Seeing him was such a relief, it was the first time I could cry or feel something other than numbness. We entered the waiting room and had to sit with other mothers who were really big and ready to pop. I was large for five and a half months, but not so big as a full term Mom. They came in with their children and the kids played. I felt to be in a surreal space.

When the doctor came in the front door of his office, I knew it was him. I leaned over to Rox and said quietly, "Look what the cat dragged in." He had been up all night with a tough delivery. He indeed looked rough around the edges. The nurse finally called and we went down the hall into the doctor's office, where dozens of children's photos were pasted on the walls. It was awful to go past them.

We went into his office and I laid down on the exam table. He put the fetal ultrasound monitor on me, another cold jerk on my tummy. Then he said in a fairly matter of fact tone looking at the monitor, "There is no heart beat, this baby is a seventeen week fetus, it is not twenty-two weeks." He measured the head with a red box that he was able to make appear on the screen, "It's a girl." He said dryly. "I am sorry, this is always the most difficult news to hear, and the worst part of my practice. We will leave you two alone for a while." Rox and Dr. Salvay left the room.

    Alfonzo and I folded our arms around each other and began to cry, as the news hit us like a ton of bricks. Still I felt as though I was watching a movie while I was in it. Mari couldn't be dead, I felt her here. Her presence was still around me, and in me.

    Rox and Salvay came back in a few minutes later. Then Dr. Salvay said clearly. "We have to get this baby out. The child is dead, and there are dangers to you, the possibility of Toxemia, among other things. "You can have a D&C, or you can deliver the baby and go through labor."

    After some discussion of the procedures, I asked, "Could we see the baby after a D&C?"

    "No." He said flatly.

    "Does she come out whole or in parts?" I asked.

    "Parts." Salvay said clearly.

    I looked at Alfonzo and said to him. "Now, Alfonzo, I want to hear what you want, forget about me for a minute. Is it important to you to see this child?"

    He thought for a long while, then he said, "You are the one that has to go through this Robin. I will do whatever you want."

    "We are going to deliver this child." I said very clearly. "I want to see my only daughter, I want you, Alfonzo, to see her too."

    I turned to Dr. Salvay. "Looks like a delivery, Doc."

    "I want to give you a prostaglandin, it will speed up the delivery. The sooner you get the child out the better for you."

    "Doc," I said, "Whatever you do, cut the dose in half, then, cut it in half again. Then you will have my dose. I am very sensitive to medication as my mother was."

He gave me two instead of six tabs, inter-vaginally. Then we were to wait. As he pulled the glove out, there was much more bleeding.

"It will take an hour maybe two to really start, you are already in labor actually. I would say be at the hospital in an hour. It should be over by mid-afternoon. It's about 11:45 a.m. now. Go to the beach, take a walk, then come back to the hospital. We will be ready and waiting for you."

Alfonzo and I went to Sea Bright Beach, not far from the hospital. By the time I got there I had to pee again. This time, I was bleeding more.

Then I got to the sand and I had to sit down. By the time I got to the water, about 50 yards from the car, I was doubled over. I touched the water and said to Alfonzo, "Get me to the hospital—now!"

We walked back from the shore, and I doubled over every other step, all the way back to the car. I held on to his knees and screamed. He was my birthing tree, just like Erena described the way the women gave birth among the Maori in New Zealand. They dig a hole at the base of a special tree where they give birth. Alfonzo stood firm like a tree while I screamed and held on. Finally we got to the curb. He pulled the car around. I was doubled over on the wall to the entrance of the beach, trying not to scream with pain.

A woman came up to me. She was large and motherly, "I am a nurse. Are you alright?"

"No!" I said curtly, "I am in labor, and we know the baby is dead, we are on the way to the hospital."

"Oh my poor girl, let me help you." she scooped me up and helped me into the car. I was so grateful for her presence. It was as though she was an angel in that moment, just like the one that had come to help Grandma when Grandpa had died, so many years before.

We were off to the hospital. I was so angry that there was traffic. It was not fair. I was in so much pain. Other people were going to the store. I was going to the hospital to deliver my dead baby girl. In the car my water broke. I squeezed Alfonzo's hand as hard as I could and screamed. My feet were on the dash.

Finally we arrived at the hospital. He opened the door as if I could walk to the entrance.

"Get the wheel chair!" I screamed.

Alfonzo got the wheel chair and by the time I got to the door, I was in major labor. He wheeled me in, and everything seemed like an eternity. Waiting for the elevator, up the elevator, down the hall, into the room. I was holding the baby in and sweating like mad.

When we got to the room, a nurse said, "We were waiting for you, come on, let's get you into bed."

As we were getting my things off, she said, "Is this your first?"

"Yes, my first and last."

"I have lost two," she said dryly.

"Oh, my God, how did you do it?" I replied. She looked at me deeply, and said,

"I had another one. My son is nine this month."

I worked my way onto the bed with her help. The minute I laid back, the baby popped out.

There was a lot of blood. As I was delivering her, I could feel Mari's presence as I had for five and a half months. She was there, and as her body came out, I could feel her spirit scream, "NOOOOOOO!!"

I realized in that moment that death was not part of her plan either. She was not planning on coming half way. She was intending to be born to Alfonzo and I.

Psychically, I called in my Mother and Grandmother, and introduced them to Mari, and asked them to take care of her, 'I can't cope with her right now, please help her.' I asked in my heart. They complied and I saw them leave with her, consoling her. I was able to focus on our baby's body that the nurse fished out from all that blood that came with her.

Alfonzo was right there, standing by the whole time. He was rock solid, and so strong. I felt, as though he was a tree, still standing by as he had on the beach. I was sure now I had married the right man. There was not a shade of doubt any more. Rox came in moments after the baby came, and so did Dr. Salvay. He looked at the cord and pronounced it the problem.

"Now we are just waiting for the placenta." Dr. Salvay said. After they dried Mari Luna's body off, we got to see our star baby. She was little, dark-skinned like her father, tiny, and whole. She was perfect. Nothing was wrong, except the cord. It was pinched and frayed, flat on a few spots. It was as though the hand of God came down and pinched it closed. She could not get the nutriments she needed. She had stopped growing at seventeen weeks. Clearly there was another plan in action other than ours.

We waited and waited for the placenta to come. Dr. Salvay left to work with other patients. We were there with the child, a good two hours, just looking at her. With our permission, the nurse took pictures of her for us to keep.

"You will be glad we did, later," the nurse said.

A few minutes later another Doctor came in unannounced. We were now two plus hours post delivery.

"Hi! I am a colleague of Dr. Salvay's, Dr. So-in-so." I didn't catch his name and didn't care. I was spread eagle on the bed. It was impossible to cover up in time when he walked around the end of the bed glaring at the mess between my legs. He went to Alfonzo and shook his hand who was standing by the window.

"I am sorry for your loss, I understand you are waiting for the placenta to be delivered."

"Yes," I said.

"Well, I want you to know that very often we have to do a D&C because there just isn't enough contraction started by the process of birth to release it. We have to have the placenta delivered before you can go home. Sorry to deliver this news but this is the way it is."

"Who the hell is this guy?" I asked Alfonzo with a fair degree of aggravation. He left as fast as he came. I was so angry. I felt so violated.

Alfonzo came to my bedside, and Rox came close too on the opposite side saying, "Robin, I know you can do this. You have to go really deep and let go of the placenta."

"I have to let go of everything?" I whimpered to Roxanne.

I thought, 'What more is there. I didn't know there was any more to surrender.' I closed my eyes and went inside. The surrender was as deep as I had ever gone. Then the placenta popped out.

"Good Girl." Rox said cheerfully.

"Oh honey you did it." Alfonzo said startled, with a little bit of awe.

"I'll show that bastard Doctor." I said under my breath. "How dare he come in here and pronounce me a case for surgery!"

Dr. Salvay came in again right after I delivered the placenta, and he was pleased that we didn't have to go into surgery. He looked over the placenta.

"It is fairly small. There is no damage to it, it looks good, but look here at the cord. It has flattened areas." he said. "What blood-type are you?" He asked for the second time.

"A positive," I said clearly.

The nurse had asked too. They seemed jittery about how much blood I had lost. The nurse kept pushing me back so I couldn't see the bloody puddle I had between my legs.

We held the baby and looked her over, every little part; her tiny fingers, her little feet that were quite large for her size, and her beautiful head. I knew it would be the last time we would see her. There were little folds of skin that were peeling off her face and back. Her thin skin was very dark, like her dad's. She was little but whole and beautiful. The cord looked like it had been pinched in areas.

Suddenly, I was so cold and tired, and felt as though I was in some sort of sea of unreality. The nurse wrapped me in another preheated blanket. I could barely get warm. This was real. It was serious. There was nothing but extremes.

Another man came in and he announced that he was

from the funeral home. We had to go through a funeral home to bury or cremate our daughter as she was too many months along for us to take her home. We had to sign these papers. We allowed him to take the baby. I gave the papers to Alfonzo. One was a newspaper inquiry.

After I rested awhile I showered, and Alfonzo and I left the hospital, I got in the car where the labor took place. We entered Alfonzo's same red RV. Everything was the same—but nothing was the same. The Universe had altered its course again.

I was devastated. It was so odd, I knew nothing, I was empty and raw. How could this happen to us? How could she be gone?

When we got home, we crawled into bed together, everything seemed like an assault. Matt came in, I was crying. He asked what was wrong.

"We lost the baby, Matt."

"Oh no, I am so sorry," he said. He touched my arm, and crawled up on the bed with us, laying across our feet. He hung around for a while and talked about his day.

"You know, it didn't seem right that you would have a baby." he said, then he went to bed. That felt like an honest statement, but not one welcome at that moment.

The next day I did not want to wake up. Instead, I was covered by a thick blanket of grief. All I could do was weep. I stayed in bed, eventually got something to eat. Got out my paints, drew something, circles and spirals, loss, I wrote poetry and painted whatever moved me. Whatever helped, drawing helped.

Kate came by, Roxanne's midwifery partner. She stayed for several hours. Kate and I talked. I felt totally raw.

"The worst thing is I don't know who or what I am any more, I am not a mother, I have no career, I let go of everything to be with the baby and Alfonzo and his kids, now I have to let go of her, and I do not know what to do next." Kate took my hand and said firmly,

"Robin, listen to me. You are a mother no matter what.

You carried that baby, you gave birth, and you labored-and no matter what-you are a mother! Don't let anyone tell you otherwise."

Alfonzo came home from work and Kate left. I hugged her and was so grateful she was there for me and that she said what she said.

A part of me felt like running off the back porch, which hung over a cliff. I did not want to live. Mari's death was uprooting my old death wish that I thought I had let go of years before. The rest of me that could not move off the couch was too tired to get up. I felt something good would come of this.

I checked inside, my faith in God was still intact. Although I had lost all faith in myself, my identity was shattered, I did not feel capable in my ability to do anything well. I felt like an utter failure. Oddly enough, I felt grace descend like a cool waterfall all at the same time. All is well, even though I am a mess. Somehow, I would survive the worst possible loss. It was such a paradox. I made a comittment to survive and carry on.

Two days later I got a notice in the mail. The insurance company would not cover the bills at the hospital, nor the doctor, nor the lab. We were looking at least two-thousand dollars of debt on top of the several thousand of credit card debt we already had. It added insult to injury. We were in the hospital from one to five-thirty-four and one half hours-that was about four-hundred and fifty dollars an hour and I did not get even a meal while there! So much for managed care.

My first grand nephew, Liam, was born on my birthday, January 3rd, that same year to my niece Lysne and her husband Craig. Another friend, Annie, had her first son born two days after Mari's birth/death on January 8th, 1998. It was a constant reminder that at forty-five, I was over the hill. Annie was ten years younger than I, and Lysne was ten years younger than her. Birth at any age is exhausting, but watching them recover quickly, with healthy babies, I was reminded how much a woman gives to have a child. It was obvious that it is much easier at a younger age. I had waited too long. Or perhaps it was not meant to be for me after all.

When the funeral home man came to the hospital, he had given us in the packet, a newspaper form to fill out, which asked for a description of the deceased. I had to draw a black line down the page, through the lines that asked for graduation dates, achievements in the military, college degrees and simply put infant at the top of the page. A few days later, after the insurance company denied us coverage, the paper's editor called to say that they would not put our daughters death in the paper.

"If she was born full term we can do it, but under seven months it is considered a fetus and doesn't count as a full human being."

I was devastated again. They wouldn't count her as a full human being. Why do they draw this line? Political correctness be damned. I just cried and hung up the phone. I wrote poems that seemed to be coming one after the other.

No Stitch in Time
How do you sew up a black hole?
Send light rays across it's chasm,
unfathomable hole left by an imploded star.
Emptiness rings across the edges of nothing
to the other emptiness and there is nothing
to tie into the lasso stretches and stretches
is sucked into the hole with everything
loose in the universe.

How did this happen?
The milky way mane is tossed and galaxies ripple,
a black hole? One more place you can't focus anymore
call it a cosmic kaleidoscope.

You cannot tie it up nor nail boards across it,
 knowing it will always be there,
You cannot replace it with another star,
it is there along with countless other stars and galaxies,
other black holes, unfathomable loss,

and you can do nothing but stare into the blackness
and know it is forever a part of your universe.

Recovering and Starting A Practice

Alfonzo was depressed for about two weeks after Mari's birth/death. But then, he seemed fine and was back to work. This was not true for me. It took me much longer. I felt I had been blown apart. I was the Scarecrow in the Wizard of Oz. My leg was over there, and my heart was somewhere over there, and my head, well that was tossed over there.

After two weeks we held a funeral service at the same beach where we labored and lost our child.

Blue Bones
We circled on the beach
with friends who came to wish us well.
Alfonzo said a prayer. I held her ashes

in a pine needle and sweet grass basket.
Alfonzo held a pale pink rose.
I blessed him with her ash. The wind howled and

sea foam spewed over our shoes
"The sea is kissing us," someone said.
He blessed me with her ash.

We walked to the shore. He took
a pinch and I took a pinch. Our fingers barely
fit inside the basket rim.

Waves hit our shoes and we were soaked knee deep.
Our pinches hit my shoes, sea foam and sand too.
I was covered in my daughter's tiny bones.

Some green and blue bits colored my white socks.
"Robin's egg blue," I thought.

We were letting go as best we could.
Take her Yemaya, Take her winds of the West.
Blow and mix her tiny body with the Earth.
Take our baby who blessed us, take the grief from my uterus

Take the grief from us both.
I emptied the lunch bag of ash into the water
mixed it with the foam and tides.

Her remains lay in tear drops on the sand.
We waited for a wave. It soaked our shoes, our clothes again.
The storm increased, wailed in response to our grief.

Alfonzo threw up his arms in thanks,
I did the same. He turned back to the car.
I stood stock still.

This is where I labored two weeks before.
This is where the pain forced me to let her go
This is where I first sobbed her loss.

Now we bring her back to sea and foam,
where she began and never touched the Earth until now.
I prayed to the waters sweet and salt,

and felt the blessing of spirit on my red cheeks
my saturated skin, my numb fingers, I turned around.
Two friends stood like centauries of motherhood,

sisters, waiting and waiting for me.
One a mother four times,
me a mother once, step-mother twice,
one a mother not at all, a step-mother four times.

I hugged them both long and hard.
We made a triangle of arms.
I shed what I knew were not the last of my tears

for our baby, Mari Luna del Sol Lopez-Lysne.
We walked all the way back,

We walked in the sand and rain,
my baby's bones mixed with sand and sea,
Her star bone bits in the sea and salt,
My baby's bones rest on my shoes.

 A storm was raging on the ocean with wind gusts ranging to fifty miles per hour. As we returned to the cars my friends held me in their arms, and we cried together.
 We had our youngest son Chris to worry about now. He had left home and we had no idea where he was. We were afraid of losing another child—this time to drugs.
 As I laid around the house, I realized I had just gone through some kind of big initiation. It is what my vision of the Goddess midwives had indicated, I had just gone through a shamanic death experience. They were not only midwifing Mariluna, they were midwifing my soul.
 Over the next few months, I walked to try and build my muscles up. One day a week or so after losing Mariluna, I asked God, "What is it that you want me to do?" I felt Divine Mother around me and she said, "You are not here to take care of one child, you are here to take care of many people. That is your job."
 I got several part time jobs, but reoccurring back spasms from the delivery or possibly from the prostaglandin, were keeping me flat on my back for days and weeks at time. My second book was out and doing fairly well, but I would not receive any royalties for some time. Most of my time was spent alone. I got into physical therapy, and into a hospice group for women who lost infants. I tried chiropractors, medication, planned our public family wedding, and finally I was fed up.
 After we had our wedding at the end of July, and ten months after Mari was born just after the first of October 1, Alfonzo's birthday, I was still looking for work. I decided to take myself out into the woods camping for four days alone. I would

create rituals, and do the rites I was guided to do to heal myself. I would make a doll, an effigy of my baby. This is all I knew that I had to do, and I trusted that the process would help me recover. It was also the first time I had gone somewhere without Alfonzo since we had gotten together a few years before.

Heading south to the Big Sur coast, I found a remote camping spot. I built a camp fire near a river bend. Over the next few days, I went deeply into my internal meditative place, my heart garden, and listened and watched and went into the pain. I listened to my guidance and it was clear to me that my guides were standing by in a circle like they had before her birth. However this ritual was mine to do, and I had the skills, now it was time to use my skills to heal myself. I knew I was being tested again.

As I left the house I grabbed odd things, cotton batting, cloth, buttons, colored thread, scissors, candles, my medicine basket. When I arrive in Big Sur, I found an empty campsite and set up camp. I began to see why I had to bring this odd assortment of items from home.

I made an effigy of Mari Luna, at the age and size she would have been if she was had been a full term baby. I held her and rocked her, and wept and wept, and made prayer ties, as we had during Sundance in Rockford with my Tiosbye community. As I meditated by the fire and then by the river, I felt in the darkness of my being for the parts that had been blasted away, the pieces of myself laying in my energy field. In my inner vision I could see them fragmented. One by one I put them back together within me, and reassembled myself.

At the end of my fourth day, I called all the remaining fragments in, and prayed, and slept under the stars, cried some more, drummed and danced around the fire. I owned the pain that no one else could heal for me. I felt, at least, stitched back together.

When a group moved in next to me, and I realized they were beginning to drink heavily, I knew it was time to go. I packed up everything, took my doll baby and held her on my lap for the three-hour ride home. That is what I missed the most, holding my baby.

At home, I was shaky, but still standing. At the same time I knew Mari was fine, she was safe, and so present to me, and I was holding these two extremes, she is fine, I am too, she is dead, she is alive, I am a mess, I am whole, the extremes holding them here and there, to bridge myself.

A week later I got a job with Lucent Technologies that I stayed with for a year, it was part-time, I could go back to my writing, I would keep writing, and healing work with clients. I started to see a few clients again with my practice developing.

Mariluna's death in-utero a year and a half after my mother died was a lot of death to deal with in a short time. Her death and birth sent me into a dark place that was very hard to recover from. If it hadn't been for my ritual in Big Sur, Hospice Bereavement groups, Umbanda, the Native Ceremonies I attended, and Alfonzo's support and that of friends, I do not believe I would have recovered. They brought me around, helped me see a brighter future, and with the help of my own rituals, I was able to recover over time.

I also had a new, more profound inner vision. I now saw the other side into the astral/etheric world anytime and anywhere I wanted. It took some work managing my abilities but they were exceedingly sharp and it was undeniable. It seemed Mari's death blasted open my mediumistic abilities to a much more profound level of sight. Slowly I was coming into my own psychic powers that were now fully turned on. I was forty-six. Jeanette Snyder was right, I was rather a late bloomer, but I was also right on time in my own way.

A few years later, after visiting Puerto Rico with Alfonzo and the boys, I wrote this poem.

White Turtle Woman, the Earning of my Name
> *"Maybe there are turtles, Maybe grief is swimming by"*
> *excerpt from a poem by Julia Alter*

In Puerto Rico, women never travel alone,
but on the Island of Culebra
I had to hike to the open sea

where thunderstorms devour green islands,
black and white and blue and green.

Up a mythic trail, I step around two snakes
it is the name of the island after all. Ascending from a gentle
inland shore to the other side, stormy waves are crashing in.
I see the storms swallowing our names,
Mari Luna del Sol, White Turtle Woman,

Sea and Moon of the Sun, piercing storms
I see your name in this hungry rage
in the sun spots on blue water.
I see my dive to the depths of the sea
A deserted coral beach greets me.

I don't have to walk through fear, but as I do
Under the surface the water is calm,
I see huge racks of stag horn coral,
Brain coral the size of Volkswagen bugs,
graceful hands of fans wave on.

I don't have to swim through her loss, but as I do,
the sun breaks open new worlds to me
invisible plankton and jellies pass by
a black and white turtle swims out and about
pipe fish, parrot fish, and clown fish dive.

How odd, my life returns after she is gone,
salt water swims in coral pools,
she gives tender turns of fishes' fins,
and offers a clown turtle that sees me now
she gives black fish with blue-eyed tails.

My child died so I could live
her spirit is a woman now,
black and white turtle swims with me,
paints, becomes and reveals more of me,
 and I am no longer an empty shell.

White Turtle Woman dives at the edge of the sea
Rises like lightening to the starry sky
and she has opened both doors for her mom.
Mari travels along with me.
She swims through joy in this vacant love,

Sea and moon of the sun remains
Mari Luna del Sol is here and not.
Black and white and blue and green,
Storms pass through other lands now.
My heart aches for those in that stormy path.

How could we forget to give earth to her name?
And the sun shines after my storm has gone.
Mari Luna missed her earth and became a star
Sin la tierra, el mar, la luna y el sol
hacen una estrella.

This moon has faded in our daylight love,
I empty my shell in this moonlit pool.
El mar y el sol y la tierra quedan.
The sea and sun and earth remain.

Chapter Eight
More Native Ceremonies
The Ogitchidaah Ceremony

One of the ceremonies Alfonzo and I began to attend was called Ogitchidaah in Northern Wisconsin. My sister-in-law, Catarina, had suggested we all go. She met a man who told her about it and invited her and friends to come. She met him in Taos, NM where she lived. It was in the Fall of 1999, just under two years or so after Mari's death that this ceremony was planned to take place in Northern Wisconsin.

Catarina explained this dance as a "nighttime Sundance", but I did not really understand what she meant. I was already attending Sundance and had committed to dance for four years, the year before Alfonzo and I got together. He had gone to Sundance with me the year before Mari died, that was my second Sundancer year. That next summer when we had our wedding, I couldn't go, I was still too broken, and we had so many people coming for our wedding, no money to do another trip to South Dakota, and I was still struggling to regain some sense of normalcy after Mari's death. Then I had returned to Sundance the following summer, and now the Ogitchidaah in the fall. It seemed like a lot. I had just finished my third year of Sundance. I had one more year to go.

However, both Alfonzo and I were drawn to go to this dance, so we booked reservations and flew to Minneapolis, Minnesota with Catarina in the Fall of 1999. After we arrived by rental car to Northern Wisconsin, three hours northeast of Minneapolis, we followed the directions, and finally found the town. Then following the road described to us out of town a few miles, we found the mailbox with a red cloth on it, and turned down a long driveway to the dance grounds. There was a house and several out buildings across the road. Beyond the out buildings, we could see a lodge and a fire as we drove in with snow dusting the ground. When we saw the lodge, we were certain that we were in the right place.

Just as we arrived, we were informed that the rocks were hot and ready. Anyone who wanted to dance was required to participate in this sweat lodge ceremony first. Snow began to fall lightly.

So we found our way to dressing areas in the house and got sweat dresses on, and the men wore shorts, and went into the lodge with total strangers we had just met a few minutes before. This was a different tribe of people, but the same experience of native customs. They welcomed us in and were waiting for us.

Phil, the leader, poured the water in the lodge over the rocks and reported what the spirits had to say about this dance. It was the first Ogitchidaah since the whites had pushed the Annishnabe people over the boarder to Canada. We would be the first to dance in such a dance since white incursions. We had no idea that we were the first ones to be there for this dance. There were about twenty of us altogether. It would begin the next day in the late afternoon. Phil asked us to watch our dreams as we departed after the lodge. Our dreams would tell us if we were to dance the next day.

The three of us checked into a motel because it was too late to set up camp. The dance would not start until late afternoon the next day. We had plenty of time to set up our tents and prepare for the dance before it started.

That night I had a dream that there were two of me. One laying on the bed of our motel room, and another me was standing over the other me with boots on. The standing me pulled the horizontal one's shoes off, and said, "Get up!" I recalled Da Free John making the same command when I had the dream with him.

When we got back to the dance grounds in the morning, I told Phil the dream and he said, "You need to dance. You should do it barefoot to honor the spirits."

Gulp. It was autumn in Wisconsin. The ground was already frozen with a foot of early snow, which had fallen that night. Barefoot? I knew better than to argue with him, as he was not ordering me to do this, the spirits were speaking through him, and while I did not logically understand it, I knew I had to comply.

"Okay." I said as cheerily as I could, and we got our tents set up and prepared for the ceremony. When we went to set up, the men were assigned to camp over beyond the dance grounds, and women on the side closer to the cars. I stayed with Catarina in her tent, Alfonzo had to use our tent. It was odd, but I had brought my Sundance dresses just in case someone else needed them. I did not anticipate that I would be the one using them at all!

We were deep in the north woods, so the dance grounds were set up very differently than Sundance. The dance was set in the forest, not out on the open prairie like at Sundance. There was a large arbor open to the sky with pine boughs on the back of the arbor making a wall to the forest. The arbor had four openings or gates, and there were cloths in each gate signifying the four directions. The one direction that was larger than the others was the east. At Sundance, the East gate is blocked off, to prevent people crossing where the spirits enter and exit.

In Ogitchidaah, the east gate was where we entered and did not exit until late into the night when Phil declared that the spirits would let us leave and that night of dancing was over. The other difference was that the drum was in the middle at Ogitchidaah, and at Sundance the drum was to one side, usually in the south. Also there were eight fires inside the arbor, while in Sundance there was only one fire outside the grounds close to the sacred lodges. Also in Sundance we danced from sun up to sun down around the Summer solstice. Ogitchidaah went from late afternoon to the middle of the night sometime during Spring or Autumnal equinox. Sweat lodges were always before any ceremony and at the end of the day, so that was the same.

Phil had explained to us that Ogitchidaah was to find

one's identity of who you are, while Sundance was to give that offering to the community. First you had to know yourself, then you could offer yourself to the world. Somehow I was doing it backwards, Sundance then Ogitchdaah, but after Mari's death, my new identity was just forming, so it made sense to me. I knew I was being guided. I needed to find my new self.

Since I had frozen my feet when I was a child in the snows of Illinois, I was extremely cautious when it came to being cold again especially my feet. The spirits had known I had this fear, so somehow they pinpointed a fear that I needed to release.

To my surprise when I began to dance barefoot on the frozen ground, before any fires were lit as it was still daylight, the earth responded to my "fear of freezing" by warming the Earth below my feet. It was amazing. I was not cold during the entire dance and my feet did not freeze at all, even though the weather was cold and snow occurred from time to time! As long as I stayed in the same spot, I was fine. When I had to move, when the fires were lit, once I stood for even a few minutes the Earth 'heated' that spot, right under my feet. I began to trust the Earth in a more profound way than ever before. I could feel that the living being of the Earth loved me.

Mariluna's spirit was dancing between me and my sister-in-law during the whole dance. We could both feel Mariluna's spirit between us.

During the third day of dancing, praying and singing new songs for this ceremony, I felt a presence like I had never experienced. This larger presence came into the South gate after the sun was long gone towards the end of that day. Catarina and I and Mariluna were dancing near the South gate just after dusk. However, this other presence was not Mari, it was something or someone else.

As I looked behind me through the South gate, there she was, towering over the trees at least 50 feet high. It was Star Woman, the Great Divine Mother, her dress was full of stars. She swayed behind us, as if the night sky full of stars had come right down to the South gate. She is the embodiment of all female deities on the planet. I was overwhelmed with joy and felt a deep reverent awe.

I called Phil over when he danced by our fire. "Phil, it's Star Woman!" I whispered.
He nodded, smiled and said, "Yes, Just keep dancing."

After about two rounds of drumming, where the dancers and drummers take a break, and we get our pipes to smoke and pray, we started dancing again, and she began to speak to me through my clairsentience. I felt love wash over me, and yet a wildness I cannot explain. She had a sense of total freedom in her being. It was a little daunting. As the drums began again, we returned our pipes to the rack and began to dance again around our small fires. That is when I heard Star Woman say to me, "I am leaving now, watch. It takes awhile."

I looked up as I kept on dancing near a small fire in front of us. That is when I saw her as a star-streak lighting up across the sky that lit up the entire arbor and the woods around us.

"Whoa!" I said, and others did too. Then it was clear, Mari was gone, Star Woman had taken her home.

It was as though the Universe had shown me Motherhood and then said, "That's enough! This life is not for you this time around. You have other work to do." That work was more psychic and mediumistic than I had thought it would be as my main interest was in healing and helping others heal from whatever ailed them. I realized then, once she was gone, that Mari had not left my side for two years. Now I was in another cycle of grief about her loss. She had completed her work with me and it was time she left my side. I had to move on without her.

After the dance on the long flight home, I thought about all that had transpired in the dance. I could see that this was right, even though it hurt a lot to lose her again. She needed to go. I had tried to let her go, but now, her spirit was gone to where she needed to be.

Alfonzo and I had his two sons to launch into their lives. So I settled into life with the Lopez family. I felt they became my own sons to some extent even though their mother was active in their lives too.

As I lived with Alfonzo, I grew my practice in energy healing and psychic and mediumistic awareness, after my job ended with Lucent Technologies that year after Mari's death. My next job was as a part-time community organizer for drug and alcohol prevention for two years. I also trained and counseled therapists in rites of passage and community drug and alcohol prevention strategies at Mountain Community Resources in Ben Lomond and several years later for Pajaro Valley Prevention and Student Assistance (PVPSA).

Later I worked through PVPSA in a junior high school working with young female teens, in jail settings both men and women in medium and minimum security, and in another school as an art teacher and art therapist. I had started my own educational center teaching classes on psychic development and divine guidance.

I was glad to be working again, and also was able to write another new book and see clients on the side. Alfonzo and I did ceremonies together as we both had been trained as mediums through Umbanda, a Brasilian spiritual community. This was great for both of us, and created more intimacy between us. (see Part Ten page 232 - Umbanda Rituals).

Troll of the Willows

For two years during Sundance, I had been running a Lakota lodge in the Santa Cruz Mountains on the property of a friend of mine. The ladle for the lodge had been passed to me during Sun Dance. I was now leading lodges both at home and also regularly during Sun Dance.

When I did not get enough people to help and participate in the lodge at home, I stopped the lodge and rested for two years. I told the Spirits that if they wanted me to do a lodge here again, they would have to give me a sign.

When I came back from the Ogitchidaah the end of my two years of resting with the lodge, I was impressed with the spirit of the head woman, Karen. So I invited her to come out to

California from Wisconsin for a workshop. When she stepped off the plane she said bluntly,

"This isn't about my workshop, it's about you getting the lodge and doing it!"

She was so emphatic. This was a definite sign.

A few months earlier, I had told her a dream I had of my pipe-bag, and I asked her help in making it for my pipe or Chanumpa, or 'Boggin' in Annishnabe. She told me to send her tobacco and she would send it to me, which I did. A few weeks later, a beautiful leather bag arrived with two white ermine hides on it just like in my dream. Initially I did not realize the fact that the pipe bag I dreamed about and the lodge were connected in anyway.

Karen had told me when she sent me the bag that the dream I had about my pipe-bag was the necessary sign that I should also get the lodge. I had been in denial when she said it the first time around, probably because it is a huge responsibility. This time, I heard her and I was shocked when she told me. It was the sign I had waited for, I could not deny it any longer.

Of course, I had to tell Alfonzo. He was angry that I did not tell him prior, discussing it with him. I understood his feelings, but sometimes if you are just suppose to do something, it isn't really up for discussion. I had given my life in service many years before and if I was asked to do something by the spirits or felt drawn to do something like a ceremony, it was my work to do. Sometimes I had no choice. It meant I would be taking on the lodge as a once a month obligation into the foreseeable future. This was what we were both resisting.

"I didn't ask for it, it just happened!" I said to Alfonzo. "I did not know she was giving me the lodge here too!"

So before the workshop, Karen and his sister, Catarina, and I went to gather branches to build the lodge. A friend had property outside of Santa Cruz, not too far from the lodge, and since I had cut willows there before, I knew there was a guardian spirit of a Troll (yes they are real) of a grove of willows we planned to cut from, several miles from the lodge. The other women did not perceive him; not because they couldn't—both were very intuitive—but because I had been in relationship with the Troll prior from the Lakota Lodge that we built, he wanted to talk to just me. Also he was kind of grumpy, and didn't know who these new people were.

Trolls are by nature very territorial. It is their job to protect areas of land and groves of trees, so they don't like intruders. (Hence all the wonderful stories about Trolls from Norway and Sweden guarding bridges and crossings.) In Scandinavia, it is very much a part of the mythology and culture to believe in and see Trolls, Divas, Fairies, as it is in the British Isles. Since my roots were three-quarter Scandinavian, and one quarter Scottish, it was natural for me to know spirits of the land.

This time the Troll made his presences known by jamming his hand into my pocket and trying to take the chocolate kisses from me that I brought for him. I had to tell him,

"Now wait just a minute, I will give them to you, don't be so greedy!" As I said this out-loud, my friends knew that he was there. Karen said to me,

"Okay, Robin, show us where to cut which trees, he only wants to talk to you."

He had stepped back after my admonishment, appearing a little bit more sheepish after that. I told him in my thoughts that I was going to guide them with his help, and he agreed.

Actually, he felt quite neglected, because the Native American people, who had lived on this land prior to white settlers, were the last ones to make offerings to the Earth on a regular basis. Native people knew the natural protocol of making gratitude offerings before asking things from the land, instead of taking without asking. The truth was that he did not have anyone offer him anything in a very long time, at least 150 years, to cut or use the willows, so he was grateful and anxious to get the offering! Trolls can live many hundreds of years protecting an area of land or a grove of trees.

He guided us to the grove and was very clear, "Take what you want from this tree, that one over there, or this grove here. He pointed out." I told Karen and Catarina what the Troll said.

"Be sure to offer tobacco before you cut anything." I said to them. "He is still a bit grumpy." Since Karen was Annishnabe (Ojibway), and Catrina was part Taino (Native Puerto Rican) they were well versed in offerings, and agreed without question.

After we had the branches cut for the lodge, we dragged them to the truck and tied them on and gathered the small ones for the lodge as well. I thanked the Troll with more chocolate and we were on our way.

When we arrived at Hilltop, the place where the lodge would go, we met some other spirits of the land who also wanted offerings. So I laid out tobacco all around the area, and they seemed pleased.

Since I was not going to be doing Lakota Lodges there, and only Annishnabe lodges, it was a different tradition, and so we built the lodge according to the customs of the Annishnabe people as Karen instructed. Once the structure of a dome was created, we prepared the lodge with blankets and coverings to keep the heat and steam in. We prepared the fire and got the rocks nice and hot.

One of the spirit guides in the lodge gave me instructions. That guide was named Kunceecha. I had met him at the last Ogitchidaah dance that I attended in Wisconsin. Kunseecha, was a spirit that came into the arbor at the last day of the dance. He was totally charcoal black, and I could only see his eyes that shone brightly and the outline of a small man.

During the dance, Phil, our leader, announced at the break, that there was a little man coming to visit us and no one had asked him anything yet. He encouraged us to talk to him. Since the little man was standing at our fire, I greeted him, and asked if there was anything he needed? All I could see was his smile, and his outline in the dark. His presence was very jovial. He said nothing but smiled more broadly. But I found that when I returned home, and began pouring Annishnabe lodges in California he was there, popping out of the fire as I laid tobacco down in the fire pit to begin the lodge.

In that first lodge he helped me with, after getting the fire going to heat the rocks, he asked that he and I go into the lodge together alone before the other people came in. So I followed him in, and he sat in the west side at the fire pit edge, where we would place the hot rocks after we had everyone come in a bit later. As he and I were there together, the pit had no rocks in it, and he asked that I sing a song before the ceremony got started, before anyone else came into the lodge. As I sang a healing song for him without any rocks in the pit, all the charcoal black he carried drained out into the pit in the center of the lodge, and he became completely white.

He had spent years at ceremonies gathering all the negative energy that people released in the dances. I gave him the opportunity to let it all go into the fire pit. That is what he needed from me, a healing lodge. After a while the others came in, Karen and Catarina sang songs with the other women. There were about eight women altogether at this first lodge. Most of us felt very happy at the end of the lodge.

After that, Kunseecha helped me with the lodges for many more years, teaching me everything I needed to know about healing with the lodge. Many people had profound transformations when they attended. I also met two young women that I adopted as my daughters in the sacred lodges. Christine from California, and Iria from Brasil. It has been a great gift, as through other ceremonies and relationships, we are still together as family and friends. I was happy to know I always felt healed, as they did, when I poured this lodge. The spirits did the healing; I just poured the water.

One never knows what really happens in the lodge, but I can say from pouring water for fourteen years, that the spirits of bear, wolf and deer come into heal people, as well as other Native Spirits that come for all people no matter what color a person is or their spiritual tradition. I am grateful I was a part of that tradition and extended it into the future through the help of the spirit I met at Ogitchidaah.

During the last year of my lodge, an Acacia tree (known for its purifying properties by the ancient Greeks) fell on my lodge. A purification tree, fell on my purification lodge. Okay, message delivered! I was afraid I had done something wrong.

But Kunseecha said it was just time to end the lodge there, and I had done my work and my obligation was over. He was going back to Wisconsin to help with other Ogitchidaah ceremonies. He hugged me, and I thanked him profusely and he jumped back into the fire pit. He was taking the "inner earth express" back to Wisconsin! Thank you Kunseecha, you helped so many people, I will never forget you.

Journey to Canada

In the early days of my marriage to Alfonzo, his sister, Catarina, acted as a guide for ceremonies we attended. She lived in New Mexico, and was connected with many Native Americans there who sometimes came through the area where she lived in Taos for ceremonies and rituals. She called one day and had heard about another ceremony from Phil and Karen in Wisconsin. This one was in Canada.

"There are others from here that are going, do you want to go too, Robin?"

After sitting with the idea in meditation, I felt a strong pull to go to this ceremony. The only trouble was it was in the dead of winter, January, and we had to rent a car and drive nine hours from Minneapolis to get to the ceremony. The ceremony was two days, and then we would follow our route back to the airport. It would be a grueling trip. The more I listened to my inner guidance and sat with it, the more it felt right. It was a struggle. Guidance said to go. "I", the practical one, the human one, the one without much money in the bank, did not want to go.

Catarina and I and three other people from the Ogitchidaah dance, landed in Minneapolis and rented a car where we packed everything into it, our ceremonial gear, and our suitcases. We were sitting with luggage in-between our legs in the back seat and feathers and fans were packed and wrapped carefully into the back window. The minute we got to the car and began to drive I started cramping.

"Oh no, I'm on my moon!" I whispered to Catarina. I immediately started to regret coming. However, I was stuck now, and would have to go with the flow, literally.

In Native American ceremonies, women were considered to be in their own ceremony during their menstrual cycle. Historically, in the Lakota tradition, women went into moon lodges where they were taken care of by other women to dream and inform the whole community. But we were in the 21st century and now it meant you could not participate in the larger ceremony. It was the same with the Annishnabe people, or so I thought.

Our long journey was punctuated with bathroom stops, lunch and dinner stops that were fast food only. We had a terrible boarder crossing where we had to take everything out of the car and repack it in the freezing cold wind. I felt that the boxes of feather fans in the back window informed the boarder agent that we were going to a ceremony, and he gave us a more detailed inspection than he might have. In any case, we unpacked and repacked the car, opening suitcases and freezing in the whirling snow wind while the inspector examined every case.

Several hours later we arrived at the motel in the dark, and met Phil and Karen and others from Wisconsin. After finding our rooms, we set out to find the grounds for the ceremony. I had no idea what to expect.

As we arrived at a turtle-shaped building, I asked Phil if it was okay if I went into the building because I was on my moon. He said, "Yes. Just stand in the doorway and don't go inside, you will see everything from there."

As we came into the turtle mouth of the building, it was dark inside except for a wood stove glowing and a few candles. It was the only light. A huge turtle shell with tobacco piled high on its shell was near the heart of the turtle-shaped building, and a medicine man sat around the entrance where I could not go. The dance had already begun. I respectfully stood in the doorway close to the door. Catarina and the others went inside. Many people had ceremonial costumes on. They were hard to see, as they appeared brown and shaggy. The dancers had transformed into creatures. People danced wildly as the drum pounded loudly.

At the end of a round of drumming, a woman came to talk to the medicine man, and then she announced that the Grandmother's could see that there was someone in the building who was on their moon, and they needed to leave immediately.

I looked at Phil, and he shrugged. I forgot he was backwards. When he said yes, it meant no. I left out the door again, and Catarina followed with others that wanted a smoke. She suggested I either wait in the car or go back to the hotel. Since it was below zero, I took the keys from her and told her I would meet her at the hotel. We had several cars so she could ride back with Phil and Karen. She agreed and hugged me goodbye.

As I left I could feel all this grief rise up. It was just three years and a few weeks since Mari's death. I felt all my hard work at rebuilding myself just got flushed down the toilet. I felt worthless. The worthless feeling was beyond the rejection I had just received from the Grandmothers. I began to cry as I got into the car in the freezing cold, and made it back to the hotel.

I got undressed and got ready for bed and lay in the dark weeping. I could not stop, the flood gates had opened again. After several hours, Catarina came back. It was the middle of the night. She saw I was crying, and came to my bedside.

"What's wrong Robin?"

"Catarina, Why the hell am I here? I spent all this money, drove nine hours in a very uncomfortable car to get here and now I can't even attend the damn ceremony!"

"I think we need to talk to Phil and Karen about this tomorrow. Maybe there is something they can do. The dance is over tomorrow night, it just is two days long." She said to me. Clearly it was beyond what she could do.

The next morning we met Phil and his wife Linda and Karen for breakfast, and I broke into tears again. I couldn't help but be full of anger about why the hell I had even come all this way for nothing.

Karen suggested I talk to the medicine elders who ran the dance.

"We will take you over to their house today, so you can meet them before we go to the dance. There is another girl in the same situation who is staying there today too. We will come back after the dance and you can talk to them. Give them some tobacco, and ask why you came to this dance. There is a reason for it, Robin, even if you can't see it now."

I felt a bit better, but I was so depressed. I spent the day hanging out at the house of strangers. I had a book with me, but I was instructed—very clearly and loudly by my guides—to pray. So I spent the day in prayer. When I wrote in my journal, or picked up my novel, I felt my guides say to me: "You are in ceremony." I appreciated the reminder though it was odd not to be 'in' the ceremony with the other dancers. It seemed my ceremony was going inside, and being with myself. The girl was listening to songs with her ear buds in the whole time.

After the dance, which went on until after dark, a group of people arrived back at the house where they prepared for a feast. All kinds of food was brought in and prepared, and we ate until we were all full. I was still feeling awful, and waited patiently for people to clear out so I could talk to the leaders.

After most of the people left, I sat down with the couple who ran the dance. I will call them Joyce and Ben. They were an older couple in their late sixties. At the time, I was in my late forties. They seemed much older than I in many ways. Certainly they were wiser than I because even though I had spent the day praying, I still felt resentful that I was not able to be in the dance itself. My death wish was raging. I wanted to leave this planet. This pain was just too much.

After handing them a pouch of tobacco, they asked me about what had happened in the last few years. I told them about my mom's death, meeting Alfonzo, and Mari's passing. They looked at each other.

Ben reached for my hand, and said to me. "My dear, why do you think you could get over the death of your only daughter in just three years?"

"But I have done everything I can and still this grief comes up and whacks me. I can't seem to recover, I just get my bearings and this tidal wave comes over me. I can't keep doing this, I don't know what to do. I just get flattened." I couldn't stop my tears any more.

Joyce said quietly, "Ben, I think you should tell her your story."

Ben pulled back and lit some cedar in a bowl. He smudged us with the smoke and then he began to speak slowly.

"My mother died when I was six months old. I was sleeping in the same bed, and when I went to snuggle up to her, she was ice cold. Now, I grew up with a big family, and my Dad did the best he could, he remarried and there were lots of aunts and uncles around. But I still felt this hole inside that gnawed at me. I married Joyce, and we had our kids, and when my son was born, I began to drink. I treated them terribly, and I beat her and the kids, and hated myself for it. We split up for a time. Eventually I got into treatment, and learned that the hole in me was from my mother's death. Joyce forgave me, and so did my kids and eventually we got back together. They all dance with me now, and we have healed through the ceremonies. But that was in my forties, and now in my late sixties, the pain still comes up from my mother's loss. It has been sixty-eight years!

"You will carry this for the rest of your life. The grief will change, it won't be so sharp, but you will have to find a way to carry it differently as you go on."

Joyce added, "Robin, you have been too hard on yourself. Stop beating yourself up for not carrying her to term. She died in your womb. It is not your fault. I know you have another purpose. Ask Gitchi Manitou (The Great Spirit) to help you."

I wiped my tears, and realized I had been beating myself up for not having the child I dreamed of, for not being a mother, for failing at this one thing that I wanted in life more than anything. I needed to stop doing that and turn to what I have, who I am truly, for acting on what I am here to do. The two of them smiled, and I smiled, and now I felt I had a reason for coming all this way. It was Joyce and Ben's help that I needed.

"Thank you so much. I am sure the reason I came here was to meet the two of you. You have helped me so much."

Some ceremonies happen whether we are in them physically or not. Besides praying all day, clearly mine was with Ben and Joyce.

After hugs and goodbyes, Catarina and I and some of the people we had come with, left the reservation and returned nine hours away to the airport in Minneapolis for the flight home. Others went on to Wisconsin.

Six months later, Catarina got the news that Ben had been killed in a car accident. I wrote to Joyce my condolences. I was so grateful I had met them both when I did. They changed my life, especially Ben. I sent thanks to him too with my prayers.

San Francisco Mountain Gratitude Ceremony 2010

Sisters and Dad in 2006 family gathering

Chapter Nine
Brasil and Another Kind of Earth-Based Ceremony

Umbanda Initiations

While most Native American Ceremonies are not to be talked about with anyone outside the ceremony, especially the details of what goes on, with Umbanda in Brasil (in North America we misspell it as Brazil) they have different rules. Babalorixa (Head Priest) Pai Carlos Buby gave me full permission to write about Umbanda and what it is about, as far as I am able. Pai had been known as Carlos de Sousa, and was quite a rock star musician in Brasil at one time. His sister Illorixa Tina de Sousa traveled and offered ceremonies around the world to offer Umbanda beyond Brasil. She is a psychologist as well as a priestess.

My first experience with the power of Umbanda was at the International Science and Consciousness Conference in Albuquerque, New Mexico in 2001. I was presenting on the Science of Ritual, drawing from a ritual explained in my first book, *Dancing Up the Moon*. I had created a ritual for healing with the Earth. After a slide show presentation, where I spoke about how earth-based rituals connect all of us, I organized the people to clear the room of chairs, and formed a circle. There were about 100-125 people in the room. After everyone was gathered, I asked certain people to read from slips of paper calling in the four directions, earth, sky and heart, depending on where they were standing in the circle. An elder couple was chosen to represent Mother Earth and Father Sky. I asked people to state their intentions for the Earth, asking for prayers, and healing. Then we did a spiral dance. I lead the group, and we snaked our way into the center and out again. Afterwards we opened the four directions and there was a definite shift in the room. We stood in silence soaking in the good feeling that permeated the room, a feeling of love and presence with the Earth. The elder couple and I scheduled a lunch date because they were so interesting to me and we discovered that they were from Ben Lomond, very close to Boulder Creek where I lived in California at the time with Alfonzo, Barbara and Jim Thomas.

Afterwards, I decided to attend some of my colleagues' seminars, one of whom was Tina de Sousa. The minute I walked into the room where Tina was presenting, I started to cry. Tina was emanating so much love I could hardly take it in. She was a bit shorter than I, about 5'5" tall with reddish brown hair and a beautiful face and figure. She looked a lot like the actress, Sophia Lauren.

In that seminar, she demonstrated what she could share about moving energy. Once the workshop started, she had us lay head to head with a random partner, and through the rhythm of the drums, she was able to the direct energy moving through us. Suddenly I felt a wave of energy swim through my body. My partner felt it too. I had no idea how this happened. Tina suggested it was the "energia do conga," the "energy of the drum."

I had to know more. I was so excited about what she taught us, I decided to go talk to her at the end of her session. She did not speak much English, but she had a woman with her who spoke several languages. Her name was Constance. Constance was founding a new temple in Santa Cruz called Temple Guaracy de Terra, an extension of the one in Sao Paulo, Brasil.

There were three temples in the U.S., Constance explained, one in Santa Cruz, one in Sebastopol, California, and one in Washington, D.C. as well as several temples in Europe and South America.

We could come any time to the one in Santa Cruz, and I was welcome to bring my husband. So the following week when

I got home, I would not accept 'no' for an answer, and Alfonzo and I went to our first Umbanda ceremony.

Now that first ceremony, which Tina was offering the week after the conference in New Mexico, happened to be an Elegbara Ceremony. The word Elegbara, means "messenger for power or authority." Eshu is the messenger and represents the primal spark of fire, where all life begins. The ceremony took place at night. I was not at all prepared for what we would experience, but I was excited to attend.

The Elegbara ceremony was held outdoors around a fire circle with the drumming on one end. Today, these ceremonies are for temple members only, but then they were open if the Illorixa intuited that we could attend and handle the energies. We were instructed to shower before we came, and wear a white shirt and white jeans. No drugs or alcohol could be consumed twenty-four hours before the ceremony. Those were the only instructions.

The ceremony calls for the two parts of the psyche—masculine and feminine—to be brought forward into the ritual and to emerge and manifest through the bodies of the mediums as Eshu or his feminine counterpart, Pompogira. He/she is the Orixá of the crossroads that helps with decisions that need to be made. The Eshu is the subconscious sexual, warrior self; and the Pompojera is the fiery, sexual feminine aspect of the Elegbara. The Elegbara is generally the primal fire and the part of our nature that sparks creativity.

What I experienced was a coming together of many things I had intuited, but not really experienced prior. The ceremony itself brings up the darkest parts of the human psyche: the prostitute and the warrior. These spirits seemed to come right out of the Earth into the mediums as part of the collective experience of everyone. There was not the same kind of "incorporation" that one experiences in a regular Umbanda ceremony where the spirits of light come down from the crown of the head into the medium. These spirits came up from within the Earth.

Incorporation is the word used to describe a spirit entering the body. This is not really possession, which implies a spirit entering a person and not obtaining permission. Incorporation is much more accurate a term. If the mediums are willing to open to the spirits of light from the other side, they will talk to the observers in the ceremony for the benefit of healing or cleansing. The specific intention is very important.

In the Elegbara ceremony, you dance as the drums tell you to move, as they set the rhythms that are played. Pretty soon all of the mediums were dancing in ways that were very suggestive and I saw them transform into the darkest parts of themselves. It was hard to tell who was incorporating at first. In this tradition, it is thought that one must go down into the underworld before one can get to a higher level of consciousness. The Elegbara spirits are of the underworld within the Earth.

The Elegbara ceremony brings one into the dark side so that the medium may evolve and go higher into the light. It is the first element of primal fire. Everything in Umbanda begins with Elegbara, or the primal fire. Tina would say that they are not only a part of the psyche, but separate spirits.

What I experienced was a shift in the mediums incorporating their entities. Once incorporated, those of us on the sidelines could then speak to the entities that were incorporated, and they would tell us of their places in the Earth and why they were there. It seemed that they had not done well in their past lives and had to be in the Earth for restitution and service to those walking on the Earth. They had lost some degree of free will and needed to offer this service to others as a Pompajera or Eshu, dealing with our energetic discharge.

When the drums start to change at the instruction of Tina de Sousa, who had already incorporated her Eshu at the beginning of the ceremony, everything winds down and the mediums come back into their bodies as themselves. It was all quite mysterious, unlike anything I had experienced.

The next day we did a regular ceremony in the Umbanda Temple where everyone wears white and you come to dance with your "Caboclo" or spirit of light or spirit guide. Tina explained that it was actually a continuation of the ceremony from the night before. When they are incorporated with their spirits of light, then the participants who come for help can talk to the spirits. That was it. I was totally intrigued. I had to follow the path of Umbanda, at least for the time being.

Umbanda ceremonies help people by bringing in spirits of light that are here to help others. These spirits come into the regular Umbanda ceremony through the mediums. The spirits are finishing their karma on Earth and the mediums are being guided to their Orixá or essence. It is a beautiful ceremony. The spirits that come in are called Caboclos. They are to help the medium get ready through a series of initiations, to embody their Orixá or essence. Cabolcos are spirits that have been on Earth before, in the essence of a certain Orixá. What's more, there is no sermon and no one preaching or proselytizing. The Elegbara ceremony is done privately with just the mediums that are in training and the leaders or coordinators of the Temple. Although that changes from time to time depending on Pai Buby's instructions from his entity, Pai Guaracy, who is basically the real leader of Temple Guaracy.

As Tina said many times: "Who knows what goes on in an Umbanda Ceremony?" When I first heard her say this, I thought, 'Sounds like the sacred lodge!' There are so many amazing things that happen during Umbanda Ceremonies, just like at Sundance, because the spirits are everywhere and most everyone is sensitive enough to feel them or experience them. However, I will share one of my experiences with Umbanda when I was initiated as a daughter of Xangô and Alfonzo was initiated as son of Oxassi.

Alfonzo and I attended the temple for two years, going to Brasil twice to attend the ceremonies at the Mother Temple outside of Sao Paulo. Both times it was quite an extraordinary experience.

It was the second time we were in Brasil at the Campo Segrada, the Sacred Grounds or Sacred Campus, outside of Sao Paulo when both Alfonzo and I were to be initiated. We had come the year before and enjoyed the ceremonies a lot. On our first trip we had only been in Umbanda for a month or two. We got to witness a "Faetura" ceremony of several people who had been in Temple Guaracy for several years. This is the highest initiation possible and there are seven levels over seven years of initiation once you reach Faetura. Very occasionally, a person is given all seven years in one year.

All of this happened on the property given to Pai by some of his followers. Pai's compound consisted of about 135 acres of land with a house built for the Babalorixia, Pai Carlos (de Sousa) Buby, and another house where his parents lived. They were also restoring rooms available for guests on a terrace below Pai's house. Tina de Sousa, his sister, lived in Sao Paulo. She also traveled extensively at the time to share Umbanda with the smaller satellite temples in Europe and the U.S. and brought people to the temple for programs such as the one we were attending.

The property had two large hills; the Campo Segrada was perched on top of one hill and the main house was on the other. The main entrance road passed the Campo Segrada, and continued down the hill and over a bridge and up the second hill where the main dining hall stood attached to Pai's house. A second dirt road met the first near the bridge. We walked down the hill and over the bridge every day for dinner.

The bridge traversed a wide creek, that eventually emptied into a pond at the far side of the property. The road followed along the creek and passed the pond and a thatched round building used for ceremonies also referred to as the old Campo Segrada. The dirt road made a large loop encompassing the property and wound back up the first hill to connect with a road that came to a back entrance and connected to the currently used Campo Segrada.

A parking lot for our busses and many cars was located at the back entrance. There were trails every where, that went through bamboo forests and groves of trees, a waterfall and terracing with dirt trails connecting both hills to make the place a paradise to walk around. There were armed guards from the Temple who took care of the fenced in property perimeter all night long, due to poverty and crime in Brasil.

At the hilltop of the Campo Segrada was this large circular temple house open air on the sides with a thatched roof. When we first got to this temple I studied it's structure because I had never seen anything like it nor as large. Log pillars held up the large roof around the outside circumference, which spanned at least forty feet in diameter. The roof was cone shaped, with beams attached to a large log hub that looked like a wagon wheel hub from underneath. The radiant beams that came from the center log like the spines of an umbrella, were also connected to each other by smaller poles that made concentric circles from the center to the outer edge of the roof like ripples in a pond. The thatch was being held up by network of flat sticks directly under it between the thatch and the poles.

The real intrigue was in the center. Inside of the temple was a large log two feet in diameter set into earth that stretched upwards at least twenty feet. The rest of the floor was a cement slab. One assumed that the log was holding up the roof until you got under the thatch edge. However, the log stopped four feet before the hub log, which looked like its continuation. This free-standing log was not holding up the roof or supporting it in any way. However it symbolized the space between the medium and the guides, the mystery of mediumship, and the grace of the guides with their invisible presence. It was a reminder that this visible world is really held up by the invisible world of spirit. The hub was the Source supporting everything. At least that was my interpretation.

We slept under this large open-air roof enclosure on our first trip. I loved sleeping under it, waking to view this free standing log, not holding up the ceiling, but still continuing to what actually did support the roof sheltering all of us, like the guides and the Creator watching over us.

The outdoor circular grounds adjacent to this sheltered temple building were three times larger than the building. This was the official Campo Segrada. The open-air circle had five smaller houses around the edge called "honkos," small round brick buildings with tile roofs. In the center of the Campo was a fire pit surrounded by a graveled area where people danced. Members of the community of Umbanda in Brasil constructed the grounds at the direction of Pai and his main spirit guide, Pai Guaracy when they created the entire temple area several years before.

Most of the ceremonies were held outside in the Campo Segrada surrounded by the honkos, with smaller ceremonies going on in the honkos from time to time. For example, we often gathered with one of Pai's entities embodied in him to talk with us about the next steps of the ritual. Nothing was prescribed, it was all directed by the entities.

Thirty or forty people would crowd inside the small building, or hang outside and peek through the windows and the door. When Pai was in ceremony embodying his entity such as when Pai embodied his Eshu or with the spirit of Pai Guaracy, we all wanted to be as close as possible to hear what the entity had to say about the next steps of what we were to do. Sometimes he shared various entities with us because he wanted us to experience them. This happened a few times on our second visit to the land.

Initiates were also sequestered in the honkos from time to time during ceremonies. Altars to various Orixás—or divine elements of nature—were set up in the honkos. Some altars were set up in-between the honkos on occasion. Oxassi, the spirit of the forest, and an Eshu altar were two that I remember inside the honkos. A Xangô altar was set up outside in a small bamboo grove.

The first of the honko contained a kitchen where food was prepared for the rituals. Often these rituals went on all night and food was necessary at odd hours for the mediums. I worked in the kitchen during the first year. I felt it was a great honor to have such a ring-side seat, especially the first visit. Pai came in to let me know it was an honor to witness these ceremonies in the kitchen in my first year. Those of us in the kitchen had a front row seat to watch the ceremonies. Pai and I spoke Spanish together, as it was a common language we both spoke to some extent.

On the second visit to Brasil, Alfonso and I stayed in newly renovated rooms near Pai's house. It was more comfortable, but I missed sleeping outside.

That year at the ceremony that Pai held for us in the Campo Segrada, we were to find our Caboclos or spirit guides. He had us make a circle around the fire pit. There were at least 25 to 30 of us initiates. Each one was called one at a time to "find our Caboclo." Cabolcos in Umbanda were to help us find our Orixá, as I mentioned before, which was our essential core or our Authentic Nature.

The drummers were set up between two honkos on the far edge of the Campo Segrada, and they played during the entire time. They had to know which prayer-songs to play at the right time. Pai spent a lot of time with the drummers because their music was the foundation of all rituals in Umbanda.

He was such a master ritualist, he would only have to nod in their direction and the drummers knew to end one song and begin another one. They never missed which song came next.

As the fire blazed in the center, and twenty-five or so of us were seated on the ground in a circle, he would call us one at a time to come to the center near the stones that surrounded the fire pit. We were dressed in white pants and a white t-shirt with the Temple Guaracy logo on it. He had in one hand what is called a "twalia," a long piece of cotton cloth about two feet wide and eight feet long. As he danced next to each of us near the fire, he wore one twalia draped around his neck, and the other one tied at his waist like a sash.

At the right moment, he would throw the twalia from around his neck over the head of the initiate to drape them and cover their face so they could get out of their heads, and go inside themselves into their hearts. He took the second twalia, which he unwrapped from his waist and placed it around our waists so that he could control the direction we were dancing without touching us. This was primarily to keep us away from the fire at a safe distance. Then he commanded them to keep dancing. "Dansa, Dansa," he would say in Portuguese. As the drums played on the edge of the Campo Segrada, we fell into a trance where we were semi-conscious and he kept the drums going as we began to "approximate our Caboclos" or draw to us the right spirit of light to guide us to our Orixá (our Spirit Essence), one at a time.

As the person began to dance with Pai next to them, they took on different movements, indicating a different entity that was entering the person, and a certain Caboclo. When the initiate made a demonstrative move towards the drum, or began to really dance hard, using particular hand and arm movements, Pai could tell what element of Earth, Air, Fire or Water, they were relating to. There were several Orixás that one could relate to: The daughter or son of Xangô, also the mountain or manifested Earth such as a volcano; Ossasi, the spirit of the hunter in the forest and Jurema, the feminine counterpart as the light in the forest; or Ogum, movement or flow of any element. These were the main elements embodied by the mediums of Temple Guaracy. They were called "lines." Other temples used some of the same and sometimes different lines.

When it was my turn to dance for my Caboclo, I stood facing Pai, who said in Portuguese, "pronto?" (ready?) I nodded yes. Then he threw the first twalia over my head and, with a nod, commanded the drummers to begin playing. Suddenly I felt myself dancing in gestures that were not really ones I would have chosen. My arms were raised up as if I had two axes or hammers in my hands and I was pounding them in the air with fierce gestures. I had never danced like this before. As my body moved, I was drawn magnetically to the drummers and suddenly I was towering over the drummers as though I was twenty feet tall! I felt I could look at them from way above the Campo and I felt the wind pick up around my body. I was not semiconscious, I was awake like I had never been before, and what energy was dancing me was not separate, it felt like me fully embodied and free. Then as the song changed, the energy I embodied brought me to the fire again where I danced like I had never danced before. Thunderstorms gathered around us. Sweat poured off of me. The wind howled and a light rain fell. All the while I had the twalia over my head. Pai kept me away from the fire with the other twalia.

Then the music subsided and Pai kept my head covered and moved me towards a honko where inside there was an altar and candles lit to all the various Orixás. He instructed me in Spanish to sit, and meditate. There was a young man who had gone before me who was inside, and crying softly. He was okay, just a bit overwhelmed. Pai checked on him but left him sitting in front of me.

As I sat in the honko and meditated, the spirit of the wind came blowing past me saying, "I am Iansaaaaa," She came by twice and I could perceive her quite clearly. She was dressed in white diaphanous robes that brushed my face as she passed. She was so full of love. She flew all around me inside the honko. Then I felt water pouring off of me and I felt the sweat from the dancing making rivers down my face and body. I felt strong and soft at the same time. Mountainous, I was mountainous. Xangô was my essence. I had become my Orixá, or spirit of nature. It was such a profound feeling I bent over and wept.

Another young Brazilian woman was brought in the honko after me, and wept softly for whatever she was experiencing. Others were brought in to sit with their Caboclo and then ceremonially brought back out again when it was time.

As Pai brought me out of the honko, the people in the Campo lined the doorway to the honko and clapped as we came out one by one. I had no idea why they were clapping. Everything was in Portuguese. Alfonzo was not there to translate for me, as he was in the group too far away to ask him anything.

Back at the large thatched roofed building, as the rain began to fall lightly, Pai gathered us and told us that this one, Alfonzo, was the son of Ossasi (everyone clapped); and that one (another woman in the group) was a daughter of Jurema (applause); another young man the son of Xangô (more applause).

When he came to me, he looked at me a long time. Then he said through a Portuguese translator, "The question with you is—what do I do with someone who is already what we are here to bring them to become?" I interpreted that as, "You are

already a medium, you have your Orixá already, daughter of Xangô. What are you doing here?" (No applause, only silence).
No one knew how to respond to his comment. Neither did I.
Later, I recalled my experience when I was two years old, dancing on top of the refrigerator. I had climbed up to my mountain top scaling the drawers as a stairway. I was dancing to life with a large knife in my hand, singing to the divine. I had always been a mountain, always here to serve. Pieces of my life were clearly falling into place.
It did not take long after we returned to the U.S. for me to realize (with my other spirit guide's help) to see that I did not need to become a medium in Umbanda, I already was one. My spirit guides, WuLan, and the Archangels began to help me by instructing me gently at first and then in more decisive affirmations to leave Umbanda. I was reluctant to do so because I loved the community and loved the ceremonies. It is always quite amazing to share ceremonies with others, but channeling my entities were not Umbanda's entities and I needed to leave to start my own center. I listened to my guides and left within a few months. Alfonzo left a month before me. While I left the Temple I kept attending workshops, and I hosted Tina at my Center for the Soul in our home for two years, offering her insights to other people.
Alfonzo and I held our own private ceremonies at home together and brought our entities into our bodies when it felt right to do so, usually once a week. We continued, on occasion, to visit the Umbanda ceremonies, as they were open to whoever wanted to attend, even if we had been in the temple before. We could still embody our Umbanda spirits inside those ceremonies.
In hindsight, Pai gifted me with that acknowledgement of my mediumship and my Orixá. Without it, I might not have realized that I was ready to begin my own spiritual center, and had to get started as I knew enough now.
In 2003, at forty-eight, I started The Center for the Soul, my educational center, where I taught classes out of my home

and held "Finding your Spirit Guide" and "Developing Your Intuition" classes. I taught those classes along with the Heart Path guided meditations for many years. Today, I still hold a monthly meditation class where I teach the Path of the Heart process and channel my guides. Some of my very first students still attend after all these years. A very loyal group indeed!

Condomblé Ceremonies

After our second retreat at the Campo Segrada with Pai and Tina, Alfonzo and I visited Salvador Bahia, a province of Brasil up the coast from Sao Paulo. We wanted to experience a Condomblé ceremony, which is different than Umbanda. We also wanted to relax a bit before heading back to the States, as the time with Pai and Tina at the Campo Segrada was not relaxing. We did ceremony morning, noon, and late into the night. We needed a real vacation before going home and starting work all over again.

When we landed in Salvador Bahia, a beautiful city with red tile roofs and white thick plaster walls on the buildings, terrific beaches and islands off the coast, we felt strangely like we had arrived home. "If we had a lot of money, I would buy a house here," I said to Alfonzo. He agreed. We loved Bahia.

We spent time in town wandering shops and fending off vendors. We had our pictures taken with women dressed in hoop skirts and took pictures of the buildings and the town square.

Next, we visited the African Museum, which had displays about the African diaspora, and slavery and about African ceremonies coming to Brasil. Alfonzo struck up a conversation with the man who took our money for the museum. In Portuguese, Alfonzo asked the man if there were any tours of Condomblé ceremonies, or Babalorixas that offered private sessions. The man resisted at first, and asked some questions of us, and then was very helpful, as he gave us two leads: a ceremony, and a ceremonial leader who gave sessions. He asked us to wait and he would call his friend who would help arrange these adventures for us.

We toured the museum where we viewed many marvelous exhibits. One of which were larger than life size Orixiás (spirits of nature) that were carved by hand, all by the same artist. They were amazing representations on wooden panels that were at least eight feet tall by five to six feet wide. After spending time learning about the slave trade and the ceremonies that developed from the mix of African and Native Brasilian, we returned to the front desk. The friend of the man at the desk gave us directions to the Babalorixa's apartment several blocks away. He would take us there immediately. I was not prepared to go so soon! He only spoke Portuguese, so he and Alfonzo struck up a conversation.

"Hold on Alfonzo, what are we getting ourselves into here?" We went to a nearby restaurant with the man to eat something and discuss what we were doing.

"How do we know this guy is legit?" I asked him.

"I feel confident that he is on the level." Alfonzo said.

"How much is this little adventure going to cost us?" I asked.

"I'm not sure, but I want to do it. You have to trust me." Alfonzo said.

Gulp, I was not so sure at all. Alfonzo could be compulsive when it came to spending money. His moods went from extreme generosity to conservative spending; he was in his generous mode on this day.

We ate our lunch in silence while I thought about it. The man was talking to Alfonzo, sensing that I was not so sure about all this, when Alfonzo turned to me and said, "You can stay here if you want to, but I am going." I did not feel safe staying at this restaurant and definitely did not feel safe going. Well, okay, l do love adventures. After lunch we set off to find the Condomblé Babalorixa.

So we followed the man through the barrio, where people were living in concrete buildings with no glass windows – just openings that were like windows, and there were children and people hanging out everywhere on the street. We were, I am sure, a strange site to them. Once we were through that area, the man directed us to a clean modern apartment building several stories high, on the edge of the barrio. We found the right buzzer and the man left us sitting in the lobby.

"What's going on?" I said nervously to Alfonzo.

"We have to wait. He is busy with someone, and he is getting ready for us."

"How do we get back?" I said.

"It is no problemo, we can catch a bus down the street back to our hotel. Don't worry, I have this!" Alfonzo was doubly irritated, as trust was an issue between us, (me trusting him) and he hated translating for me. He spoke five languages fluently, while I spoke English and a little Spanish. I also hated being dependent on him, which I had to be because of the language barrier.

Soon we heard the buzzer and the door unlocked and we were let in. I followed Alfonzo up the stairs, and we found the apartment. There was a palm mat outside the front door, with jars of various kinds of offerings. This was the place for sure! The door opened and a woman greeted us. She signaled for us to step over the jars.

Then she seated us in the living room on a couch. The Babalorixa came in from an adjacent room, and without speaking to us, he opened the door to a bathroom, took a mouse out of the bathtub, and put it outside the back at an altar on his back deck to Eshu, breaking the mouse's neck as he traveled to the back deck. I grabbed Alfonzo's hand, as we looked at each other. "He killed the mouse, Alfonzo!" I whispered. He just nodded. "Si!" Alfonzo said looking at me.

Animal sacrifice was not done in the Temple Guaracy, as far as we knew. However, we had heard of this practice done in other temples. Some sacrificed chickens or other creatures would then be prepared and eaten by the community afterwards. The offering was to the Elegbara, the spirits of the underworld, for their information and advice.

The Babalorixa disappeared then came out of a backroom and greeted us, and ushered Alfonzo into the back. This is where he would caste the bijous or cowrie shells for a reading. The priest only spoke Portuguese, and I could not understand a word he said, as he spoke very fast. I could sit on the couch and wait for Alfonzo.

The woman sat with me watching videos of the priest's ceremonies. It was all very strange being in a high rise with more high rises outside the window, and a statue of Elegbara spirits staring at me from the balcony, a dead mouse at their feet, while I watched videos of ceremonies. It felt like I was in a time warp. However, now that I knew we would not be the sacrifices, I felt better, and began to relax.

After an hour Alfonzo re-emerged, and I could see he was happy with his reading. He paid the man $140 and asked if I wanted a reading. "Not at that price," I said, "unless you are paying." I knew Alfonzo was tapped out, and I could not justify a reading with my money as I did not have that much with me, and I certainly did not want a mouse to die on my account. "No, I'll pass," I said.

So we said our goodbyes, and found our way down the street to the bus stop. Alfonzo was fairly silent all the way back to the hotel. He did tell me the mechanics of the reading, the circle with the equidistant cross in the center where he spread the shells, and what the man had to say generally. But I had a feeling there was a fundamental shift that had taken place and I wasn't sure what had happened. I wondered how much of his future the Babalorixa had shown Alfonzo.

The next day we were told there would be a bus coming to the hotel at a certain time to pick us up to take us to a Condomblé ceremony after dinner. This was with other people from the hotel that had the same idea. It would cost us $100 each. It all felt very clandestine, as we were told not to tell anyone in the hotel where we were going. Just to wait in the lobby. I am sure there was no arrangement made with the hotel about this.

"Whee! This is getting expensive!" I said to Alfonzo. But both of us were excited to go, though I wasn't sure that we wouldn't end up left for dead in the back-country somewhere.

I relaxed when I got into the van and saw other passengers from other hotels, also very nervous, some of whom spoke

British English, others spoke French, and some Spanish. There were about nine people in all.

As the van pulled away from the hotel, a woman turned around and spoke to us in very clear English. She told us the etiquette of the ceremony and then told us a bit about the temple and what we were to expect. We were invited to witness the first part of the ceremony, but at a certain point the ceremony was private, and she would signal for us to leave the temple. We were instructed to watch for her signal.

When we got to the village, at least a forty-five minute drive out of Bahia, we found ourselves being ushered into a building that was like a large community center or hall made of cement block. The building was painted white. Inside there was a large wooden floor. On one side was a small bandstand, and in the center on the floor was the symbol for Ossasi, the warrior of the forest, made of eucalyptus leaves.

"I'm in the right place!" Alfonzo said smiling, as he was just designated as a son of Ossasi.

"I can see that!" I said chuckling.

We were herded into seats on the side of the room behind a low railing that divided the ceremonial space from the spectator space. Other people came in too. We waited and waited, and waited. Then at a certain point the woman who spoke to us in the van, our tour guide, ushered us to seats around the ceremonial space. Everyone had good seats as we were all along a wall with no second rows. Shortly after we were seated, drummers came out and began to play.

Coming slowly from the back, dancing in the off-rhythm beat of the drummers, women dancers moved onto the floor of the ceremonial space. The women wore the dress of their particular Orixás; that is, large hoop skirts, and heads wrapped in the Brazilian plantation style. The men had brightly colored shirts and pants with large sashes. They were dressed in the colors of the various Orixás.

The dancers did not seem to be in a trance. They would dance and then stop, and then dance and stop. Things were said in Portuguese, then they would start again. We were not informed of what was going on exactly, we just watched them dance in a circle around the large leaf symbol on the floor. This went on for a long time, maybe an hour. We lost track of time. One loses all sense of time and space in many indigenous rituals.

Then the music changed and I could see various dancers embody their Orixá. Their faces changed, and were ushered into the backroom one by one. Once they were all gone to the back, they came out again, this time embodied and dancing in different arm movements that expressed their Orixá. These were not Umbanda songs, but we recognized the cadence as Eshu or Pompajera, spirits of the underworld.

After some time, as we all swayed to the drums. A woman spectator next to me began to sway more ecstatically and fell forward, and then got up to dance. It was not my place to do anything for her, as she had just been embodied with her Orixá for the first time. A group of helpers came and scooped her up and brought her to the back room. I could see she was in a deep trance. This was how the Orixá or spirit of light connected with their mediums in Condomblé.[8]

Once the new medium was taken away, the woman who was our tour guide signaled to us to leave the room. So we stood up in unison and were ushered out to the vans. Inside our van the tour guide told us that the woman was in trance and had received her Orixá, and that the ceremony would go on for sometime, probably all night long. We looked at our watches; it was already one a.m.

Alfonzo and I were quiet all the way back to our hotel. We realized we had witnessed a ceremony that few people experienced unless they became part of a Condomblé Temple.

I had made sure my crown chakra was closed up dur-

---

[8] It seemed that it was not that different than in Native American dances. The Spirits of each tradition run the ceremonies. In Native American dances, once you prayed for them before the dancing in ceremonies, spiritual 'tools' such as the Chanumpa (sacred pipe), feather fans, or staffs are given to you if you were to have them. After receiving a vision, the dancer would receive the Chanumpa (sacred pipe), feather fans, or staffs or get instructions to make them. Some people made them after the vision, others received them from someone else as a gift.

ing the ceremony, so that I would NOT incorporate anything during the ceremony we witnessed. I had my Orixá, now I had to live out into the future what I had received from our time in Brasil.

During one of the retreats at the Campo Segrada, we were told by Pai's brother, Anthony who is a Condomblé Babalorixa in Sao Paulo, that once the Orixá comes into a new medium in a Condomblé ceremony, it is a six-year commitment on the part of the medium to learn what had just happened from other mediums and the Babalorixa. This is very different than Umbanda, where the learning is up front, and then you get your initiations to your Orixá very gradually over years. I was an exception to this in Umbanda. I got my Orixá right away.

I was extremely grateful to be only a witness in this ceremony, as I knew what was required in Native American ceremonies. Once you received your vision to dance, you are committed for four years to Sundance or Ogitchidaah. It was a total way of life, not just something you did once a year. I was glad mine came the way it did. Now I was on my own with my own center, and my Orixá, Xangô, manifested Earth or the Mountain. I was to become my own Mountain.

Umbanda cermonial grounds with the five honkos (small temples) in Brasil

Section Three: Mediumistic Work

Chapter Ten

Stories from this Medium's Work

Readings and Healings

One day, wanting to expand my practice beyond Santa Cruz, I looked "over the hill" (the Santa Cruz Mountains) to Los Gatos and San Jose. I discovered there were several bookshops where I could work doing readings and healing sessions.

On one trip I drove to Los Gatos and discovered Inner Journey, a meta-physical shop and bookstore and the owner happened to be there. This shop was a part gift and part spiritual shop where regular visitors came to get readings, healing work, tarot readings, incense, sage, earrings, Tibetan tankas, books and a host of other items of a spiritual nature. We made a nice connection, and within a few weeks I was working there one or two days a week offering healing, mediumistic sessions, and Energy Medicine.

Mari Luna's loss had blasted open my psychic awareness, and I was now able to read the energetic and astral world as though I had a hand in both worlds. Two worlds are my reality and have been most of my life, but more intense now then ever.

I was officially calling myself a medium, and I really felt I had earned it. Every session was a test of that. This next story was one of the first and most challenging sessions I had while at Inner Journey.

Stacy's Story

It was a day like any other, at Inner Journey waiting for clients to walk in. I regularly saw people of every walk-of-life and in every life situation from Silicon Valley engineers to new moms, to grandmothers, to hairdressers. Some would come in with one issue or another and I was there two days a week to help them sort out their lives.

A woman I will call, Jane, who I had met several times, made an appointment. She was asking about her spirit guides. I had begun teaching classes on the guides at Inner Journey and at The Center for the Soul, my educational center in Santa Cruz that took place in my home with Alfonso. I had done a painting of Jane's guides because she had a Hindu Goddess above her head, and I had never seen anyone with this guide so firmly implanted in her aura. At the end of the session, she asked about a neighbor whose husband had just died.

"Send her in I would be happy to talk to her. "

"He didn't just die, he shot himself." Jane said flatly as she told me the story.

That tug in my belly said it was tragic, but there was nothing I had not faced myself, I thought, so I suggested she come in anytime and gave her my hours and when I would be available.

A few days later, Jane brought Stacy (not her real name) in to visit me. Jane had been through the whole ordeal with her. Stacy was a small pretty woman, with large eyes and brown hair. What struck me was how young she was. She couldn't have been more than 31 or 32. She looked extremely shaken, and had a wad of tissues in her hand.

The first thing I wanted to do was make her feel as though she could tell me whatever she wanted to about the incident. Instead she asked me to read the situation.

"Could you tell me what happened?" Stacy asked. "I wasn't home when he ...."

After getting her husband Burt's full name from her (Burt is not his actual name), I saw him clearly, sitting outside their house on the corner of their property, shaking his head, and asking the universe what just happened. I reported what I saw to Stacy. She could not hear my conversation with Burt, nor see him. "I am going to go silent for a minute while he shows me." I said to Stacy.

I sent my spirit to him, and introduced myself, and told him that Stacy had sent me to help him. He was so glad to be able to talk to someone. Clearly he was stuck between worlds.

"Show me what happened," I asked. He took me into the garage, and showed me the gun, then he said, "I was just cleaning it, like this." he said, placing his imaginary finger barrel to his chest, "And then it went off. I found myself standing there, and seeing my body on the floor of the garage here. I have been wandering around the place ever since."

"You died, Burt. You shot yourself accidently. You are in the spirit world now."

He was so angry with this information that he kicked the air, and we were suddenly back outside his house on the curb.

"Stacy, it was an accident, he was cleaning his gun, and it went off."

She started to cry, and wailed, "I was sure that was the case." This would help the police report, as she and her family were taking it to court. The police had it listed as a suicide, which meant she would get no insurance money, which she desperately needed.

Then she asked through her tears if there was a sign or anything he could give her to be sure it was him.

I turned to Burt, "She wants a sign, could you tell me something only she would know?"

"Tell her I wasn't really mad at her, and I am sorry for everything. I am so sorry. This was not what I wanted at all."

"Did you and Burt have a fight before he died? He says

he is sorry, and he didn't mean to kill himself, and he is sorry if you thought he was angry at you."

Her mouth went slack with recognition, then she said, "We weren't getting along right before, anything else he can tell me?"

"I turned to him, Burt, help me out here." I said.

"Earrings, I gave her earrings recently, for the holidays." I reported this to Stacy, and she agreed. "Yes, they had diamonds in them."

"What else?" Stacy still had a great deal of skepticism.

"What do you want him to say? He has given you two clues, three really. This is really him." I described him, she was more convinced now.

"You don't understand. I don't really get this stuff. I don't really believe in all this. But I guess now, I have to."

I smiled and said, "You should, you know, you are highly intuitive yourself!"

She knew this, but had repressed it to a large extent. Then I asked if there was anything else she wanted me to ask him.

"The boys, what should I tell them, other than what I already have told them?"

"How old are they?"

"4 and 6."

I shook my head. "Too young. Just tell them Daddy went on to help them as their Angel. That is all they might be able to process. It is too hard for them to understand. All they know is he is gone. I am so sorry Stacy, I can't imagine what you are going through."

Our session lasted an hour, and I felt that this would not be the last time I would see her.

A few days later, she came back with more questions.

"Could you see how he is now?"

As I tuned in, he seemed more accepting of his situation, but still angry at himself. He wasn't leaving this earth plane though and that worried me some.

"Burt, there is a reason for this, why don't you ask your angel why this happened now?" I said to him.

A large Angel stood behind him, and he had not seen it until that moment. I could see him turn to the Angel and ask why.

"You have a lot of work to do over here for your family," the Angel said.

Then a few more days past and she called and asked if I would be available for a phone session after the funeral for the whole family.

"I'll warn you, Robin, there are many skeptics in this family."

Now that was a challenge. I agreed to do it because I love challenges. However, it was the hardest group reading I had ever done at that time. The first part of the job was to get clear enough myself so that their collective grief did not interfere with my own insight. I had to hold my emotions steady and not get swayed by all the emotions flying around in the room. As an ultra-sensitive, clairsentient (feeler), that is not easy at all for me to do, which I empathized with Stacy immediately.

Having gone through the sudden death of my daughter, I could only imagine how difficult it would be to feel such a huge loss with a spouse and so very young! But I had to reign in my emotions. At the same time the second part of the job was to "tune into" what Burt had to say.

She called me from the house of his parents after the funeral. Stacy put me on speaker setting so the whole family could hear Burt's answers to their questions as I received them. On the other end of the phone were family members on both sides of the family, Burt's brother and parents, her father and mother, and his brother, several generations of nieces, nephews and cousins. There were twenty or so people, all of them in great pain with Burt's sudden loss. He was the oldest brother and much admired on both sides of the family.

Then she asked if I could bring Burt into the room, or come into contact with him. I felt him show up right away; actually he was already there. Then there were the questions wanting me to prove that it was Burt. It was a phone session after all, what could I possibly do? Then I thought, 'It is his job to convince them, not mine.' So I asked him;

"Burt could you give them a sign please."

Just then the lights flickered in the room where they were all together.

I heard a collective "Whoa!!!" on the other end of the phone. There was lots of nervous laughter. Stacy told me what happened.

Then someone asked if there were any messages.

"He says that his younger brother needs to get his act together, and he is here to help him do it! A kick in the butt from the other side!"

There were peels of laughter and sniffles too. That was the sign they all needed. This was Burt for sure. There were many more questions.

He said his "I love you" to everyone, and they asked questions here and there.

But when it was done, I remember being exhausted. The reason was the sense of double pressure first of all proving that it was Burt and then, that the experience would be a good one for so many people who were all grieving his loss at the same time.

While it was challenging for me, it was doubly challenging for them. There wasn't a person in the house that day that walked away skeptical any more. All of them felt somehow transformed by being able to communicate and say their good-byes to a man who simply left too soon and too suddenly.

This, I came to understand, was another part of the purpose of him leaving early, that is to change skeptics into believers or at least ones willing to entertain the idea of the other side. After that phone session, I found myself asking Burt to let go now. "It is safe to leave, you have to go before you can help your boys." Burt left with the help of his angel who escorted him towards the light. He waved good-bye and said a big thank you to me.

Over the years, I have continued to talk with Stacy. From time to time, Burt will come to her and she feels his presence now without my support. She knows when he is trying to tell her things, and when she can hear them, other times she can't, but she often checks in with me about their communication.

Burt has accepted that part of his role now is to help Stacy and the kids. They are older now, and enjoying life in a different part of the country. His death has helped his entire family believe in something beyond death, and know that each of us has a guardian angel. Burt is a guardian angel for his boys and for Stacy, and I know he always will be.

Several years after working at Inner Journey, we heard that it was in danger of closing, so I began to look for other places to work and offer readings. Soon after I found East West Bookshop in Mountain View. I had done book signings at East West with both my previous books and offered workshops occasionally too. I interviewed and began working in both places. Some of the following stories came from readings I did at East West as well as Inner Journey as well as in my own private practice.

An Unwanted Visit

In once case, two young cousins in their twenties came in to talk to me and wanted to know about their Uncle Reggie (not his real name). 'Did Uncle Reggie go to heaven or hell?' was their question.

"Heaven and hell are constructs. They are separate parts of the astral world, lower and higher vibrations of the same realm." I said to them. They looked at each other and shrugged.

While they did not tell me anything but his name, they knew who he was. When I made contact through the vibration of his name, he crawled out of a very dark and dense realm. He belonged there. He hadn't changed at all. Actually they did not like him much when he was alive. He had been in jail and died there. He had done criminal activities for his whole life and was a hit man, murdering many people for money. When they asked me about him, I felt a very creepy dark feeling that he would just as well slit my throat as well as to say hello. I stopped the session. "I do not want to make contact with him. He was up to no good when he was alive, and you girls shouldn't be asking after him either. You know who he was." Their questions were not out of grief but curiosity. I sent Reggie back to the place he crawled out of and sealed the door. These girls are an example of the wrong intention to contact the other side.

When to Call on a Loved One who has Died

These two stories taught me a lot. The first thing I learned was not to contact loved ones right away after they pass. It should be done months after, or a year after to be on the safe side. In the case of Burt however, he needed to be contacted because he was stuck, and his wife's concern for him helped him too. But normally, I ask people to wait one to three months.

This is because when someone dies, they have to cross over as if they are traveling over a bridge or a river (like the River Styx) for a period of time before they can come back and serve humanity, if they choose service. They are in a process, and the process takes Earth time. So it helps to give them space.

You wouldn't expect a new baby to walk out of the womb. Pulling the dead back to stave off the pain of grief for those left behind is not helpful to those who have transitioned. They have to cross fully to the other side and get their 'sea-legs'. Also if they are coming back disoriented, it doesn't help the persons they left behind either. It can often cause more concern.

I have also learned the lesson of not contacting the dead right away from my Native American teachers, and other teachers. Through the spirits of light that I channel have also instructed me through my mother's death to give her time. Of course there are exceptions to this.

In some indigenous cultures, the ones remaining do not say the name of the deceased (it is called holding the spirit) for one year. On the year anniversary the family has a give-away of their things, and then they have a feast in celebration of the deceased, where they share stories and enjoy the memories, being assured that the loved one has fully crossed over.

When people are very sick, I have experienced that sometimes they cross over in bits and pieces. That is, some part of their consciousness is already gone while aspects of their body and mind take a long time to let go and inch their way across. Sometimes there is an energy body left, like a blob of energy that is attached to a house or property. In that case, that part of the spirit needs a little help, and prayer is the most effective way to help.

Praying for the soul of a person to cross is a very good thing to do, and helps the souls of all beings immensely. It is something most churches do for those who have died. I recommend it for anyone with a loss.

One time I was offering a class in Felton, CA where Alfonzo and I lived for two years. During this particular nighttime class, close to Halloween, someone had lost a friend in the group, and that loss had prompted the question. We asked WuLan, 'What it was we could do for the souls of the dead?'

Wulan instructed us to pray for them. So we created a circle both physically and psychically with our intention. We made a circle or vortex with our prayer and our clasped hands. We dropped our hands once the circle was set. Then we asked the soul of the friend who was struggling to cross over, to go to the other side through the vortex we had created. Suddenly I perceived him fly through our circle like a bird, then I perceived hundreds of souls who had died in the nearby area standing around us. We could feel them whoosh past us as we held the circle with our intention that they could go into the light. As the tide of spirits subsided, we opened the circle, and reflected on what just happened.

Through the intuition of several of my students as well as myself, we collectively perceived hundreds of beings crossing over in the span of about fifteen minutes. Some beings had died a very long time ago, both Native Americans and white people who had once lived in the area. After that, every year around Halloween, when the veils between the worlds are thinnest, my students and I made the circle and released spirits that were ready to leave.

Sasha and Her Lover

Many of my clients come in wanting to talk to relatives that have passed away, and often they want to ask questions that lead to issues of their death. The most difficult for me are when tragedy has hit a family hard. Take Sasha, (not her real name). She came in with a gun shot story that broke my heart.

She had fallen in love with a good guy that became a drug dealer. We will call him Tony. The true story of his death is unknown to this day, but whether it was gang related, a drug deal gone bad, or a self-inflicted Russian roulette—a bad bet at a drunken party—he was living on the edge of a very dark world and just fell off into the void. They found him in the street with a gun-shot wound to the head, and the gun in his hand. It was winter, and raining in Northern California the night he died. Any evidence was washed away or compromised.

There was no way the rain would stop for this young woman in love with him. She came into my office after returning home from Santa Barbara to find out what happened.

A few days before he had told her to find someone else, that he was not good for her, and he wanted her to have a better life. She was smart and good at school, and he was not. But she loved him, and knew he could be a better man, so she refused to leave him behind.

She got the news at College, four hours away from San Jose. Two weeks after school started, she got three calls, one from a friend, another from his mother, then her mother, telling her that Tony had been shot dead. The police were involved, as this looked like a faked suicide—the scene was set up as though he died of a self-inflicted gun-shot wound—but actually it was made to look like it and was actually an execution of some sort.

Sasha, just nineteen years old, was devastated. A friend of hers, Monica, who also knew Tony, brought Sasha into my office. It was less then a week after his death. She was such a pretty young woman, and her face was twisted with grief, tears streamed down her face. She asked Monica to sit in with her in the session. Sasha was shaking.

As we began the session, I gave her a tissue and asked her to take a few breaths, as this would calm her nerves. When she was ready, she said very calmly, "I have to know if he killed himself or not." As I tuned in and looked back on the scene, I could perceive what happened.

He was playing a version of Russian Roulette with a friend. Both were very drunk. They played with the gun and it went off. I didn't see an execution. I saw a stupid act that was more a kin to a game. I could see that there were men after him. He was in too deep and owed them money. This was his way out. Tony had not intended to kill himself, but playing with a loaded gun while your drunk was beyond stupid. In a way, he was hoping the gun would kill him. He was in very deep trouble. The drug dealers might have killed him anyway. He was completely careless about his life. That much was clear.

The hardest part of this story for me was that there was no peace for the families nor for this young woman. Tony was smart, and almost too smart for his own good. He just hated authority and could not reconcile teachers, nor principals telling him what to do. His own father was unknown to him, and his last contact with him was in jail. He did not see a way out of the violence and stress he lived in everyday. He had not just fallen into a bad crowd—he was leading it! He had stolen the money from the wrong man, as a game, that ended badly.

Sasha was at a crossroads with him anyway. She knew their relationship was coming to a breaking point. In some ways, when I contacted his spirit, he was glad to be out of all the chaos and really wanted her to move on. He loved her enough to really let her go. She needed to do the same.

When I described him and his actual death to her, she felt it was him. He gave her information about the situation that was true enough to her, and confirmed his recklessness. He wanted her to move on, but he had broken her heart, and she could not find peace, she felt he died so that she would let go. To some extent that was true. He wanted her to have a better life than the one he could have offered her. She was still broken hearted and bent over as she poured out her tears.

Then I suggested that when she was ready to look down the road of her life, I would be able to help her see more of a future for herself. But right now she just needed to grieve. I took her hands in mine and looked into her eyes.

"Sasha, no one should have to go through this at your age or any age. I can see that you mothered Tony." She nodded affirmatively.

"Stuff happens for reasons we can't always see right away. What I can see of your spirit is that you are very strong and you know that things happen for a reason. Tony loved you, but he couldn't get past his own limitations. He knew you saw his potential, and he knew he would never meet it in this lifetime, because he was too far in with all he was involved with, the drugs, and the money. Some of it darker than you will ever know. I don't want to tell you all I saw. He was in big time trouble. He may have ended up dead anyway. But I want you to know that you can do this, you can heal. When you're ready, come back and we will look down the road together."

A few months later, Sasha came back, and she was smiling. That was a big surprise. This time she came alone.

"I wanted to thank you for your help right after Tony's death. It was so good to know I could get past his death. But I feel guilty. I feel that he died to save me. I have such a hard time forgiving myself …" Then the tears started again. "I feel like I killed him."

"Sasha, listen to me." I took her hands and looked into her tear soaked eyes once again.

"Tony made bad and careless decisions. You did not kill him, he killed himself or someone else forced him into it through his own bad choices. You have to move on. Your intelligence did not kill Tony. Tony's lack of ability to move in his life is what killed him. He made bad choices partly because he had no father to guide him. His poor mother was overwhelmed with other children. He practically raised himself."

"Do not feel bad for being smart and wanting something better in your life. You deserve it, and so did Tony, but he didn't know he could better himself."

After contacting Tony, she asked him some of the same questions over and over, he finally said to me, "How can I get her to move on!" I turned to Sasha.

"What is it you need to hear from him to let go and move on?"

After a long pause, she said, "I need to know we can try again in another life. Can we meet again, and can he make better choices? I love him so much, I need to know he would be willing to try something different down the road."

What I could see on the other side was a young man, hands thrust deep in his pockets turning his back to her to pace, then turning around suddenly, as if she had hit him with a question he was not prepared to answer. Then he broke a grin that said yes and said to her,

"You mean you would try it with me again?"

"Yes, I would love to. Please, Tony, find a way to love yourself enough to choose better parents. You deserve a father who will be there for you, instead of the one you got."

I could see the way he was standing, that she really challenged him.

"Okay, if you promise to move on." Now he had just challenged her.

"Okay, I agree." Sasha said with some reluctance.

"Tell her I love her, and I will work on loving myself more." Tony said.

"You have to forgive yourself Tony. Do this for both of you." I said without much hesitation.

"Deal." Tony said. "Tell her I love her so much."

"I love him too, and I am so angry, I don't know who to punch." Sasha started to cry.

Tony had to leave. It was as though his time with her was up. As he left, and told Sasha of his departure, then I turned to Sasha.

"Do you think you can look ahead in your own life now?"

"Yes, I think I can."

I guided her into her own heart. Then I asked her to see a golden road unfurling out in front of her. It was a beautiful bright path.

"I want you to see this for yourself, Sasha. What do you perceive coming down the road to your heart?"

"I see a man coming towards me, he is older than me, and wants to have children. He, he is really smart and loves that I am too. He encourages me in my own pursuits." Then she paused. "Wow, he is so different than Tony. He is really kind. He loves kids, and wants to be a good father. Tony had a mean streak. He was never mean to me, but he could be cruel to others."

"You got it!" I laughed. "Eventually, Tony would have hurt you too out of his own frustration with himself. You deserve a man like the one coming towards you, and he is quite close actually, but you have not met him yet. He is on his way. Just pray for Divine Order, and he will show up at the right time. I see him about six months away."

She broke a grin for the first time since I had met her. Dimples punctuated her beautiful cheeks. "That is just after I graduate. I see him. Wow, he is really handsome too!"

When she opened her eyes, she was smiling and it was as though a cloud had lifted from her.

"You will know him when you see him." I told her.

I didn't see Sasha for a while. But about a year and a half later, she came in to show me her ring. The man I had guided her to see, was now in her life and they had just gotten engaged.

She wanted to talk with Tony again. This time, to tell him that she had moved on. As I set up the space by imagining the circle of light and healing and tuned into the other side, Tony came right in. Then she shocked me with her question.

"Ask him if he would come in as my son. I have found a really good man for his father."

Tony said that he would consider it. He needed more time over on the other side. "I'll let you know when I am ready." he said. "I can't forgive myself, that has been the hardest part."

Sasha grew sad, "Tell him, I have forgiven him, his

mother has forgiven him, even his friend Rolo, who watched him pull the trigger, has forgiven him. What does he need to forgive himself?"

I could hear her frustration.

At that I stepped in. "Sasha, let me talk to him for a minute, you won't hear anything, but it will be just a minute." I turned to Tony.

"Tony, listen, you gave your life away because you loved Sasha, as well as trying to find a way out of the trouble you were in. Nothing is black and white. You made a hard choice because you couldn't see another way out. What you did was not all bad. It is time you realized that. You are a good man, and you are being given the opportunity to come in with Sasha as your mother, and a good man as your father to help you. But you have to let go of your pride, and you have to get humble to realize you need help. If anyone can help you, it is Sasha."

At that Tony's spirit got brighter. He seemed to get what I was saying. He was really taking it in.

"Just forgive yourself that you don't know it all. That is why you come to Mother Earth for the lessons. Maybe your death was to teach you humility. That is a huge lesson."

"Got it. Okay. Tell Sasha, yes."

After that session, Sasha was relieved and said. "Here I thought we would meet in another life as lovers. But things come around more quickly sometimes than any of us could imagine!"

"You will fall in love with your child, that I can guarantee. And if it is Tony, you will know it right away, the minute you conceive. But choose his name carefully. Give him a new name, one that gives him strength. One that will help him meet challenges and over come them. One that will give him humility and help him learn from others."

As Tony's spirit left, I could see him ascend into a golden light that seemed to absorb him. It was so beautiful, I knew he was getting ready to return and try again.

Ninja Healing - Takuma's Story

Takuma (not his real name), who was a regular client at East West, came in one day. He looked nervous and sat down across from me. After setting the space with an affirmation that I always say to help sent a clear intention I asked:
"What's going on Takuma?"
"I've just been diagnosed with prostate cancer." He said. "And I want you to help me heal it before it gets worse."
"Oh, I am so sorry, Takuma. Sure what is it you want me to do?"
"I need to get to what is underlying this disease for me. There are things I have not told you about my family line." Takuma rearranged himself. "Please take a look at this and see what you see."
As I tuned into his second chakra, his sexual chakra, I could see a red dot, which seemed to be the cancer, and under it, holding a large space in his 1st and 2nd chakras, was a dark energy that looked like a swirl of a cancer. Then I saw two eyes that reminded me of a Ninja warrior. Takuma was of Japanese descent on both sides of his family.
I tried to coach my words carefully. "I see a dancer dressed in black. I can only see his eyes, but he has a knife. He seems like an assassin. He sits underneath the cancer."
Takuma took a breath, "I knew it! Going back in my family line, all the men were trained as Ninja's, my grandfather, and my father, but after the war my parents moved to Hawaii, and I was born there. My father did not want to continue the practice and the empire had fallen into disrepair, so it was a good time to move on. I need to release it all, but I don't want to dishonor my ancestors. I am stuck, can you help?"
"Sure. Lets do some Heart Path[9] and see what we can do on a soul level."

---

[9] Heart Path is a process I developed with my guide, WuLan that helps people love themselves more, and resolve blocks from the past that hold us back. See *Heart Path, Learning to Love Yourself and Listening to Your Guides*, Blue Bone Books, Santa Cruz, CA 2007, or *Heart Path Handbook*, BBB, Santa Cruz, 2014.

After guiding Takuma into his heart and gathering his inner family inside his "heart garden" I asked him to bring this energy, that I saw in his 2nd chakra, to the outside of his heart garden gate.

"What do you see, Takuma?" I asked.

I see my Grandfather and Father and a line of ancestors stretching back. They are standing by waiting for me to carry on, all dressed in black."

"Can you give them something to honor your ancestors, and then tell them that Ninja period is over. In this time of the 21st Century, it is no longer necessary to be the Emperor's assassin." I suggested. "Give them a history lesson."

I watched as Takuma was in an internal conversation with his ancestors. After about five minutes, I could see them resigning to the fact that their time was done. His gift was a bridge to their understanding. I could see these very proud men, dressed in black kimonos, shuffle around like they had lost a game. Then I saw them huddle, and turn to him and burn a contract with Takuma.

"They are releasing me from the ancestral obligation!" He said.

I saw the energy lift, and he just had a small shadow left attached to his testicles. I reported to him what I saw. I also could see how exhausted he was.

"I think we need another session or two around this Takuma. But I don't think today is the day."

"I know." he said. "I have to talk to my son about this. I've never told him."

At the next session, Takuma and I released more negative energy around his pelvis, and I could see a curse lift from his family from a commitment made centuries ago for his entire line of sons going into the future. That was the dark energy remaining.

At the next session, Takuma reported that his cancer was gone, and that with my help, he had reversed his disease.

He gave me several gifts, which I wanted to refuse, but I could see it was important to him. One was a ring with two black dragons holding a black pearl in their mouths. It seemed an apt gift. I wrapped it up, and put it somewhere safe in my jewelry box.

Irma's Pain

One day a client brought her mother into see me. The mother, Irma (not her real name), had a headache that would not be cut by any drug on the shelf. Immediately I was concerned.

When I looked at her energy field, I could see a mass pressing on her brain causing the headache. After questioning her some more, and seeing that she was a very self-sacrificing woman, who put everyone before herself, I took her hands in my hands, and looked right into her eyes.

"Irma, I can see that you love your family very much, and that they love you too. You put everyone before yourself. But right now you HAVE to take care of yourself. I want you to promise me that you will go and see your doctor, or go to urgent care immediately. Will you promise me this?"

Irma tried to pull away, and make an excuse, when I wouldn't let go, she saw that I was very serious.

"Okay, I promise," she said.

"I don't make diagnoses, but I want to be sure you have many more days with your loved ones. If you don't go immediately, I am concerned that you would not have many more days left with them at all."

She got it. But for extra assurance, when her daughter came back to pick her up I told her to take her to the doctor today, and no excuses.

"Go to Urgent Care if you have to, don't wait for an appointment."

Two weeks later her daughter came back to thank me for impressing on her mother that she needed to go immediately. She had a scan and it showed a benign brain tumor pressing on her brain. They had admitted her immediately and she had surgery on Monday following our appointment.

"You saved my mother's life, thank you so much." Her daughter said.

"I am so glad I could help. I could see she had more time here with all of you, but only if she got this handled. The lesson is that she needs to take care of herself first, then everyone else. Otherwise she might not be here to love all of you in the flesh."

Carl's Request

Sometimes it is not fun being a medium. This comes up when I have to give a message to the living—from the dead—that are not asked for by the living. I have a strict rule in my private practice that I only serve those who ask for my help, otherwise the ego gets in there and I do not feel the ego has a place in spiritual healing or mediumistic work. Integrity is the most important quality for this work, the ego gets in the way.

As a medium, all sorts of spirits ask for help when you least expect it. Most of the time I can send them to the light, or connect them to their angels. It is not my job to help everyone. This I know from experience. Just because I can see spirits doesn't mean I have to help those who randomly float around.

However, I always know when a message is mine to communicate, so it isn't always my choice whether or not to help. It is a feeling I get, like I have a job to do and I am the one to deliver it and there is no one else for this particular duty, whether I get paid for my services or not.

But this night was my night off. I wanted to have time to listen to the author presenting his poetry book at Bookshop Santa Cruz. I have found that I need to turn it all off at least once a week for a couple of days, so I can rest and disconnect from the spirit world.

There I was, minding my own business, listening to a poetry reading, when suddenly the spirit of Carl was upside down, hanging from a trapeze to get my attention. Then, he kissed me on the mouth, to make sure I could not ignore him.

"Carl!" I said internally to him, "What are you doing!"

I knew Carl's younger brother, Jeremy, as we dated for two years in high school. Then we broke it off. Carl had asked me out on our first date once when I was in college several years later. We had a nice enough time going out to dinner, and then at the end of the night, he turned to me and kissed me and then became aggressive and started attacking me. He was groping and smashing me up against the passenger car window and I got scared. I ran out of the car and I never saw him alive again. I realized he was more attracted to me than I was with him. His kiss was the same now as it was then, even though he was in spirit! I didn't like at all his attack, but couldn't forget his kiss! Anyone watching me would have thought I was listening intently to the poet, but I was really carrying on a full conversation with Carl.

"Robin, I need your help!" Carl said urgently.

"Can't you see that I am in a poetry reading, trying to listen to the author." I said to him psychically.

"Sorry, I need your help." he said.

"What can I do?"

"I need to get out of here!"

"Where are you?"

"I can't stand it any more."

"Stand what?"

"I can't stand being in a place where I have to look at myself all the time. I can't get out." Carl said desperately.

"Oh, well, you have to forgive yourself, Carl."

"Oh no, I can't do that! You have to ask my mother for help."

"No way! You want me to ask your 89 year-old Mother to help you? Don't you think you have hurt her enough!" I found myself still being angry at him for killing himself.

"I know she can help," he said desperately.

"Carl, she is old and misses you terribly."

"You have to ask her for help!" Carl pleaded.

"It could kill her!"

"No it won't she would love to help me if she could."

"I will think about it. Now leave me alone so I can have my night out."

Carl disappeared into the night sky. At least I could hear the poet now. But I was still thinking about Carl and his request.

I knew he was right. The one person that could help him was his mother. His mother was a very dear friend of mine, and I did not want to call her about this. She and Carl were very close. I was also very close to her, as I visited whenever I went back to visit my father in my hometown.

I was resistant to his request partly because I felt he was one lucky guy who threw it all away. To me he had everything; he had a loving wife, he was handsome and very rich.

He lived in an upscale neighborhood in Chicago with anything he wanted and had a second house at a nearby lake resort. His father bought him a seat on the Chicago Stock Exchange so he had lots of money besides his inheritance. I was angry that he would throw it all away, and hurt people so much, just because he was bored and didn't want children. He had committed suicide instead.

Just when I dismissed the whole idea, a few days later, he popped in again.

"Please Robin, I need your help, I have to get out of here. Call my mother, pleeease!"

Begging was against his nature. Even though I was angry at his death-by-suicide, I always liked Carl a great deal, and admired his sense of adventure, even though he had attacked me on our date. I knew he was in trouble. He hardly ever asked anyone for anything when he was alive. It was against his sense of independent pride. I was surprised at his insistence and knew he really needed help, or he wouldn't have come to visit me twice. I had to forgive him for leaving so suddenly before I could really be of assistance.

It took me a while before I could get up the nerve to call his mother. Janelle was a wonderful Midwestern matriarch. She had taken me in when I dated Carl's brother in High School when I so desperately wanted to go to prep school. She was the one who gave me the Lovejoy's directory of prep schools.

Afterward, after high school, Jeremy and I broke up. Yet, I still visited her almost every time I returned to my hometown for 30 years! She and I talked about art, about the boys and their lives. She showed me art acquisitions she had acquired, and told me secrets of her boy's lives. She hired me to create a rite of passage for her grandson that was Jeremy's child when I moved back to Rockford after mom's illness. Then she patterned other grandchildren's rites of passage from the one I created for her first grand son for all her grandchildren.

One time, after I was married and so were her sons, she invited me to lunch at her lake house. After lunch she said, "Do you want to go see the boy's houses?"

"Sure," I said. "Aren't they away?"

"It's okay, we'll peek in the windows!" She was so much fun! I could see where Carl got his sense of adventure. She bought all my books with a sense of pride and was so glad to see me when I visited.

She often caught up hearing about my family, and loved hearing about my life and adventures. She was a fun, adventurous, mother figure to me. She was the one who had helped me get into prep school, and had supported me with encouragement when my own mother would not or could not do it.

So it was very difficult to call her, because I loved her and out of respect had never brought up Carl's suicide, unless she wanted to discuss it in our conversations. We had talked about it from time to time when it was right for her to speak about it. But here I was caught between an insistent Carl and a duty I knew I had to perform. I really did not want to jeopardize my friendship with her.

As I dialed the phone, I realized I had never talked to her about what I did for a living. She knew anyway, and was happy to discuss it from time to time because she 'kept an eye on me' as she would say. But we had never had an official conversation about it.

When I finally did make the call a week or more after Carl came in, I began by wishing her a happy holiday, as it was just before Christmas. She was very glad to hear from me. Then I said to her, "Janelle, you know what I do for a living, right?"

"Yes, you are a psychic and medium, isn't that correct?" she said.

"Yes, dear, it is. Sometimes I get visits from people unbidden. The other day Carl came in. I am so sorry to tell you this, I know it must be difficult."

I took a deep breath, as I was hearing her sobs on the other end of the phone.

"He, he is asking for your prayers. He needs to get out of the place he has been in since his death."

She paused from crying then said. "Do you mean to tell me that he has been in hell for five years?!"

"Well, it depends on your world view. Do you know the movie with Annabella Sciorra and Robin Williams, "What Dreams May Come?" It is kind of like that. He tries to rescue his wife after her suicide because she had locked herself in with guilt and shame. I would call it a kind of purgatory, but basically, she has to reflect on the gift of life that she threw away and forgive herself. The love was the important thing."

"But I always felt it was his choice to do what he felt he needed to do." She cried.

"Yes, and no. He was given a great gift of life, and he ended it for no reason really, just that he did not want to continue, and he and his wife wanted different things?"

"Yes, that is what I understood." Janelle said sadly.

"In any case, he needs your prayers now. He has been pestering me for weeks, and I just had to call you. I am so sorry to bother you with this, but I do believe it is urgent."

"Well, of course I will pray for him."

I told her I would pray also, and we said our goodbyes and I promised to call her with any 'news.'

As I hung up the phone, I sat down and prayed for Carl immediately, and could see her stream of light and my stream of light open a lock to a place he was in and he flew free almost immediately. Within minutes, he flew towards me, and shouted, "It worked, thank you so much!"

It took me a week to get the nerve up to tell her he was fine.

"Merry Christmas, my dear." I said cheerily. "It worked! Your prayers released him. He is fine now."

"Merry Christmas, and thank you, Robin. I am so grateful you called me, God bless you."

Janelle was crying again, but this time tears of joy mixed with grief. I was glad I had done what Carl asked me to do.

Seven months later, I got the news that Janelle died of a heart attach. She was 89. I happened to be going back to Illinois for Fourth of July, and her funeral was just before our family reunion. It was an opportunity to see Jeremy again, and his other family members. It did not seem appropriate to tell Jeremy about his brother's visit.

I felt Janelle was meant to live that long so she could help her son. I felt a great release when she died, as though it was the end of what we needed to do together for our karma. It was part of the reason I felt compelled to maintain the connection with her, besides the fact that she was so supportive and wonderful to me all those years, and we cared for each other as a mother and daughter. She was a wonderful, loving surrogate mother. I will always honor her memory and her spirit if she ever wants to come visit. Carl can visit too if he has to, but no kissing! I know he has moved on.

Flight # 237

Sometimes I find myself in the right place at the right time. Such a meeting took place when I met a woman I will name Dolores. On a flight from Dallas to Chicago I sat next to a woman who at first ignored me. She was Latina, and I am white.

"Okay," I thought, "She thinks she can't relate to me." Then we ordered drinks, I got my virgin snappy Tom, and she ordered a beer and a glass of wine.

My notebook cover kept falling on her tray.

"Oh, I am sorry, I can't bend it back, it is a hard bound."

"That's okay, I don't care, you can leave it open, I've got

plenty of room."

Embarrassed at her drink order, she said, "You must think I'm an alcoholic. I have had a rough day. I just left my ninty-one year-old father back in Roswell, and my daughter and granddaughter, who both cried when I left. She never does that. She kept saying, "Mama, come back. Come back. Please come back."

Dolores' hand was visibly shaking. Her scarf was black with pink skulls on it. Her hat was a fancy baseball style with a rhinestone skull off to one side.

It's okay, I understand. I am just on my way to visit my ninty-eight year old Dad. Every time I leave I think it is the last time I will see him."

"I know what you mean!" she says tapping my arm with her hand.

'Now we are connected,' I thought.

Over the next hour she poured her heart out about all the losses she'd had.

"You go to the Roswell Cemetery and there are my families' graves lined up. They had to put my brother across the road, because my whole family is there and takes up the whole cemetery.

"I don't know what is wrong with me, but I can't go through any more deaths. My Dad was sleeping in his chair, and I am poking him." She pokes me like she poked her Dad to see if he was awake. She narrates the scene.

"Dad."

"What's wrong!" He says,

"Then he wakes up." She is poking me over and over.

"Don't do that!" He shouts at her.

"Oh Dad, I was so worried that you were dead!"

"My Mother dropped over, just like that. So suddenly, I can't take anymore. "

I could see the tears in her eyes. I put my hand on hers.

"Your okay, you have PTSD from all the losses," I said to her softly. "I know how it is, I lost my mother and daughter within a year and a half of each other. It was so sudden for my daughter. She was an infant. One moment she is kicking then next, ella esta muerta." I said to her in my broken Spanish.

"I know, I know, my brother's family, the whole group of them were killed in a car accident, nieces and nephews, and my sister-in-law and her sister, it was awful!"

I was in awe at how this woman wasn't consuming more alcoholic drinks. I said to her, "How do you bear it? Do you have a grief group to go to?" I asked.

" I have a psychiatrist and a counselor. They help some," she said looking down into her plastic wine glass.

"That is not all, my nineteen year old nephew died of cancer and he was in so much pain. You know, he was so scared. And my mother said, 'I'll be there for you.' Six months later my mother dies and six months after that to the day, (she polks my arm again) he dies. I knew she was there on the other side as I was with my nephew on this side. Just like that." She snaps her fingers.

We had already landed, and were stuck on the tarmac. As we talked about all the losses she had I could feel her soften. I missed my bus to Rockford, but I would get the next one. She needed this.

She talked about her mother's death some more. I felt as though there was a hand holding the plane where it was. Finally she looked at me again.

"What do you do?" she asked.

"I am a professional medium," I told her. "I do readings and healing work. "

"Get Out! Give me some of that healing, I think I really need your help!" she said frantically pawing my arm.

"Please give me your card. I feel so much better. You really are a healer!" As I handed her the card, the plane lurched forward and we were on our way to the gate.

"Wow, now this was meant to be!" She said poking my arm again. "Did you see that, the plane is finally moving again!" Now she was smiling through her tears.

"I might be able to help you understand more about death. I have learned a lot over the years. I would be happy to share it with you." I said to her quietly. "You could talk to your mom if you want to."

I knew she wouldn't call me, but at least she had my card, just in case. And I was also happy that I could be of service to her without any payment. She had gone through so much. I had gotten so much help in the transitions I had gone through, it was really wonderful to pay it forward to a woman who really needed it.

"I just know this hour long wait at the tarmac was meant to be. I am so glad I met you, I know this was perfect, meant to be!" Dolores said poking my arm again.

"Yes, me too—you," I said.

We both took each others hands as the other passengers began to move about, as the plane had finally reached the gate.

"Thanks for traveling with us. Sorry for the delay." The pilot said over the speaker.

She got off first then I followed several passengers behind her.

I was struggling with my suitcase, my purse and computer case. I saw her out at the end of the ramp to the airport waiting for me. When I reached her we hugged.

"I'll call you," she said.

"Okay, I would be happy to help anytime." I said.

'Thank you, thank you, thank you!' I said to my self and my guides, as I checked the time. I'll have to wait for the next bus. But it was okay, This meeting was DEFINITELY meant to be.

Chapter Eleven
The Awakening

During this time, in the early 2000's, I was running my lodge in the Santa Cruz Mountains, and meditating every morning as I had for over thirty years. I was working part time and starting my practice. Alfonzo was working for the county as a counselor, and we had just launched his two sons to be on their own. After I began to teach classes for several years, and wrote my third book; *Heart Path, Learning to Love Yourself and Listening to Your Guides*, I went through an experience that I will attempt to describe, I call it now, my awakening experience.

Somewhere between the Umbanda Initiations and writing my book, I had the realization that God or All-That-Is, is both positive and negative in the world. All that occurred, whether we understood it or not, was part of God's plan. We have free will, to choose whether we would be guided in it or not.

I had reconnected with Brenda Morgan when Alfonzo and I had first gotten together, as she was scouting places to live around the country. She had met Alfonzo when I was living with Roseline and held a workshop with several people. Roseline and I had gathered the people for Brenda. I had shown her our new house in Boulder Creek, and invited her to return when it worked for her.

Now several years later, we had moved to Santa Cruz, and I invited her to come again to my Center for the Soul, to speak to my students about enlightenment, and Self-Realization. She did not come herself but sent one of her students Tom. Tom was amazing and had been a student of hers for several years, and had learned a great deal from Brenda. One thing I remember him saying to me was, "You don't have to die to know God. The All is here now."

I am sure that his stay with us, and the work he did with us in workshops and classes, was somewhat the catalyst for me breaking through my death-wish, or my desire to live in the spirit world. After he left, about two weeks later, I was home alone as usual, trying to write and taking calls scheduling clients. Alfonzo was at work.

I was suddenly so restless I did not know what to do with myself. However, in my mind, I was sure I was about to die. I was panicked, and felt crazed. I tried to call Alfonzo, and could not reach him. Somehow I knew he was not the right one to talk to about this anyway.

This had never happened to me before. Panic was not familiar to me, as I was a pretty calm person generally speaking. Even with Mariluna, when I felt broken, and distraught, I knew I was sane. This anxiety was fierce, and I had no reason for it. It just came upon me like a red irritating cloud.

I wept with confusion. I could not concentrate on writing or anything else I normally did during the day while Alfonzo was at work.

Suddenly the phone rang and it was Brenda, assuring me that I was fine, and to keep breathing. I thanked her for calling me, and we talked for a while but not long. As soon as I hung up, I felt a bit better, then the anxiety returned and I was crying again, my mind was sure it was dying, panic and extreme stress about nothing was all around me.

The phone rang again out of the blue, and it was Tina. I had no idea how she nor Brenda had gotten my number, but she called from somewhere in the states. I was so relieved!

"You are fine, there is nothing between us that needs forgiving, I love you, you are fine." she said.

When I hung up the phone through my tears, I was somewhat relieved. Then I felt the great need to just sit down and try to meditate. It was as though a hand pushed me down. Sit now! Perhaps that was Da, I did not know.

As soon as I did, I felt my mind drop out. It was as if it

just went away. I was floating in a star-studded reality—everything was the Universe. The sun was setting, and I knew that, but inside my mind was emptiness. It was wonderful. No-thingness was delicious. I felt the happiness that Michael Silverman had promised so many years before. I felt blissful. The bliss has not stopped ever since.

    I did not relate much to ordinary daily life after that. I was more interested in Being than doing. I had to understand how it works now in a body, being in the flow rather than checking off tasks. Instead of making my 'do list' every day, I 'felt into' what needed to be done and followed the flow of energy through my body. It was like following a scent, and I was in a graceful state. Sometimes I got more done that way, than being a good Capricorn and checking things off my perpetually long "to do" list. I still wrote out a list and followed what felt right.

    After my Awakening, my interests became centered in divine communion. Love was raining love all around me all the time. Sometimes it brought me to my knees, and I just sat and wondered in the love that perpetually bathes us. This raining of love has not stopped ever since. I just have to tune in towards the flow, and return to this love stream moment to moment. Sometimes I still get angry, or sad, or scared, but the over ridding experience is joy. Just Joy for Life. No more death wish! Blue Girl has integrated within this being of Robin just after this experience as my Divine Essence or Star Essence that descended after my awakening. She was happiness and glad to be fully expressed.

    I realize now that the Blue Girl within me was sad before primarily because she was not acknowledged by me to be divine and was certainly not fully expressed in any way. She was shunned by my own lack of understanding internally for being blue, which I related to depression. The truth today is I am living my Divine 'Blue' Print—Krishna Blue Print— lover of hearts! Medicine Buddah Blue, and my job now is to help others awaken to their reality of being love. We are each unique and magnificent, truly!

We threw a party that summer and hired a band that we loved, Dandaro, the same one that we had heard when Mariluna was alive and kicking inside me. We moved from that wonderful house that we loved, (because the owner sold it) to another house that was not so wonderful a few blocks away. This was two years before the 2008 crash and two years before the crash and burn of our marriage.

Transition - 2nd Saturn Return

After moving to our new house, and after launching our boys, Alfonzo and I enjoyed life together until we didn't. Our needs diverged as his retirement approached. We were fourteen years apart in our age difference. He wanted to retire at 70, and I was just getting started at 56. I had been an official medium and intuitive for about eight years at this point. I had worked hard to get my practice started and it was working.

Alfonzo was preparing to retire and wanted to go back to Puerto Rico where he was from. The boys were on their own and getting married to wonderful spouses. Between the new house that we both disliked, to our diverging directions, our age difference and differing desires for our lives, and the fact that two of my family members were critically ill, making it impossible for me to go so far away, we decided to separate and divorce before he moved back to Puerto Rico into a house we had bought together.

The confusing part for both of us was that we still loved each other and lived easily together. We liked our life, but it was wearing thin too. Our needs had changed. No matter the love, it wasn't enough to keep us together.

I set up a book tour with Heart Path, my 3rd book just before the crash of 2008. Suddenly, no one was buying anything, and the crash had begun in the middle of my tour!

As the economy collapsed that September, so did our marriage. We divorced, and Alfonzo moved to Puerto Rico, and I moved into a friend's house in Santa Cruz. My income was decimated, two jobs had ended, and I was not attracting students and only a few clients because I was a mess. It would have been too hard to start over with no support from Alfonzo in a country that primarily speaks Spanish. It became clear he wanted to start over without me. This was due in part to the fact that he was bi-sexual, which I knew, and he wanted a male partner, which I did not discover until later. So I held onto what little I had, and stayed in California. Somehow, with all the confusion in my life, I was still happy and sure that I would be fine. I was just going through my second Saturn return. That astrology period happens every twenty-eight years. Ugh!

Kisti's Crossing

Six months after my mother passed away in 1996, my sister Kisti was diagnosed with breast cancer. It had already gone to her lymph nodes, and that meant that it was in her system-or stage three. She did the usual western treatment of a mastectomy followed by chemotherapy and radiation. I decided, since I was already back in California when she got diagnosed, that I would set up book tours, lectures and talks so I could visit her regularly in Brownsville, Texas, which made traveling down there financially possible. She helped a lot by setting up programs with her Unity Church, as she was on the board. I presented and held workshops, and offered sermons and sessions during a long weekend, while during the week I was free to enjoy time with her.

I was closer to Kisti than most of my other sisters. We shared many things, we were both artists, and we attended the same Unity church in Michigan where we lived close to each other for many years before moving to different parts of the country.

In 2009, one year after Alfonzo left, and eleven years after Kisti's diagnosis, when her cancer was back and she was getting closer to her demise, I found myself flying back and forth to Brownsville, Texas, where she lived with her husband Sid, to visit her—seminar or no seminar. I had flown down as it turned out, three weeks before her death to have quality time with her after they took her off the chemo.

    She was so thin and pale, and jaundice from her liver disintegrating from the drugs. She had enough energy to go to lunch and then visit a gallery, but she had to lay down on the gallery bench while I went looking around at the art work. When we got back to her house she had to lay down and sleep.

    After dinner, which she made with help from Sid, she and I did what we had done since I was small. We sat together holding hands, her on the couch, me on the floor beside her and I played with her rings.

Kisti's Hands #2
Remembering her
long thin fingers, nails

cut straight across; she wore two rings
one turquoise with small dots of silver around the stone

the other three gold rings worn as one
for each child on her wedding hand.

She often drew pictures in the air,
then erased it as she struggled to speak,

how the red poppies in the blue vase
shook the stillness.

In her last days Kisti and I sat
as we always had, me playing
with those rings

comparing spots to spots
her fingers expressing what
she could not say.

As I told her I didn't know

how to be here, on the Earth,
        without her,
we wept together.

For an hour or more
she lay on the couch,
me on the floor holding her hand in my two,
her fingers traced tears around my eyes.

Then Grandma and Mom popped in,
        They're here with us Kisti
Grandma says in her Southern Drawl:
        "Now, what   do   we   have   here?"
They'll be there for you.

I will always remember
        playing with her rings
        as she wiped my tears,
as her relief
        filled the room.

    Just as we finished talking about her illness and how I would miss her, Mom and Grandma Lysne (Mom's mom) showed up for us from the other side.

    "Mom and Grandma are here Kisti." I said softly.

    She began to cry. "Thank you, you have no idea the gift you just gave me."

    "They said that they will be here with you every step of the way. Grandma says in her Southern Drawl, "Now what do we have here?" A phrase she often said when one of us was hurting or sad.

    We both laughed then cried. They had some more messages for her. Then it was time for her to go to bed, and me to try to get some sleep before I had to turn around again and go home to California.

    Three weeks later, I got the call, and found myself on a series of airplanes to get to Brownsville before she died. My other sisters were there already except for my sister Sara who was coming in from Singapore. Dad was too fragile at this point to make it down. He was in his 90's and living independently, but airports were too much for him any more.

When I finally got there after missing a flight and getting delayed, I arrived about 10:30 p.m., Kisti was barely alive lying in a hospital bed in their bedroom. Her kids and grandkids were there, as well as two of the three other sisters. As I went in to see her, she recognized me, I kissed her and held her hand and whispered, "I'm here!" Almost immediately she began cheyne-stoking her breath. Her feet were going cold already.

The rest of the family had been there for days and were punchy and tired. I called them in because I felt they might want to be present when she passed. All of them gathered, sitting on the bed, next to Sid.

I could hear Kisti's spirit cry out saying, "Look at this body! What do I do with it?"

"Go to the light Kisti," I said out loud, "It is okay, you will be fine. Let go."

At that she turned her bodily face to me one last time and we locked eyes. Her spirit elegantly and slowly left her body and went into a bounty of spirits, angels and guides, all full of gold light dancing on the other side. As she left the spirits began to applaud her and danced with her as she crossed over. It took some time. Her spirit moved rather slowly witnessing every one she was leaving behind. She danced over through a "hole" between worlds that her transition opened up.

"They are dancing over there!" I said through my tears to the rest of the family. "They are celebrating her arrival!"

I watched her dance for the longest time. After hugs from my nieces, and sisters, everyone left the room and I was alone with her body with another sister, Kisti's daughter Lysne and niece Laura. She died at 11:05 p.m. about thirty-five minutes after I arrived. I was glad she waited for me.

A few days later friends sent emails and texts of condolences. One of the messages from friend Sherrie in Rockford, said that a mutual psychic friend in New York could still see them dancing two days later! I was astounded, and it confirmed what I had seen at the time of her death.

Kisti's death was the hardest next to Mariluna's and my mother's. Kisti had been my emotional Mom when our mother could not be there for us. She comforted me when I was sad, as I did for her, and we helped each other through a great deal in our lives when we were younger, and through the eleven years we lived close to each other in Michigan. It did not matter that we were eight years apart, she never treated me as a younger sister or 'less than' in any way.

It was doubly hard because I had been divorced from Alfonzo the year before and was feeling doubly alone. South Padre Island, where we spent a lot of time when I visited Brownsville, was the closest point to Puerto Rico. When I looked out of the Eastern shore of South Padre Island, I was looking towards Puerto Rico.

Since her death, she visits me regularly and is probably more available than she had been in life, due to her illness and her involvement with her own children and husband. We were so close, and now I get to have her visit me when it suits her, or when I have a question. I miss playing with her rings, but she is ever present in spirit. I read the following poem at her funeral.

Kisti
Fine lines defined you
a twirl of your charcoal or the
touch of blue shadow on the apricot.
"The two-ness" you would say,

how you placed things in harmony
and discord to express the
cage of your body you felt you were in.
The nakedness of form, the expression

held in clay of the shaman who was holding
a vision, how he knew something
deep and vulnerable when the

ravens spoke in your sculpture.
How your water maiden came out of the
ocean. Was that you?

And beach glass broke the surface
that you scattered around her.
And those drawings of your children as they
slept, with a few strokes of your pen,
how you could swear they were breathing?

How every since I was born I was in awe of you
as my older sister, who never treated me as younger,
the art we shared, your support for where my heart
guided me. You were always there,
cheering me on. I was always there to hold you too.

This day, gratitude spills over for the deep trees
you sketched with me. How you knew what
I was saying in my drawings, in the words I wrote, and knew
what I wanted to say, then edited for me.

The way you called me baby cakes when you loved me
and deary when you got mad. How you
took so long to say things, then made your point,
how it could be for you but wasn't

when you knew for yourself
that the sedge grasses lay down when the
long summer days were dissipating into autumn,
as the weather turned again to frost.

When you finished the drawing you last made,
how the colors were not right,
and you had been working on it all afternoon
then one more day, one more hour of almost finished,

When you went into your own heart, sat with your body

by the fountain. Realizing you could not do this chemo any more,

How you could simply say this is enough.
You said you needed to eat fruits and vegetables now.
Clean yourself out. Yes, I say to you,
build your immune system,
I say to myself, love yourself home.

Starting Over-Back to School

After Alfonzo left, I had moved into a temporary home in Santa Cruz with my Chiropractor and another roommate. Then in December of 2008, not knowing where to go next, I was on my way to a meditation group that I was running and driving with a friend. Another friend, Dana, had offered me to come stay with her and her family who lived on the other side of the Bay Area in Alamo. As I asked that question in the car, "Do you think I should move to Alamo?" it was as though the voice of God came through my friend I was riding with, "Go to Alamo!" She was quite insistent, and I was glad she was so clear.

So, on January 1st, a few weeks later, I moved to Alamo, an hour or more from Santa Cruz. It was good to get away from the place where Alfonzo and I had lived for thirteen years together as there were too many good memories that I had to wade through now as a single woman. I had to start over, and I had to do this alone, though I loved being married and missed being paired.

I returned to Santa Cruz for clients every week, using another friend's apartment in the back of their house as an office, and spent most of my time writing, and offering phone sessions from Alamo.

While there, I also communed with Mt. Diablo, a misnamed mountain that rose high and dominates the towns of Danville, Alamo, Walnut Creek, and Concord. It is a huge sacred mountain near Danville just behind the house of my friend. The Mountain taught me a great deal. The main lesson was, "Stand as your own Mountain." I am doing that now, and have been since that time.

As I was recovering from Alfonzo's departure, I spent a lot of time sleeping and waking up late. I would lay in bed, praying, asking what I should do next. Thoughts came in, then questions.

"What do you want to do?" I heard from my guides. I decided to make a list of what I wanted to do. I asked myself, what is it that I needed to do before I die? I needed a bucket list. I was in a very different state of consciousness, Kisti's early death at 64, focused my attention on what was left to do with my remaining years. So once again, I asked, "Show me what you want me to do." I surrendered and followed the flow.

Slowly I began to realize that there were many things I had set aside to be married to Alfonzo. While I helped be there for his kids and share a life with him, there wasn't much room for Robin's deepest desires. While I had always done the work I was guided to do, and recovered from Mariluna's death within the marriage, there was no way I was going to be able to go back to school when both his boys were beginning college. As Alfonzo was ready to retire shortly after his kids were graduated from their respective colleges, he would not have been willing to take on more debt, nor another school tuition.

Over and over, it kept coming up in meditations for me go back to school get my M.F.A. in writing or art. It had been a dream of mine for years, ever since I had gotten my B.F.A. when I attended undergraduate school in art. Now that I was free, I chose to go back to school.

After applying to several places, one school chose me, and I finally completed Graduate school for a second time, earning an M.F.A. in poetry from Mills College. I also decided I would complete my Ph.D. in Energy Medicine, which I had started several years before. I completed my doctorate in the summer between my Master's program years, defending my thesis the summer after graduation. I graduated from Mills College and from The University of Natural Medicine in Santa Fe, NM. This on-line university along with attending Mills, helped me fulfilled my need for more education. It also brought

Energy Healing into sharper focus, along with being a medium. The doctorate also gave me more clout to offer energy healings and clearings.

After school was finished, I return to Santa Cruz to live as well as work. I had begun offering healing work through East West Bookshop in Mt. View several years before. Inner Journey had closed, and my private practice that I had set up years before, was still going in Energy Healing, counseling, and mediumistic work as I had maintained my practice throughout school.

Working six days a week, I did homework on the seventh day, I was exhausted from the hard work, and needed to recuperate. I also needed a new place to live. So I moved back to the Santa Cruz area off Summit Road, where I could access both sides of the mountain, and it gave me a quiet country place to rest, and it was also closer to Bay Area poetry readings. As I rested, I once again surrendered to what was in front of me. After turning my thesis and dissertation into books, I set out to find a way to teach others what I knew about healing and kept writing and making art.

Now I was an intuitive healer as well as a professional medium and I consider myself a practitioner of nature-based spirituality too. Writing had been an on-going process. My publishing house was launched before my divorce and the market crash. In 2007, I started Blue Bone Books to self-publish my books and also publish other people's poetry and spiritual books.

Channeling

A medium can offer services to people in a variety of ways. One of the ways, I have been guided by my angels and spirit guides, is to bring them into my body so they can speak directly to others through me.

Whether I am presenting in a group to offer channeling, as in my monthly meditations, or when I am by myself and I am ready to write, I feel a spirit next to me. I always ask them to identify themselves, unless I know their spirit intimately, like WuLan or Star Woman. My intention is always for the highest and wisest good of all beings. Then, surrendering, my crown chakra opens, and that entity enters my body and begins to talk. If I am writing, they enter my hands, and start to write words I would never think of. Sometimes they reflect to me what has been confusing to me and they clarify the order of events or what they are suggesting next as part of my work.

This is one thing that a medium does, embodies spirits for others to talk to. It is my choice who or if I wish to embody other entities. My choice is always to embody a spirit of light for the highest and wisest good of all, including me. In the Umbanda tradition they call that spirit their Caboclo. This embodiment often happens in other mediumistic traditions as well.

Early on in the nudge towards channeling from my guides, I made a clear statement to them. Help me evolve and I will channel.

So I did. And I have. That is why I only channel the wisest beings: Archangels, Star Woman (Divine Mother), Wulan (A Tibetian teacher and my main guide) and the Ascended Masters.

After I left Umbanda, in 2001, and shortly after creating 'The Center for the Soul' I began to embark on a work that the guides asked me to create called Star Gate. Star Gate was originally a group of souls that came together to create a vortex into the Earth to bring more light to the planet. We created "Pods," small groups of people that then brought in light to the Earth, like a funnel. After the initial meeting, where about 25 souls came together for an initiation into Star Gate, we were to meet once a month in our "pods" or groups, for a year at various people's houses. I met with each of the four pods once a month, and I would channel my guides who gave us specific directions in our meditation together. The guides gave us instructions, and teachings. We formed four different pods together and brought in light for the Mother Earth once a week for a year. At the end of the year, several of the groups dissolved, or condensed, and I continued doing Star Gate as an initiation for the general public once a month for four years. The single group continued for several years and others were brought into it as I initiated more people each year, one by one. Eventually the group became my Wednesday night Mother Earth Meditation Group, which still exists to this day. We were told that Mother Earth was suffering under the weight of humanities dense consciousness. She was shifting and needed assistance. We were ready to help.

Today after years of gathering since 2003 when the first initiation occurred, we continue to meet until 2012 when the guides gave us clear instructions not to give Mother Earth light, but to receive the light instead.

In our 15th year, January 18th, 2018, Star Woman and Wulan gave each person from the original Star Gate (four women who come every month) the gift of knowing themselves as Star Woman. She stood before them and gave them each a great blessing, that is: feeling their Divine Core.

I have channeled many times for public events prior to this. But this night was the most profound. The irony is that I did not channel Star Woman or Wulan as I usually do, instead, because a part of my soul was in the process of integration, or had just arose into my consciousness, the guides wanted me to integrate the blessed energy that came in. So they stood by my side, and explained what they were going to do, as I would not channel tonight. I gave the group the information without channeling through my telepathy.

Star Woman said, "I will come to each one of you." And she did. She stood before each one of the group, and they received the light of her shoal of stars.

It was an amazing experience and each one of them could feel her profound blessing. None of us could talk after. We felt profound peace, unconditional love streaming down everywhere. When we opened the circle and ended the evening, we sat for a long time. Star Woman said to me, "This is what we (the Divine beings of light) have been doing here all these years, to get them to this point." I shared with them what she said to me. There was not a dry eye in the house, including mine.

Chapter Twelve
What I learned from House Clearings

Settling in again to Santa Cruz County after graduate school, I began putting more work into building my practice - seeing clients for all sorts of things, including psychic readings, Akashic record readings, energy clearings, healings and house clearings.

Years before I had started doing house clearings. That is, I would clear ghosts, negative energy and other entities out of houses for their owners.

One day I got a call from the sister of a client. She needed a house clearing and wondered if I would travel north to Marin County. She had a difficult marriage that had gotten worse since they moved into this new house. She reported to me that she and her husband were fighting constantly, more so than usual and she wanted to make sure that the house was not making it worse. She felt odd things and spirits there at certain times of the day and felt that there was a Native American spirit who was angry at them for living in the house at all. Obviously, she was quite intuitive herself.

When I drove up to Marin from Santa Cruz County, and into their driveway, after driving up a steep roadway and around several curves in a remote part of San Rafael, the woman who I will call Sheryl, greeted me on the deck of their beautifully designed home. It had a long drive and then a stairway to the main part of the house where there was a large triangular deck. The house was based on triangles and was designed by the former owner who was an architect. Sheryl and her husband were the second owners.

Sheryl showed me around, and immediately I felt all

kinds of negative conflict in the house. It was thick with turmoil, as though a bad fight had happened just before I came into the house. However this conflict was all over the place, and worse in some areas than others. I went outside to see what was going on outside, and to get some fresh air. I offered up some tobacco for the spirits of the land to help me with this one. That is when I saw him. A very distinguished Native American male spirit in full war paint. He did not want this house on his sacred grounds and was definitely on the warpath to get this couple out of the house. A lot of the anger was his.

I introduced myself, in my Native American name that I had received as part of the Ogitchidaah Ceremonies, White Turtle Woman, and asked him if he was willing to share the Chanumpa (sacred pipe or Baggin in Annishnabe) with me. He knew I was honoring him as well as offering a peaceful solution.[10] He agreed.

We shared the pipe together as if we were in each other's physical presence. I was actually smoking the pipe, and then I handed it to him. He took it to his mouth as if he were in a body, and thanked me for this opportunity to touch a sacred pipe again. He was quite moved by this gesture.

When the pipe was smoked with prayers for healing the land, and for us to find a way to make peace, I asked if he would speak to me about the land, and he agreed.

He was a guardian spirit for the burial grounds up on the ridge, and this was considered part of that whole area of the sacred lands where the house had been constructed. People had come here to pray and bury their dead for centuries. It was not to be built upon. The house was set on the trail to the burial site. It was blocking the path to the ridge where the actual burial grounds were located.

I asked him if the house was actually on the burial site. He said no. I asked him if he could understand that the present-day people had no idea that it was a burial site, and if they had

---

10 Since the Lakota path in 1988, I have been a pipe carrier or Chanumpa carrier. The pipe is a commitment to pray for others and a lifetime commitment to carry the pipe for those who ask.

known perhaps they would have chosen another location. At this point, it was not possible to take the house down now that it had been here for twenty years or so. He agreed.

I suggested that his people were no longer here to mourn their dead, and wondered if we could consecrate another route to the grounds for the spirits. There was plenty of land that was untouched by any construction and too steep to access anyway. He agreed, that it was possible to consecrate a new route.

So I asked where he would like that trail to be? We designated it with our intention and by a tobacco offering line around the property where I knew that no one in a body, except the deer, would be able to go up that trail anyway.

I made a line with the tobacco all the way around the house. I asked if he could honor that tobacco boundary to designate their home as a place for them only. He agreed. Then I asked if he was at peace with our new agreement. He said yes, and said that he would be willing to leave the house to the present day owners. He appreciated my approach to him, and I offered a prayer of protection for his sacred grounds. He left as I saw his spirit rise and stand on top of the hill where his people had been buried. I put my Chanumpa away, and began to look at what else was needed by the house and it's owners.

Then I started on clearing the house. I found that between my intention and the thick "skin" of conflict that layered the walls, I needed to use all my medicine.[11] Owl medicine is very powerful, and it ends things decisively. Owls see in the dark through conflict to the original Self, so I felt the Owl feathers were important to really clear everything from the past. It took two passes with a smoking sage wand and an owl feather fan to clear the house! There were two layers, the one of their marital conflict, and the other angst of the designer and first owner of the property.

I sat on the deck with Sheryl and told her about the Native American Spirit and told her of our new agreement with him. She was glad to know he wouldn't be coming back through

---

[11] Medicine in this context represents all the powers of inner world, including animal natures, such as owls, bears, wolves, or mountain lions, as well as intuition that contacts spirits, and sage.

the house and that I had made peace on their behalf with the guardian spirit.

I then talked to her about her marital conflicts and how they were drawing negativity to the house with their fighting. I also shared that there was a lot of negativity from the former owner. He was very angry at losing the house, and having to sell his "baby." He had completed his dream to live in a house he designed himself. Then he lost everything and had to sell it.

I learned several important things from that first house clearing. First, that it was important to clear property back to it's origins with the First Nations People. First Native Americans who lived on the land for centuries before white intrusion were still on the land in spirit in many cases. It was really important to make sure the land and property was not a burial site, or that it wasn't ceremonial grounds, or something else important to the people that had lived there before. It was also important to honor their lives and existence. This honoring created peace in the land and on the property.

Secondly, I learned that conflict attracts more conflict, and that if you are going to clear a home it should be all former owners and occupants, that means clearing back to it's foundations. You wouldn't construct a house with old nails sticking out from previous sheet rock or boards that had been attached to the studs of a house, so why go part way?

I also feel that clearing a house requires my physical presence. I feel it is more effective that way. I have cleared houses remotely, just as I do readings remotely. But when someone is there physically, it is deeper, like cleaning anything with an actual scrub brush as opposed to a cursory rinse. If you actually are there in a body, it makes all the difference.

The other important thing I learned was that architecture impacts the house. I use Feng Shui, or energetic redesign. This house had multiple angles and exposed beams that tend to sever a house or fracture the energy of it. I was able to suggest "remedies" such as crystals, and Feng Shui mirrors to help them. I have studied the Chinese art of Feng Shui for my own benefit. This house had beams everywhere in strange groupings. One joint had seven beams that were randomly attached together. It was an obvious design flaw. Because this house was designed and built by an architect in the beginning of his career, he did not have as much experience as he needed. The house had strange junctures that would likely not be in a house he designed for someone else.

When I was done with the house, the obvious anger was gone. I talked to the owner about ways to resolve their conflicts. She agreed that counseling would help her and her husband. I shared that clearing the house was a start, not the completion for the two of them.

A San Francisco Apartment Building Nightmare

Most of the time I really enjoy making a difference with house clearings for clients. There is such a dramatic difference from when I arrive to when I leave, that even the most skeptical people can feel the difference.

One of the worst buildings I cleared was an old apartment building in San Francisco that was full of ghosts. I was really there for just one apartment, but because the whole building was afflicted, I had to do the whole building. The owner of the apartment was willing to pay me whatever it took to shift the energy in the building, which seemed dense, dark and full of unwanted spirits.

Unknown to me, she had sent out an email to all the other apartment owners telling them that she had hired someone to clear out the ghosts that everyone knew were haunting the building. That was probably a mistake, as one of the residents was clearly into some dark tradition, and defended their apartment with a horribly negative energy and symbols of skulls, and dark drapery on their door! So I avoided their apartment and worked around it. Obviously, I did not clear other apartments, only this owner's and the hallways up to the doors of the other residence.

I started with the owner who hired me, which took about ten minutes as it was a very small place. Her father had owned the apartment and had just died. So before she moved in, she wanted it cleared. He was still there in spirit, but he was very compliant and moved across to the other side and to the light fairly quickly. His spirit was just relieved to know where to go into the spirit world!

Then I went to the roof, to get a bird's eye view (literally) of the whole property. Since it was built on a busy street, there really wasn't a place outside where I could go to "view" the apartment building. Besides, there was a lot going on outside between traffic, pedestrians, and shop owners.

The roof perspective sounded like a good idea and the best option, especially because the spirits seemed to be traveling up and down the elevator shaft, and the stair well. Really, it was like they were using these holes in the building like a freeway!

When I got to the roof, I could see the problem more clearly. Besides the elevator and the stairwell ending there, there was also an internal light well that brought light to the interior rooms. This huge window well started on the first floor and ended on the roof. There were four stories. The spirits traveled through all three corridors in the building, the light well, the elevator and the stairwell!

I put on my Umbanda regalia of beads and a white dress for protection that I made for the occasion, and began to talk with the spirits. I told them they needed to go and it was not their home anymore. Some of them had been former tenants and some were ghost from other areas in the neighborhood. With my intention and the help of my guides, we opened a "window" to the light as though creating a hole in the clouds, and sent them on their way.

What I was not prepared for were the dozens of spirits who had died in the neighborhood over generations. These were homeless people and other tenants who had crossed over in other buildings in and around the structure. I quickly designated, with my intention, just a two-block radius around this particular building to limit how many spirits could go through. Some had been there a long time, as San Francisco had a huge Earthquake (7.9) and fire in 1906 and there were many who perished, some of these spirits were people who had died then.

These spirits had been trapped in San Francisco, and they were literally running to the light through my energy field. It was like getting trampled by hundreds of spirits in a stampede! My energy was just not large enough to handle the numbers of spirits coming through. I should have done this with a group of mediums.

After the numbers of them lessened, I closed the "hole" to the other side and proceeded in clearing the whole building with my intention, sage and my trusty owl fan. The halls and whole stairwell were heavy with negativity. After the roof clearing I began to travel up and down the elevator a few times with a lit sage stick. I felt I had done all I could do. All of the other spirits had left through the light hole I had created in the clouds at the beginning of the clearing. I talked to the owner who had hired me and told her what happened. She could feel the difference and gave me my check.

When I got home, I found myself feeling awful, as though I still had foot prints all over me from being trampled and I also felt I might have a few hangers on. I was not feeling well at all physically, kind of moody and lethargic. I called a friend who also sees spirits and asked if she would help me clear my field. She did, and it took quite a while, as I had a few spirits that liked my energy so they were stuck to me. I did not need that!

"Don't do that again!" my friend Amita said, "There were all sorts of spirits that you released. Some good, and some not so nice, I just took three off you."

Being forewarned is to be forearmed, so the next time I would attempt to do a clearing in the middle of any city I would just intend for it to be with the energy in the building only. It did bring up the idea and need for neighborhood clearings, and area clearings where war had taken place. I agreed with Amita not to do such a thing again unless I had an army of seers with me so we could effect change as a collective vortex, instead of just little old me.

Beach Boardwalk House

Back in Santa Cruz, the owner of two large Victorian houses was remodeling them. Their realtor called me wanting me to come clear both properties that were occupied by ghosts near the Santa Cruz Beach Boardwalk. One house was facing the water up on a hill, and the other was down the block towards the beach. All the tenants had been evicted, and they had to find new places to live. (An all too common story in Santa Cruz, as well as in California.) I was part of the clean up crew, along with the many contractors and people hired to clean and fix up the two old houses.

The first house had at least five apartments within three stories. Not only were there ghost, there was also the energy of reluctant tenants who did not want to leave their homes after many, many years. In room after room, I found their energy still attached to the property. I couldn't blame them. It was a charming house.

In one case, a man had lived downstairs in the largest apartment for over ten years. The floor to the living room was oak and it was decorated with walnut inlay. A large bay window over looked trees and the backyard. It was a gorgeous place right in the heart of Santa Cruz. No wonder he was attached to the place.

Inside the apartment, I could feel his anger and resistance to leaving. The actual man and his things were gone, but what hung on the walls was a thick layer of brownish black goopy energy that anyone could feel the minute you walked into the room. The beauty of the architecture did not match the feeling of it.

So I began with a prayer, as always, and started at one end of the room, and "peeled" the layer of goopy energy off the walls and ceiling with sage and my feather fan. It took two passes, as the first layer was about the eviction, and the second layer was definitely his personality. The energy remaining was angry to begin with, and since he lived there a long time, he paced back and forth and his negative thought forms layered onto the surfaces. I cleared the apartment, sending the goopy energy into the Earth, and then sent his energy back to him in his new house. He had split himself in two, so the part still in the house had to go back to wherever he now lived.

Upstairs from this apartment, was the spirit of an old woman who had originally lived in the house. She was very elderly and died on the second floor. I chased her out of the upstairs hall, and kept trying to talk to her, but she would not have it and kept running away and hiding in various rooms. Finally after clearing out one room after the other, as well as other spirits more easily persuaded to leave, I had just one closet left. I discovered that in the closet the previous remodeler had left a hole into the attic that was never filled in. The hole allowed the spirit of the old woman, and other ghosts, to move from room to room and haunt the whole house without coming out into the open except through the closets.

I solicited the help of the relator and decided to trap the elderly lady's spirit in that room. The relator stood with her hands up at one end of the room with the intention of blocking her way, while I cleared and smudged out the closet. That is when I could see her instead of just feel her. She was probably in her late 80's, white hair, tall, and very angry.

"MY house, This is M-MY-Y-Y HOUSE!" she finally screamed at me.

Through my mind I said to her with as much compassion as I could muster, "Dear, I know it is hard to lose something you love. But you are dead. Your children, who inherited it, sold this house. Now someone else owns it. So you must go on, or you will never be able to comeback in another life and live here again."

"MY house." she said a bit less stubbornly turning away, moaning.

"This WAS your house. It is no longer yours. You died, and your children sold the house."

"I don't want to go," she whimpered.

"That is okay, I know you don't. But it doesn't do you, nor the people trying to live in peace, any good for you to haunt them like this. It is not helpful. Do you have a husband or your mother who might want to help you across?"

Just then I saw an angel come to get her. The angel brought with her a passageway through to the other side.

"Go on dear, it is safe, the angel will help you across, your family is waiting for you. There is a new house waiting for you over there too, just like this one." I gently fanned more smoke in her direction, and she suddenly lifted out of the closet and decided to go with the angel."

"Goodbye, have a nice time over there." I said in my mind very sweetly, so as not to aggravate her.

"Wow! I can feel that she left! All that aggravation is gone!" The realtor declared.

"I just told her the facts, and she made the choice to leave." I said. "She was stuck between worlds. She couldn't leave and couldn't go forward. Poor thing."

Upstairs in the attic, there was another woman's spirit from the 1930's. By the clothes she had on I could tell she was not from this time. She was angry and upset at losing her daughter. Her baby was only a few months old when it died of pneumonia. A baby carriage and a crib frame were still in the attic resting along the wall. Especially around the carriage, or pram, I could feel the mother. She was sobbing over the empty pram, as the child's spirit was not there. At first, I was not sure if she was a fragmented part of the old woman I met downstairs, or if she was a different soul. As I touched in more deeply, I felt that she was a different personality altogether. She died of grief after the baby died, or perhaps she committed suicide.

"Hi," I said, "I see you lost your baby."

The mother wailed.

"I know what that is like, I lost my child too. It is the hardest."

The mother stopped wailing and looked at me.

"You did?"

"Yes, and I wanted to die too." I said.

"I planned it, executed it, and I am still HERE!" She shouted.

"Yes, you are in spirit. You died. You just don't know you are on the other side. Perhaps you thought you would leave behind the emotional pain?"

"Yes, I did."

"That doesn't work, it stays with you until you chose to let it go."

"Oh, I – I didn't know." she said looking down at her hands. I could see that she realized how much pain she had caused her husband too. The guilt suddenly washed over her like a wave.

"You know, you can move on and meet your daughter on the other side."

"I can?!" the woman said, losing all signs of grief.

"Yes, here she is." I said calling her spirit in. "She has been waiting for you."

At that the woman saw her child and embraced her. The "baby" had grown into a woman in a flash, and the woman who now escorted the mother away was more like a friend. The two woman left together through the portal that the spirit of the deceased child had made when she came into the attic. I could feel her husband waiting for her too at a distance. All the pain of that life washed away as she and her daughter moved into the light to greet her husband. I could hear her say how sorry she was. And I saw him open his arms to her and the child. I found myself watching the scene with tears running down my cheeks.

In the other Victorian, there were also many spirits. In the downstairs, a stubborn teenage spirit who had died of a drug overdose near the boardwalk had found this house to hang out in. She was goosing the contractors that were trying to work around the place. She would wait until they got busy on something, and then she would come up behind them and grab their buns or in some cases, their crotch! This was disturbing to the men to say the least. Since all of them were Mexican men, they were not used to being attacked by a girl, and especially not by a ghost! Most Mexican women wait for the man to approach them. The remarkable thing to me was they ALL felt this teenage trickster, as each one had been assaulted by her.

After trying for several times to talk to her about her actions, she refused to listen to me. She kept running back to the house, to be inside this one electrical box, but I chose to keep her feet to the fire and when I found her missing, I would grab her again, like the stubborn child she was, and bring her back outside. She kept her energy up by running through the electricity in the box.

For her bad behavior I had to call in the Supreme Council. The Supreme Council of Spirits is like the Spiritual Supreme Court. They are wise beings who put on trial the actions of another spirit that overrides the free will of others. Spirits that do whatever they want, in violation of others universal rights and free will are brought to the Supreme Council. This was the case here. So while I held on to her spirit tightly, I called in the Council. They were happy to help. Several times, I had to grab her by the scruff of her neck, and bring her back to the Council until she finally surrendered. Then the Council took her away to some sort of school for beings that do not understand free will and how it works. She was young emotionally as she acted as a mischievous five year old with very bad manners. She was only fourteen or fifteen when she died, but never had much parenting to begin with. However this wild child would not be back to this house.

The moment I witnessed her with the Supreme Council of Beings escorting away with lots of compassion and love, the guys fixing the electrical boxes in the house stopped their work and came over to shake my hand.

"Muchas Gracias, Senora," they said, "That girl was mucho loco!" One of the men added.

"She was a wild child, and very willful." I added. "But she won't bother you again."

Burial Ground House

One afternoon, I got a frantic call from a man and his wife. The house they lived in in the Santa Cruz Mountains was

FULL of Native American spirits. The couple was living with a whole tribe in their living room! The poor people were dealing with them every day - all day and night.

Now imagine your house wall to wall with people sitting down weeping all the time at the graves of their relatives. There is no place to move. Everyone is jammed cheek to cheek. This is what it was like walking into their living room. Two parellel dimensions were active in that house at the same time. The wife was able to see them and the husband could feel them.

It seemed the first thing necessary was to find a way to move the burial grounds to another designated area, like the ridge, and release the spirits that were hanging around the house.

After a tour of the house, I began a ceremony with the occupants of the house and the Native American Ohlone Chief who was leading the spirits. I asked what happened to his people, and he told of the stories of how they were chased and hunted down by gold miners and white settlers. Then he showed me the people who had died there in this clearing in the Santa Cruz Mountains. They had no place to go, and were mostly murdered, and some died of diseases and lack of food.

I wanted to weep too, but I could not let my emotions take over. The occupants of the house, who I will call Barry and Darlene, were weeping softly as I told the story of these people. Then I offered to help these spirits go to their ceremonial burial grounds on the other side.

"Your relatives are waiting for you." I said to the leader through my mind.

The Chief was happy to hear this. He looked up at me, and said, "Yes, take us to our tribe. My people and I have been stuck here in our grief with all the sadness and tragedy that has taken place here for long enough."

"I can help, please, follow me," I said.

I used tobacco starting at the front door, and showed them where to cross the driveway. Using an old brick wall that pointed to a Redwood grove of trees outside the house. The group of Native people came to rest under one of the Redwoods.

The spirits followed me out of the house in a long line as I sang a grief song for them.

Then I asked permission of the tree's spirit if it would be willing to help the people reunite with their relatives on the other side. The grove was very happy to help. In the same line, led by the leader, they moved up the fir tree limbs, using the tree branches as a "ladder." The branches were like a spiral staircase. The people found their relatives waiting for them. The spirits climbed the tree into the sky, and joined the rest of their people who had perished before them. There was a big reunion on the other side as they found people in shelters and t-pees waiting for them.

Somehow, some of the spirits of the deceased had crossed over to the other side before this massacre had occurred and set up camp on the other side in the spirit world. It duplicated the one they had lived in before the white settlers came.

As I returned to the house to clear it, the couple who lived there, were waiting at the front door. They explained that their drug-addicted daughter had slept in the front room, and had left behind several negative spirits that had been attached to her.

Darlene was also full of entities. I asked if she wanted me to clear them. She did, and I cleared her field as much as possible after clearing the energies in the house. She was greatly relieved and felt grateful for the help.

Clutter was a big challenge for them. They had been storing stuff from several deceased relatives as well as their own storage. So I suggested that they handle this as soon as possible because the house was attracting negative entities with all the clutter.

They agreed to work on it, as it was an on-going project. I finished smudging the house to stop other entities that had been left behind by the daughter, and other spirits who had wandered in. I led them out of the house.

Since Darlene was so sensitive to spirits, she was to some degree, attracting them. She was not fully understanding her own power with this attraction, so she thought it was just the way it was. She had been seeing them since she was a child and inviting them into her being to keep her company.

Sometimes if spirits see that you can see them, they are attracted to the person and want to communicate. Some are not respectful of boundaries and try to enter the medium. This happens with newly awakened mediums or those who are first starting on their journey as mediums, and it used to happen with me in the early days.

In the two plus hours I was there, I must have cleared out over 200 spirits, as well as cleared the couple. I gave Darlene some ways to help her set some limits with her psychic abilities so she would not be so inundated with those who were trying to talk with her, especially when she did not want to talk with them. They had been around her from the time she was a small child and to some degree they kept her company. But she was a woman now, and I find that teaching boundaries with one's intention is part of my job with those who are also psychic.

I found myself making a list of things that helped me during house clearings.
1) Protect myself with gold light and ask for help from the spirits of the land before I start clearing anything.
2) Clear the energy fields of the person that hires you. Be sure to clear them of issues related to the occupation of other spirits. What were their conflicts? How were they related or not related to each other?
3) Always ask the owners to de-clutter their house so they won't attract negative entities and energies before you get there!
4) Make sure the entities are not aspects of the owner that have split off from them. Sometimes you may be dealing with a person with a split personality, although through the processes I use, this can also be healed. I will talk about this in "The case of Harrold."

Spirit Possession - Jane's Story

Jane and Boe were living in Montana. They helped me on my first book tour by connecting my publisher with a local bookstore. I was traveling from Seattle to South Dakota, and was glad for the stop and to stay with them on my way to Illinois.

Jane had been dealing with a spirit possession since she was in her late teens or early twenties. She had a spirit in her body that did not belong there and wouldn't let go. This spirit that was in her was very negative.

I met Jane in graduate school in 1987. At the end of that year, we did a weekend with Louisa Teish, an African Voodoo Priestess, who is well known in the Oakland area for her cultural rituals and support for teens. She taught at our school when Jane and I were attending Mathew Fox's program through Holy Names College. Luisa taught there with Buck Ghost Horse, and Starhawk, Brian Swimme, and many other outstanding teachers who were also authors.

A group of us woman really wanted to work with Louisa in a longer weekend workshop. So we organized it and gathered fourteen souls to experience a weekend with Teish. We rented a house on the beach in Santa Cruz, and drove in carpools from Oakland where the school was located.

There were many things that occurred that weekend, which we all agreed to keep confidential. We witnessed things I cannot explain to this day, including a de-possession. I knew, right then and there, that I was to do de-possession work someday. Whatever Tiesch was doing, I knew I was also suppose to do that work.

Eight years later, I saw Jane and Boe for the first time since we graduated during my tour. This was after Sally Aderton had taught me a lot from my own guides, and before Umbanda where I experienced myself as a medium, so I knew enough to know I was on the right path. Boe and Jane were dear people and I enjoyed them a lot and wanted to connect with them again.

As we were getting ready to share dinner, Jane asked me if I would help her with this spirit. When she was a young girl in her teens, she opened a portal she was not prepared to go through. She made a deal with the dark spirits that she wanted to experience the dark side. She was only eighteen at the time and realized ten years later that she had learned enough and wanted to end this exploration.

She asked if I could help her break this self-imposed curse. I knew I could, but because at the time, I was newly into my mediumistic work, I prayed first and asked my guides if I should do this. They said yes, that it was time I stepped up to help her and others like her. She was my first de-possession client. My guides would guide me.

I had brought my massage table on the journey, and felt it would be best to start with a massage to help her relax. So I asked her if I could give her a massage, and extract the spirit from her through the massage. After giving her back and legs and arms massage, I asked her to turn over so I could work on the front of her body. When I got to her belly, I felt this nasty entity curled up inside her. So I asked her if she was ready to let it go?

"YES! I am," she said. "I am done with this contract. I want to end this relationship once and for all." At that, I could see a large spirit rise out of her navel. He was very stern and mean. He scared me, and I knew I had to hold my emotions steady, so I could act as an impartial interpreter between her and this entity.

"It has been ten years since I entered you to teach you what you asked to learn. Are you sure you are done with me now?" He said in an alluring manner.

"Yes, I want this to be over." She said flatly.

"Jane, what did you learn?" I asked her.

"I learned that I was a fool and that I should not have opened that door. I learned that I don't want to have him be a part of me any more, that I am the one who should occupy my own body and no one else. I think I wanted to abdicate this life at eighteen, I was scared to live my own life. This entity 'took over' for me, literally."

"Are you ready to live your own life and take responsibility for it?" I asked.

"YES! Absolutely," she said.

"Okay, here goes," I said, as I heard the word "sage" from my guides. I picked up the sage, and lit it until it was smoking profusely. Holding it over her body, while I fanned it over her, it 'loosened' the spirit. The spirit lifted out of her and said goodbye. I saw it leave and enter the earth through a portal that opened up. I made sure to close the portals around her in her aura. The words came to me from The Great Invocation, "I close the door where evil dwells."

The grandfather clock chimed. It was ten o'clock at night. She said to me startled, "Oh, my God! It was EXACTLY ten years ago tonight, at 10 p.m. that I made that deal. Now it is finally over, at ten p.m., ten years later."

"Jane, while that spirit was dark, he was also benevolent. He did what you, yourself, asked for, and when you were done, he left as you requested. He was attached to you as if in a contract. It seems the contract is over." I said to her.

"Yes, and I am SOOOO grateful!" she replied.

Over the years, what I have learned from offering many spirit de-possessions, is that most spirits are there by the person's own invitation. Whether there is a part of their unconscious or an aspect of them that they do know, some part of them opens the door and invites the spirits in. I also learned that some aspects of the self do this as a self-hating act. They don't like their lives the way they are, so they want to make them more exciting and dramatic, other times they want to 'kill' them selves by inviting negative entities in, abdicating responsibility for their own occupation of their adult selves.

For years, I used to try and help people, no matter what, with entities. But today, unless they ask sincerely, and are willing to give up the high drama of it, and the attention getting benefits of spirit possession, and are willing to take responsibility for what they have chosen to create in their lives, like my friend Jane, I will not work with them very long.

In contrast to Jane, in another case a woman in her 60's was doing just that, not taking responsibility for what she was creating. She had a husband that did not give her enough attention in her mind. So having entities in her and around her, was a way that she made him pay for his lack of attention. Finally, after giving her all sorts of tools to help her, over several sessions, and dealing with her stubborn nine-year old inner child who wanted more and more attention from everyone outside herself, I told her I would not come back.

"But, I need you!" she cried.

"Are you willing to own your nine-year old that keeps opening the door for more attention to other spirits? You have to discipline her."

"But I have, I just did," she said.

"Well, then be the adult and hold your own inner child and discipline her, and stop trying to extract attention from me and from your husband. She takes over for you and you are not handling her at all." I said to her bluntly. "This is the fourth time we have done this, and unless you do this yourself, you will never be free of other entities."

She was so angry at me that she called one more time and then broke the appointment, as if to say, "F-you." It is fine with me if people want to play games with the spirits, but I will not be there to help them, unless they are sincere in wanting to be depossessed.

The Case of Harrold

Once, while living in Alamo, CA, before attending graduate school, a client, who I will call Harrold, called me to clear his house of an entity that kept him up at night. It was a nasty spirit who was trying to attack him. Every night between two to four in the morning, this spirit would start making noise and scare my client to death.

When I got to his small house in Hayward, CA, I could see that the first thing wrong was that this man never cleaned his house. The clutter was piled high with a train set sitting in one corner of the living room and with stuff piled high on every surface. His brother had dumped stuff for him to store in one bedroom, while his own clothes, dirty and clean were piled high on his bed and spilling onto the floor. Dishes were in the sink from days before. When I asked for a glass of water, he had to hunt for a clean glass and wash one out because all the glasses were in the sink.

"Your first issue is the clutter here. " I said. "Negative entities love clutter and chaos."

He looked at me as though it had never dawned on him that he was living in a very dirty house. He looked around with a sense of disbelief.

"Seriously, they attach to chaos. They are drawn to it."

I don't think he took me seriously at a first. So I tried another tactic.

"Lets start and see where we go." We sat down in chairs where I had to remove magazines to sit. In a few seconds as I tuned in, I could feel the negative energies floating around. I told him what I saw and then set about to clear the whole house with sage and my feather fan. It felt much better, and as I was doing the clearing, the one who woke him up at night, refused to leave, and said he was not leaving because he belonged here. Period. He had a few expletives added to the end of his statement that I will not repeat here.

I asked this spirit to go to the light, and the spirit refused. More swear words.

After telling my client what was going on, I told him that I had not had this happen before, and I suspected that this spirit might be a part of him, or an aspect he did not want to claim.

Harrold had not done any work on himself, except that he was having an experience of awakening. In a previous session, he had called me to his house to clear it. The awakened part of him had split from this second more negative part that was trying to get back into his body. However this second part was really pissed off. He did not like Harrold's awakening one bit and was letting him know in very fierce ways. His ego was fighting him furiously for possession of his body. The awakening had basically kicked out the ego, and said "Enough!"

As I presented this to Harrold, he was surprised, and

admitted that he was suppressing thoughts he did not like and tried to get rid of them. At that point I took him on an inner journey to his heart garden, a technique given to me by my guide WuLan that works very well to integrate split aspects of the self. He got to meet the part of himself that he did not like very well and did not want to own.

It was a bit of a war between the two. A battle royal for control for Harrold's Being. This aspect of him that wanted to dominate him was mean and quite nasty. As we sent that aspect love, it began to soften, and eventually he released his anger at himself. It took several sessions to integrate this difficult, and opposite aspect of who he identified with, which was his loving self. His opposite aspect was more violent and more angry than Harrold ever appeared to be.

Any man or woman, trying to embody their loving more divine nature might come up against this matrix of the negative aspects of the self fighting for control. The angry or fearful aspects have to let go and surrender to Divine Love. In Harrold's case, love finally won. After a few sessions, he was sleeping through the night and did not have this aspect waking him up at all hours. He was able to have the angry one integrate and surrender to his love, eventually.

Today, he recognizes and honors his anger when it arises and loves himself and his total being unconditionally. Much of who he was, dissolved or surrendered into the love that he truly is. We still talk once in a while when things arise for him, even though he now lives in Arizona.

Since that time there have been many people who come to me for help with their awakening consciousness and their own psychic abilities as well as parents navigating parenthood with their psychic children. Having psychic gifts does not mean one is awake, but one tends to have those gifts open as one evolves.

It is not the same at all for everyone. Sometime people have their psychic awareness open up all at once as Harrold did. At other times they come to their awareness more slowly, as small dawning explosions in the mind. Sometimes the Star Essence wants to embody the person whose reality and consciousness are necessarily shifting and awakening after the person has released enough fear and anger.

I am happy to report a number of people who I know and have helped, who are experiencing this shift for themselves as they have embodied their Star Essence, that is their Divine Essence. For a time I had a small group of awakened people gathering once a month. But for now, I work with individuals one on one. I think it is starting a small Love-olution of those embodied in unconditional love! Divine beings for sure send out their light to those around them.

Dad's Family Funeral at Unity Church in Rockford, IL

Family Dinner after Dad's Funeral

Chapter Thirteen
Conclusion

Dad's Crossing

"Dad, Come on!" I often said to him as a teenager, pulling on his arm when we were trying to get him away from conversations with others and into the car. It was hard to go anywhere in Rockford with him, because current or former patients were always stopping him to thank him. Sometimes they wanted to talk about their current aches and pains and wanted some free advice. This was especially true when we attended church. It generally took us twenty or thirty extra minutes once we were in the car for him to join us. We often would draw straws as to who would go in after him to remind him that all of us, five girls and mom, were waiting for him, again.

Despite this, my father was a remarkable man by many accounts. He was a family physician in Rockford, IL, one who truly cared about his patients. It showed, as most of his patients were extremely loyal. Hence, our frequent stops when we went anywhere around town were prevelent.

He was also quite involved in civic leadership, such as being president of various boards, including the Chamber of Commerce, the County Board of Health, vice president of the American Association of Family Physicians, and state president, among other things. In his retirement years, after age seventy-two, he gave free talks to the senior residences in Rockford advocating for them to "Manage your symptoms, don't suffer them!"

He was one of the initiators with Dr. L.P. Johnson of the Rockford College of Medicine established during his years of practicing and where he later became a Professor Emeritus.

Rockford College of Medicine is a family practice medical school that is connected with the University of Chicago Medical School. Later he and a group of other people began the Center for Learning in Retirement, where he often taught classes and brought innovative ideas about medicine to Rockford seniors. All of these institutions are still going and growing today. Rockford College of Medicine just added two years to make it a full four-year medical school program.

He practiced at a time when sending anyone to a chiropractor was looked down on by his own profession. Yet he sent people to my Grandfather Lysne, his father-in-law, a chiropractor, especially if there was a possibility that surgery could be avoided for his patients.

He sent one person to Grandpa Lysne, with sever paralysis from neck injury. The man was in a wheel chair, and Grandpa's adjustments helped the patient walk out of the office on his own steam without his wheel chair. Dad's car or farm accident patients recovered more quickly when Dad sent them to Grandpa.

Dad's maverick nature got him into trouble occasionally, but for the most part it was a matter of integrity for him. Needless to say, I was very close to him. Since I was small child he was always supportive of me, and what I have become over the years, even if it went against his scientific sensibilities. We had a special connection. We just got each other with very little conversation about it.

So when he grew very old, with macular degeneration and congestive heart failure, I dreaded his demise. At 98, we knew it was getting closer.

When my father became unable to drive from the macular degeneration, he simply declared in his no nonsense way, "Well, I've had a good run!" Always positive he became the example to all of us for living well into old age. When asked how he was, he would often reply; "Fantastic!" no matter what was going on in his physical body.

My sister Nancy was visiting him at least twice a month from Northern Wisconsin, a three-hour drive. I was supporting as best I could from California. So were my other two sisters, Sara and Jill, when they could visit from over seas. Both were teaching and counseling in international schools. Sara was in Singapore, while Jill and her husband Dave were in India. The last few years, they moved to Bogotá, Columbia, where my brother-in-law finished his career in the international school system as an educational psychologist.

The last year of my father's life due to his declining health, I visited him five times. Our two other sisters came when they could, and my sister Jill often spent several weeks with him as she was not working the last few years of his life. Nancy and Ralph were visiting almost every week especially that last year.

The first trip that year was for a post-Christmas holiday with my sister Sara and Dad. We knew it was probably our last Christmas with him.

The second was in May, the week he went into assisted living on his own. He was quite aware of everything that was happening, even as he was declining, because he was a physician. He monitored his meds, and kept a checklist.

I wanted to help him transition to the new senior housing environment. It had been twenty years since he had moved into his condo that he had shared with Mom, and this was a really big transition for him, as it would be for anyone.

My sister Nan, and brother-in-law Ralph, had helped him move in to assisted living, and I was there the week after to help him with details, and to just hang out with him. I also started tearing the house apart and started to initially sort items to see what we had to get rid of and what we might keep or auction. Since he rented the condo, we had deadlines for clearing it out.

The third visit was to see him two months later at his birthday the 2nd of July, and to spend the 4th of July with the family. We had cleared out most of his house as best we could and used part of our vacations to help each other organize the last of his stuff from the condo. All of my sisters were in the states helping out that summer, and two of my sisters who had been over seas did the big movement of junk with trash bins that were as big as a car. My parents kept everything. There were boxes in the basement from their move twenty years before that were untouched from that move.

In September, two months later, Dad was ready to sell his car. My sister Nancy needed me to come finish the final clean out of the house, and I wanted to spend one more bit of quality time with him alone. By this time we had divided his stuff and my sisters, who were living abroad, put their part in storage. I also packed up the items I was taking from the house and put them in one corner of his living room.

The weekend prior to leaving for Rockford from California, I had to move myself, out of my house in California, because the owner was selling it. I sold my car, moved into a very small temporary place, and got a one-way flight to Illinois. Part of the estate agreement was for me to buy Dad's car from the estate. Then I would drive it back to California. I had looked forward to the drive, but this added stress of moving that took it's toll on me.

During the few days I was in Rockford, we signed the paperwork for the car. Then we took Dad, the old lion of Rockford College of Medicine, with two of my sisters and brother-in-law to the school to watch him offer a history lesson to the new incoming director. Dad and his friend, L.P. Johnson were the initiators of the college. L.P. took the lead, while Dad lobbied for the school with L.P. initially, then while L.P. took an active leadership role, Dad taught and mentored students. The two doctors were like brothers and since L.P. had died a few months before, Dad felt it was important to give the new director the "scoop from the horse's mouth!" as he would often say.

After an hour or so, when he was done speaking with the new director, telling him many stories about how the college was started, finally, he was ready to go home. As he got seated in his car in the passenger seat, he announced to anyone that could hear him, "Well, now I'm done." He had just passed the torch to the new lion of the medical school. We knew his time was drawing close.

On that trip back to Rockford, we also finished cleaning out his house, and closed the door the final time turning the keys over to the landlord. Then saying my goodbyes to Dad and my sister Nancy and Ralph, I drove across country with his old and my new car.

Three weeks after returning to California, I got the call. This time Dad was dying. So in October 2014, I flew back to Rockford for the fifth time that year, and went to visit him.

Two of my sisters were already there. The three of us had lunch together with him in the dining room of the assisted living facility. He was able to walk, but was quite weak. I found him and two of my sisters in the dining room of the assisted living facility. As I sat with them, I noticed he wasn't touching his food. Knowing his preferences I asked him,

"Pop, do you want mustard on that brat?"

"I sure do." he said. His hands were shaking, and he did not have the strength to squeeze the bottle. So I squirted mustard on his brat, and he ate it with glee.

"I can't even squeeze the god damn bottle." He said disgusted with himself.

"At least you have four gorgeous women to help you!" I quipped.

"I sure do." He chuckled and managed a slight smile.

We all knew how hard it was for him, or anyone, to get old, and loose their abilities one by one. He was a self-made man, blazing a trail into college for his brother and sister, and contributing so much around town. He had been so independent for so long, living in his own home for eighteen years after our mother died. He was his own pioneer on so many levels, and now to be dependent for any reason was very hard indeed. Of course he had help as he aged.

Nancy and Ralph were great at helping him out along with taking him to the doctor. Ralph was a doctor, and Nancy a Physician's Assistant. Along with all the caretakers who were in and out that he hired, that gave him endless help. He also had all of us to help, even though we lived far away.

Over that final week we took turns in shifts visiting with relatives, and friends, who came in and out to say their goodbyes. About Thursday of that week, knowing that he was dying he said in exasperation, "This is such a conundrum!" He was so angry that he couldn't just die. He had been seeing his family members on the other side, as if they were in the room, his father, Joe, who played the old banjo, and his brother, and sisters, but he couldn't seem to leave and join them.

"Pop," I said to him, sitting next to him as he sat up right on the bed in his shorts, legs slung over the side, "Pop, I think it's more about surrender than anything you need to do." He looked at me as though a light had gone off and said, "Ohhh! I get it."

The next day, he was slipping in and out of consciousness. Someone on the other side, an angel or guide, was showing him a journey that he narrated for us half in and half out of awareness. It was the death of a woman who was dying down the hall. He gave us a blow by blow of her leaving. He talked about a bridge, and how the angels helped her across. I was sure at that moment that he would go with her. But he didn't.

He came back into present time, opened his eyes, got up, and walked to the bathroom in his boxer shorts as if nothing had happened out of the ordinary.

Then he turned to me and said, "Who is that woman with Kisti?"

"Probably Mom." I said.

"Ah-uh." he said with a tone that was as though he did not believe me.

My two sisters, Sara and Jill, were on duty during the night shift and stayed with him that last night. I had been there the night before, and Nancy and Ralph, the night before that.

In the morning, Nan called to say that I should get there as soon as possible, and came back to his apartment to find him very close to death. He was cheyne-stoking his breath and ready to leave.

"Pop, I'm here." I whispered. A few minutes later, I watched his spirit begin to lift out of his body.

"He's leaving." I said to my sister, Nancy, "Call the others."

As I held his hand, resting my arms by his feet, his fingers grew cold. Ever the scientist, I watched his spirit leave his body. His spirit turned around within his auric field to observe himself dying as his body stopped functioning. His spirit was by my shoulder as we watched the process together. Then I saw him lift up and float near his head, and turn and say to us all, "I'm done."

His spirit walked up a 'spiritual hill' to where my sister Kisti and Mom were waiting for him. He slowly walked toward them. His body stopped breathing, and he was gone.

I fell on his body in tears. Nan and Ralph, who were there, also began to cry. They checked his vitals and he was indeed gone. Within minutes, my other two sisters and brother-in-law arrived. Then a few others came in to say good-bye unexpectedly.

That week others came and went as we cleaned out his things, and closed out his apartment in the assisted living facility and made arrangements for his memorial.

Each of us did our part.

When he was dying that last week, we had asked him what he wanted us to do for his funeral.

"I don't care. Surprise me!" he said chuckling.

So after talking with my family, I decided to make him a Viking boat from balsa wood, wax and paper to set his ashes in to float down the Rock River. It was about three feet long and a foot wide. His initials went onto the paper sail!

After the memorial service we gathered at the Rock River and the boat held his ashes in the hold in a beautiful biodegradable box the funeral home gave. As we lit the boat, and pushed it down stream of the Rock River, the boat fell to one side and continued to burn. His half burned Viking boat floated out of sight. About twenty minutes later, miraculously, the burned hull came back to us from down stream up stream, on it's side to the dock where we were standing without the box of his ashes in it. The boat had dumped his ashes. Part of the sails and boat were sorched.

We scooped up what was left of it out of the river, since in any Native American tradition, you do not want to leave ceremonial objects to float around or haphazardly get left behind.

After his launch, my friend Marco and Sherrie, who I was staying with, agreed to burn the remains of the boat in a small ceremony in their back yard after I left Rockford. Later Marco sent me a picture, the boat in flames in his backyard wood-burning fireplace. This was a good solution, since I was leaving the next morning, and we all went out to dinner with the whole family that night after the boat launch.

At the end of that very long two weeks I arrived home in California. After my first night in my new loft in my tiny apartment, I woke up suddenly in the morning. There at my feet was my Dad, smiling at me with Mom and my sister Kisti by his side. He was fine, glowing bright and golden and so happy to be with Mom and Kisti again. All of them were grinning.

I was happy too, as he was out of pain. His decline was hard to watch but now he was in his bright spirit body and was free. He was fully transitioned to the other side. For the next few weeks I kept myself somewhat cloistered, seeing only a few clients.

A month or so after his death, the most surprising thing for me was that I have not grieved much at all. I know he was where he needed to be, and I was happy for him. Perhaps this was a result of my awakening, perhaps it was because he lived a very long life and really tied up all the loose ends. Perhaps it was also because I know we are not separated. That is something I learned from his death: That grief is in part, due to a belief in separation. Once we see that we are not separate, grief is much reduced. In fact sometimes the grief actually keeps us from connecting with our deceased loved ones. This is something I found myself doing with my daughter, Mariluna, until I realized that my grief actually kept me from feeling her presence. Grief is also a result of the love we have for someone. It takes the time it takes and no one can shorten that time for us.

In my Dad's case, I was helped a lot by driving his car for two years and two months after his death. I felt he was wrapped around me in that car, protecting me.

He is with me, just over my shoulder watching and helping me with the things I need. Many of us have our ancestors watching and just waiting to help. We just have to ask.

Just recently, a little over two years since his passing, he helped me get a new car. His old Camry was totaled when a drunk driver hit it while parked. I was in a movie, and very glad I was. I bought my new car two weeks after the accident, with all the bells and whistles on it, and I am grateful indeed for his help in finding the right one. Thanks Pop! I wrote this poem for him and read it at his funeral.

A Perfect Flight
For my Father at 99

If I could give you words as a gift
They would be,
You are enough.
The time of proving yourself is past.

If I could share with you my observation
of a life well lived   I would say,
you are the thunder and the rain
and after the storm   the stained-glass sun.

If I could sit with you by the lake
lace my arm through yours
as we watch the geese glide away
I would say to you,

Pop, look how the geese
practice their formation over and over
how they teach their young the art

of family moving together

When they have accomplished
their rehearsals   we would see them
take a running flap
and an awkward pounding of wing

To become
one with the dawn
one with a distant
star.

Finding my Teacher

      One month after Dad's death in 2014, I was traveling to Los Angeles from Santa Cruz to share Thanksgiving with my nephews and nieces and my nephew's wife's family. I decided to take a much-needed retreat for myself before the holiday. I booked a room at Lake Shrine Retreat Center near Malibu, CA run by the Self-Realization Fellowship for two nights. As I was meditating in the retreat center's meditation room, I felt Yogananda's presence.
      "Now what do we have here!" He said with a smile. "Very good, now sit up straight, that's it." It was as though there was a thrumming running through my body, and all during that 48-hour retreat at the center I felt him walking with me, talking to me, and mostly laughing. Such joy was emanating from him and through me for the entire retreat!
      After I got home, I realized that for eight years, I had been sitting in my office room for sessions at East West Bookshop, in Mountain View and his picture was right across the store, looking at me. A few months later I discovered that Ananda, the organization that was started by Swami Kriyananda in the 1960's and has run East West for over 36 years, had a sunday service center near Santa Cruz in Scotts Valley. I had prayed for a group of Ananda devotees that would be closer to my home, and here it was! Becoming a devotee was an obvious decision.

Still, in early spring after this trip, I attended an Umbanda service to help me clear unwanted energy from my energy field. At the Umbanda service, when I went up to receive support for the next phase of my life, I was told by the spirit guide, embodied by the leader of the temple, that I should go find a new rock for my altar. In Umbanda, one's altar at home has a rock, a glass of water and a candle when you pray or meditate. The instruction was that I should find it in a waterfall and I needed to do this immediately, that very day if possible.

The same day, while attending the same Umbanda service, after I had the instruction from the leader of the Umbanda temple, I felt Yogananda standing next to me, and he said, "This is a very good spirituality, and it teaches people how to live on the earth. However, it does not teach you how to leave this planet!"

I had been praying for a way to move on to another realm of higher consciousness for many years. His statement rang in my heart as truth and I felt his path of Kriya Yoga would be the next path for me.

So that afternoon, I drove up into the Santa Cruz Mountains off Highway Nine, and found a trail that eventually led a long way down to the river. When I found a place where the water was rushing over a line of stones in the San Lorenzo River, I balanced myself on a few rocks, and plunged my hand into the freezing waterfall. The rock I picked up was so dark, I did not like it, "That is definitely not my rock," I said out loud. I surprised myself at how emphatic I was.

So I threw it back, and as I turned to look in another place for a rock, my foot slipped, and I fell onto all fours, landing hard on my knees on the rocks in ice-cold spring water up to my waist! It was so cold I felt numb, but in my shocked state, I looked up and there was Yogananda floating above me just on the other side of the river. His light was so bright and his spirit was huge.

"I am the only rock you will every need!" He said and smiled his broad grin. I was humbled, and grateful and struggled to find a log on the shore to sit on. On the log, I wept with gratitude. His love was overwhelming. As I looked up again from the log he was still there glowing.

I smiled and said, "Okay, I am yours! But you will have to help me back up to my car, my knees are a wreck!" I sat in his glow, feeling his love and support. When I was ready to go, and my knees stopped aching, I felt assisted by him and another guide or spirit, and I somehow walked a mile up the steep hill. I got back into my car, with scrapped knees and hands, with a very happy heart.

Since then, I have been a part of Ananda, a spiritual community of souls on the same path of unconditional love with Yogananda as our guide and friend. In my daily life, I serve my clients, make art, and write books like this one, write and publish poems, stories and enjoy my poetic and spiritual communities.

Of course, I continue to listen to my guidance. When they speak to me and ask me to do a project, like this one that I just finished, I listen.

Yogananda has helped me immensly. Most recently, I was able to release an entity that was connected to my past death-wish. While I had released my death-wish long ago, Yogananda helped me perceive it from many other lifetimes, and release the entity who was sabotaging me in various ways. Now I feel free and open to All-That-Is around me.

Killing the Death Wish

A white cloud death wish
was wrapped around my light
to disconnect me from the Sun.

The cloudiness hid
her betrayal of my life. She wants me
only in the spirit world.

While a cloud reflects light everywhere
It was not in her inner world.
only fury and hatred lived in her essence.

I am not meant to be over there.
This is an expanding
time of joy in this world of Mother Earth!

The raincloud hid a furious betrayal spirit
who wants me to die
from Schoolhouse Earth.

Her puff was there before I was born.
An old belief that union with God
only exists in the Spirit World.

One near death after another,
sick throughout my childhood,
spinal meningitis at age 17

a close car crash into a train at 21,
the death of my daughter at 45,
loss of two husbands, and three lovers

and the illusive cloud wants
me to leave
after each trauma.

Lately that dark cloud gave
my money away, and
pushes me to leave this plane

Yet now
I demand
that she leave forever.

She is "live" spelled backwards
Her evil presence disguised her hatred
in a cloud of illusion.

Finally, I bound her fury in a cage.
I tell her: *We live in a sacred world
whether here or over there.*

You are not welcome back here, I tell her.
Mother Gaia take her from me! She does.
As I am here in my own heaven.

    I hope you have enjoyed these true stories and poems from my life. May my life lessons resonate with yours, and help you become all that you are in this new Golden Age that is dawning now.
    Namaste.

Ananda and SRF Guru's Teachers: Lahari Moheshi,
Baba Ji Krishna,
Jesus Christ, Swami Sri Yukteshwar,
Paramahansa Yogananda

Robin H. Lysne, M.A., M.F.A., Ph.D.

As a medium, intuitive and psychic, Robin Lysne has been working with clients for over thirty-eight years. She started as a massage therapist and moved into mediumship after 1995.

Her work helps a variety of people from those with losses, to those with inner and outer conflicts that need to be resolved and can be helped through shifting fear-base to love-base, and self-love to Self-Love. She also heals folks.

Since 2004, she channels Divine Guides, including: Divine Mother, Star Woman, WuLan (Tibetian Buddhist Master Teacher), Archangel Gabriel, Michael, Arial, Mother Mary, Jesus, and others who are here to help humanity. She offers Mother Earth Mediation once a month open to anyone who wants to come on-line or in-person. New participants are always welcome.

She is the author of twelve books; two poetry, five non-fiction, two novels and a narrative non-fiction, *Kisti's Royal Garden,* and a channeled book: *The Mother of Us All: Divine Mother Speaks: The Way Forward.*

Recently, she has launched a "Legendary Women Ancestor Series," with three books of historical fiction and a narrative non-fiction book that brings to life the courage and wisdom of her Norwegian women ancestors.

Her previous books are: *Ceremonies from the Heart, for Children, Adults and the Earth, Mosaic: New and Collected Poems, Poems for the Lost Deer, Heart Path, Heart Path Handbook*, which contains some of her drawings and paintings, as well as poems. (all published by Blue Bone Books, Santa Cruz, CA)

Earlier works are: *Sacred Living, Dancing Up the Moon*, (Conari Press). Her poems have been published in: *Fog and Light, North American Review, Catamaran, Porcupine Literary Arts Magazine, Monterey Bay Poetry Review, Rattle, Phren-z online Magazine, Porter Gulch Review, Samizdat, Awakening Consciousness Magazine*, and others.

She is a member of: Poetry San Jose, Poetry Santa Cruz, and the Emerald Street Poets group who critiques each others work in Santa Cruz, Daughters of Norway, The Santa Cruz Art League and member of the Mountain Art Center in Ben Lomond, CA.

Her websites are: www.thecenterforthesoul.com, www.RobinLysne.com and www.bluebonebooks.com. On her days not writing, she sees clients, paints, dances, and enjoys her friends.

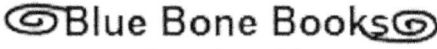
Santa Cruz, CA

Blue Bone Books Publications:

Narrative Non-Fiction
Kisti's Royal Garden

Novels
The Legend of Randine: Entering the Sisterhood
The Legend of Randine: The Laerdal Letters

Poetry
Mosaic: New and Collected Poems
Poems for the Lost Deer

Non-Fiction
Ceremonies from the Heart, for Children, Adults and the Earth,
Heart Path, Learning to Love Yourself and Listening to Your Guides
Heart Path Handbook, for Therapists and Healers
all published by Blue Bone Books, Santa Cruz, CA

Sacred Living, 365 Meditations and Celebrations
Dancing Up the Moon, A Woman's Guide to Creating Traditions that Bring Sacredness to Daily Life
(both published by Conari Press)

Two Worlds One Light, A Memoir of a Medium

The Mother of Us All: Divine Mother Speaks: A Way Forward

and *Luminaria* a new poetry book ready for publication

Some endorsements for previous books:

Legendary Women Ancestor Series:
Book One, Two and Three
Kisti's Royal Garden
The Legend of Randine, Entering the Sisterhood and
The Legend of Randine: The Laerdal Letters

Lysne celebrates the lives of her forward-thinking Norwegian ancestors, especially the strong and capable Kisti Lysne, who understood early on the injustices done to the native peoples of Wisconsin where she and her family settled, and found, through her kindness and courage, that learning from her new neighbors was of benefit to all. The narrative is rich in detail and a poetic sense of the hearts of these pioneers.

    Elizabeth McKenzie, author of *The Portable Veblen* and *The Dog of the North,* Editor for Chicago Quarterly Review and Catamaran Literary Reader

  Lysne's remarkable personal history of a family's journey unfolds with kindness, grit, wisdom and a triumphant energy to turn the hardships and fears of the New World into a land of acceptance and hope for a future that is free of bigotry and hatred and one that that embraces us all.

Wilma Marcus Chandler, author of *The Night Bridge-selected poems*, *Kiss or Kill*- a practicum for stage actors, Editor of *The Muse,* Annual Women's Poetry Contest

Kisti's Royal Garden is a fresh, at times startling, account of Native Americans and immigrants interacting on the Wisconsin frontier in the mid 19th century. Based on diaries and historical records, this is a true story of Kisti Lysne, her Norwegian family and the native Winnebago people. In Kisti, you will meet one of the most memorable women in frontier literature.

Willa Cather's *My Antonia.*

Thank you, Robin Lysne, for a picture of the past that inspires our future. This is a powerful, hopeful, invaluable contribution to history, or more accurately, herstory.

Rich Flanders, author of *Under The Great Elm*, A Life of Luck & Wonder - Finalist, American Writing Awards.
www.richflanders music.com

I so enjoyed reading your new book, *Kisti's Royal Garden*. The stories, names and locations, felt so familiar to me.
Having grown up in the Midwest, my Lutheran Norwegian ancestors were pioneers in similar communities. You brought life to what seemed like my own family history.

Joy Cook
Daughters of Norway Grand Lodge President

Robin Lysne transports us to nineteenth century Norway in this beautifully written story of the spirited midwife Randine. I admired this atmospheric and carefully researched historical novel immensely.

Elizabeth McKenzie, author of *The Portable Veblen*, and *The Dog of the North,* Santa Cruz, CA Editor for Chicago Quarterly Review and Catamaran Literary Reader

My own Norwegian ancestry initially drew me to *The Legend of Randine*, and I was quickly engaged by the story of Randine. I highly recommend this beautifully written novel, not only for its compelling characters, but also for its previously untold drama of the development of midwifery in rural Norway.

Ruth Olsen Saxton, Professor Emerita of English, Mills College, Oakland, CA

Heart Path and Heart Path Handbook:
"Learning self-love is something everyone needs to learn.

Heart Path offers readers a way to love themselves without limits."

John Gray, Ph.D. author of *Men are from Mars, Women are from Venus*.

Poems for the Lost Deer

"*Poems for the Lost Deer* is much more than poems. It is a tract that is, at once, lamentation and praise song, dirge and testament and manifestation. And an inquiry into values and hierarchy and a series of addresses to the faces of power. ... *Poems for the Lost Deer* invites readers to try to comprehend the scope and scale of the hillsides and of "what humans do."

C. S. Giscombe, author of *Into & Out of Dislocation*, Professor at U.C. Berkeley, CA

"*Poems for the Lost Deer* is passionate, compassionate, skillful, meticulous, graceful, vital, and heartbreaking..."

Heather Nagami, Editor of Overhere Press, Professor Northeastern University, Boston

This engaged and engaging sequence of poems by Robin Lysne sees permeable borders where others see boundaries.; it is a kind of wordsmithery that is at once committed to changing our given worlds and to imagining spiritual worlds we have not yet reached.
Though the subject is ostensibly the historical destruction of te white deer at Pt. Reyes peninsula between 2007-8, the reach is broader. When a voice speaks from one of the poems to say: "We sing/our ghost/dance for/the fallen," deer and native and poet sing together of the past to question our future.
Through drawings, prose fragments, and lyrics, the poet

deals in weighty matters, but with a deft touch that always allows the mysteries of nature to seep in and color everything. Let us listen hard to her singing.

David Allen Sullivan, Professor Cabrillo College, Author of Strong-Armed Angels, Every Seed of the Pomegranate.

Echoing Blake's Songs of Innocence and Experience, Robin Lysne's Poems for the Lost Deer documents the recent systematic slaughter of "non-native" Axis and Fallow deer from the Point Reyes National Seashore. Presenting "what happened" in an assemblage of overlapping voices -- factual "evidence". ..."Packing Slip Contents: / 20 dead assorted deer ñ minus racks"); and throughout it all the deer themselves -- first innocent ("Across this / field an apple tree / full of blossoms / run to it, sniff / stretching our necks / rub antlers on bark / scratch ears with hooves, / nuzzle young / we live / one more spring") then experienced ("Humans came / to stop the / hunters // They gave us / three more suns / before the massacre") and now forever gone ("thank you / for loving us / so well // We / forgive // Just know / love / is all / that / remains". This is a glimpse of the book Robin Lysne has given us, one whose time has come not a moment too soon.

Stephen Ratcliffe. Author of *Real, Portraits and Repitition*, and over 20 books of poetry and criticism, and was a long time Professor at Mills College.

www.ingramcontent.com/pod-product-compliance
Lightning Source LLC
Chambersburg PA
CBHW070050080526
44586CB00013B/987